T0335024

The Architecture Machine

The Role of Computers in Architecture

Birkhäuser
Basel

Teresa Fankhänel and
Andres Lepik (Eds.)

A.M.

Contents

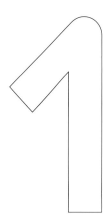 

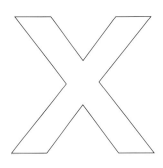

Foreword from the Working Group for Architectural Informatics

The Working Group for Architectural Informatics (AK:AI) is a committee of professors from German-speaking countries that was founded in 2003 at the Bauhaus-Universität Weimar. Demonstrating the potential of new digital technologies for applications in architecture, urban development, and urban planning is a major focus of interest for the AK:AI.

The members of the AK:AI are delighted that the *Architecture Machine* exhibition in the Architekturmuseum der TUM, Munich, is presenting an informed overview of the development of the role of computer technology in design and planning. The exhibition explores several key themes of the AK:AI, which concerns itself with current and anticipated developments and the potential for changes in digitalization in architecture, urban development, and urban planning within the group's remit of teaching and research. The exhibition echoes the interests of the AK:AI in many respects. Because it depicts the historical context of digital design, planning, and construction, the exhibition prepares for the challenges ahead and actively helps shape and drive forward innovations in digital design and construction. Building on developments in other disciplines such as film and aircraft construction, the resulting 3-D programs have enabled architects to find new languages of form, but it took some time before these could be adequately realized using new construction technologies. Today, complex buildings are normally completed based on a digital chain, the interaction of various programs and computers, from preliminary design all the way to the building site.

Members of the AK:AI are particularly interested in how new computer-based design tools, from building information models to completely virtualized buildings and building processes, will develop and go on to influence architecture. These developments lead to questions such as how the interaction between humans and machines or the use of augmented- and virtual-reality models will take place. New methods in the field of parametric modeling and artificial intelligence force architects to consider the possible future effects on their profession of the design and construction process's partial automation and the use of building-related data. At the same time, and independent of this, the presentation of design projects has always been of crucial importance for architects, who have turned to using animation, renderings, and film, which can be created at negligible expense and effort on modern notebooks.

A look back over the developments of the last few decades gives some idea of the potential upheaval that may be caused in architecture by new technologies such as virtual reality and artificial intelligence. In particular, the education of the next generation of architects must reflect the potentials and dangers of the new technologies, without losing sight of the important task of architects, which lies in shaping a viable, livable, and sustainable environment.

Foreword

Andres Lepik

Echoing the industrialization that took place in the nineteenth century, today's so-called digital revolution counts as one of the most important technological turns in human history. It began at the start of the 1990s with the introduction of the Internet for private use and since then has moved at great speed to capture key aspects of work, business, research, communication, and leisure, while fundamentally changing global society. However, the digital revolution is not yet complete and will in all probability continue for decades to come. This rise in networking between humans and machines, and between machine and machine, also extends to architecture. Digitalization enables design, calculation, and implementation of increasingly complex forms and leads to an acceleration of building processes, as well as higher rationalization. At present, architecture is not one of those professional fields profoundly threatened by the digital revolution. However, many processes in key areas such as the preliminary and detailed design of projects and their depiction have been revolutionized by computer-aided methods. These changes have also opened up unimagined possibilities. Further fundamental changes in the field of architecture can be expected in the near future: Artificial intelligence is already able to develop alternative floor layouts in preliminary design, building information modeling (BIM) changes the workflow from design through to completion, digital renderings of projects have achieved such high quality that their results can hardly be distinguished from real photographs, and virtual reality allows buildings on plan to be completely perceivable in the third dimension. Will computers soon take over the remaining areas of architecture?

With the exhibition *The Architecture Machine: The Role of Computers in Architecture* and this catalog, however, we do not wish primarily to speculate on the future but to cast a glance above all from the perspective of historians on the not so remote past. We ask: How have electronic, digital computers changed and influenced architecture? And how have architects helped in shaping this change? Our intention is to trace the interactions of computeraided systems with architecture and vice versa in several succinct phases of development. This is because the extreme speed with which the changes of the last two decades have taken place has meant that up to now there has been little opportunity for differentiated observation and reflection on historical developments by the architects themselves—to say nothing of the fact that the software companies that develop the programs for architects maintain hardly any research-relevant archives of their own, nor do they get involved in reappraising history. So while the scholarly, methodological examination of architectural history in general, such as architectural morphology, the history of building, and architectural theory, is a cornerstone in the education of architects, there have been and still are very few studies or even public exhibitions on the subject of how the relationship between computers and architecture has developed historically. We want to make an academic contribution to filling this gap by presenting some of the significant steps in these developments.

The evolution of new technologies has always caused controversial reactions in society. On the one side there are the advocates, people who perceive opportunities in innovation. On the other side stand the critics, who see mainly danger and risks arising from new technologies. Architecture is one of the world's oldest professions and, having such a long history, has always had the tendency to be rather conservative and skeptical of innovation. No wonder it took some time for the computer to arrive as a design tool in architecture. From the very start, these devices were met with great reservations, as Malcolm McCullough noted: "Gentlemen did not operate machinery." This conservative tendency in architecture is also evident in our university: while computers were being used in many faculties of architecture in the 1990s, it took until 1998 before students at the Technical University of Munich were permitted to create their final-year project drawings with the help of computer programs. Here too, the opportunities were recognized rather late. It was only in 2009 that the TUM established a Chair for Architectural Informatics, which now acts as a permanent bridge between computer scientists and architects.

It seems to make sense to present the complex interactions between the centuries-old discipline of architecture and the new technology of the computer right here, in the Architekturmuseum der TUM. As a public museum, we are on the one hand committed to historical research—i.e., a discipline in the humanities—and on the other hand we see it as our mission as an institution of a technical university to actively promote the productive interaction of architecture with the other disciplines represented here. This consideration of the digital in architecture also offers the opportunity to fundamentally reflect on the future of our archive and allows us to do justice to this mission in the future on a historically sound basis. The fact that increasingly more work processes of architects are shifting to digital space inevitably has consequences for the preservation, cataloging, research, and public dissemination of architectural history in a museum. We are meeting this challenge for the first time with this exhibition project, which also raises many new questions for us.

Introduction
Computers and Architecture

Teresa Fankhänel

New Solutions, New Problems

Hopes and fears about the impact of computers on human life are as old as digital computation. "Will computers greatly extend the capacity and freedom of choice of the individual? Or will they destroy our privacy, generate a new and powerful priesthood, and reduce the individual to a nameless ten-digit number?" asked a flyer for the 1968 Alumni Seminar on the Computer in Service of Society at the Massachusetts Institute of Technology, almost fifty years before the European Union introduced the General Data Protection Law to regulate an individual's rights on the Internet in 2016.[1] Like no other invention of the twentieth century the computer has stirred people's imagination. It has captured their darkest fantasies and their most noble aspirations—so much so that, at times, computers themselves seem to possess human qualities. Just think of HAL 9000, the malfunctioning and malicious yet strangely humanlike, artificially intelligent operator of the Discovery One spacecraft in Stanley Kubrick's movie *2001: A Space Odyssey* (1968). Or consider Kevin Flynn's antagonist in *TRON* (1982), the Master Control Program, a rogue digital dictator who ruled over ENCOM's mainframe computer system. Less bloodcurdling but no less omnipotent, Deep Thought finds the answer to the "Ultimate Question of Life, the Universe and Everything" in Douglas Adams's *The Hitchhiker's Guide to the Galaxy* (1978). Whether good or bad, computers' actions deeply impact their human partners.

Today, computers are far from being a tool that can easily be returned to the shed. They pervade all aspects of our lives. They run home appliances, fly airplanes, execute calculations that we are incapable of computing ourselves. They help us communicate with each other and store vital information. They are becoming ever more powerful and intelligent. And for the last sixty years they have been involved in creating architecture on all levels, large and small, beginning with two-dimensional drawings on cathode-ray tubes in the 1960s and ending with immersive, full-scale, real-time virtual environments today. Over the years, computer hardware has changed tremendously. From room-filling apparatuses, they have evolved into intimate objects that can be used anywhere in public or private, and that fit into the palm of a hand or sit on your lap. As objects, they have adopted the look of unobtrusive, opaque household items. Yet this should not fool anyone into believing that technology is ever neutral.

Time to Take Another Look

In 2018, the Architekturmuseum der TUM initiated a research project to study the impact of computers on everyday practices in architectural offices as well as on the larger image of architecture as it is presented to those commissioning, judging, and appreciating it. For the museum this has been a challenging undertaking. Architectural archives are just beginning to learn how to store, catalog, and preserve digital media.[2] This means that too often material that was created only twenty or thirty years ago is already inaccessibly entombed on floppy disks or CDs that are no longer readable. Often we are forced to hark back to older forms of storage: analog photos and slides, printouts and offset prints, or 16 mm films. Research into digital media is still in its infancy. With terabytes of files available from younger offices, what exactly is it that we are looking at when we study digital archives? Large numbers of versions show minute design changes in an unprecedented way. Old software, if it can be reanimated using current technology, creates another barrier to understanding. This means that, parallel to the architecture, we have to study the programs with which it was made, their underlying design philosophies, their tools, and their limitations. Unlike pencil on paper, software is not a neutral means of working. It was often built to deal with specific problems such as solid modeling, ray-tracing, or animating and it became imbued with its creators' understanding of design ▶ Fig. I. Over time, commercial enterprises incorporated these disparate solutions in packages and plug-ins that cover all design needs in one program. Still, archives often include a myriad of proprietary programs used for different purposes and design stages.[3] Making sense of these files and selecting the most important ones thus becomes the task for technically savvy researchers, often with significant help from the files' creators.

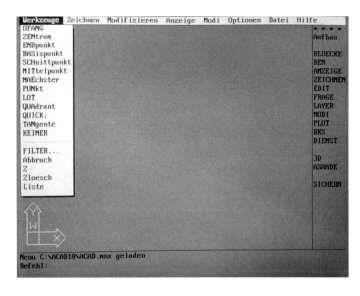

I   AutoCAD was originally designed for 2-D drawing.

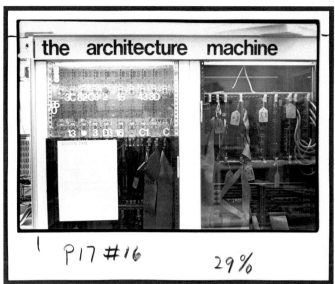

II   The Architecture Machine at the School of Architecture
and Planning, MIT

In the history of digital design, we are therefore at a crossroads. The first generation of architects who started designing with commercial software in the 1980s and 1990s is approaching retirement age. As we are inevitably going to lose some of their memories, access to their archives will become more complicated. In the future we might rely on even more technology to sort and select, using search engines to make sense of the avalanche of information bequeathed to us. Buried underneath is the question of what form original architectural ideas assume in the age of computation. Do they still take the form of an initial sketch on a napkin? Or is it an algorithm or a mathematical equation, a morphological concept rather than a fixed 3-D model?

Architecture Machines

The switch was flicked on the world's first universal computer, the Electronic Numerical Integrator and Computer (ENIAC), at the University of Pennsylvania in December 1945. Its successors, from the Manchester Baby to the IBM 360, from the Apple II to the Commodore 64, and all the way to the MacBook Pro on which this introduction is being written—to name but a few of its most prominent offspring—all follow the same basic logic: they are electronic, digital, and universal computers that can be programmed to execute any operation desired, following a binary logic of 0s and 1s stored in bits and bytes.

Two decades before computation became accessible to the wider population in the 1980s, researchers started to consider the computer's potential for architecture. Among the most well-known research projects was the Architecture Machine Group at MIT's School of Architecture and Planning in Cambridge, Massachusetts, founded by Leon Groisser and Nicholas Negroponte in 1967. Sponsored by military, public, and private organizations, they were using a do-it-yourself computer based on an Interdata Model 3 driven by a remote IBM 360/67 time-sharing mainframe computer ▶ Fig. II.

The team at MIT envisioned computers as more than an assembly of switches and circuits to facilitate tedious calculating tasks.

Instead, the computer was meant to emulate human attributes. It should be able to listen, to talk, and even to worry about design problems. Their goal was to break down the barrier between human and machine and to achieve what Negroponte labeled "Humanism through Intelligent Machines" in his eponymous book *The Architecture Machine*.[4] Another main focus was the exploration of human–machine interfaces to facilitate the use of computers. This was meant to open up design to nonarchitects and to achieve a truly "participatory architecture" created through the "cohabitation of two intelligent species."[5] MIT's Architecture Machine underwent a series of challenges that were supposed to evolve it toward the ideal goal: the computer as the designer's equal partner, an intimately personal and intelligent device. From learning to recognize hand sketches to understanding the human voice, to obeying orders and executing basic design rules, the machine mastered many experiments but failed at the most important one: it could not learn. Today, despite rapid advances in artificial intelligence, Negroponte's techno-utopian ideal remains unfulfilled for architecture.

Many pioneers of computing had equally ambitious hopes for the machine in architecture. Ivan Sutherland, who wrote the first vector-based drawing software, Sketchpad (1963), viewed the computer as a "design assistant." His mentor Steven Coons referred to it as a "computer slave" that "will be as useful and flexible as the lead pencil [...] and certain to find applications we've never even considered."[6] Christopher Alexander, author of the influential book *A Pattern Language*, called it "an army of clerks," hinting

1   "Computer in Service of Society," flyer, alumni seminar, MIT Museum, 1968.

2   Martha Thorne, "Collecting, Archiving and Exhibiting Digital Design Data," *Icam Print 1* (2005): 36–39, accessed January 8, 2020, www.icam-web.org/data/media/cms_binary/original/1349346870.pdf.

3   Greg Lynn, *Archaeology of the Digital* (Berlin: Sternberg Press, 2013). This book was published as part of the seminal research and exhibition project on digital architecture at the Canadian Centre for Architecture.

4   Nicholas Negroponte and Leon B. Groisser, "The Semantics of Architecture Machines," *Architectural Design*, August 1970, 466.

5   Nicholas Negroponte, *The Architecture Machine: Toward a More Human Environment* (Cambridge, MA: MIT Press, 1970).

6   "How We'll Design Products Tomorrow," *STEEL The Metalworking Weekly*, January 6, 1964, 126.

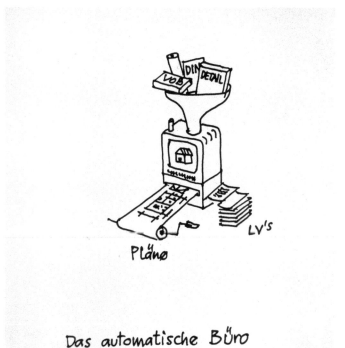

Das automatische Büro

III Cartoon of the automatic office generating plans
without human intervention

IV Diagram of a building

at the computer's ability to master tedious and repetitive tasks. Not everyone was so optimistic, however. Architect Charles Moore regarded the computer as "a very efficient money-making dead end—the opposite of innovation."[7] And Louis Kahn went even further, stating that "the machine cannot create, cannot judge, cannot design. This belongs to the mind."[8]

When architecture schools started introducing mandatory computer classes, they were met with equal measures of enthusiasm and resistance. Malcolm McCullough, Autodesk's product manager for architecture in the mid-1980s, remembered how much of the faculty at Harvard's architecture school believed that "gentlemen did not operate machinery."[9] Likewise, when the Technical University of Munich, to which the Architekturmuseum belongs, installed the first computers a decade later, they were meant for drafting, not for design purposes. At the heart of these debates around the computer's potential as an architecture machine are basic questions that are as relevant today as they were fifty years ago: What is good design? How does design work? What exactly is it that defines an architect?

Digital Evolutions

With six decades of developments behind us, we have chosen forty exemplary cases for the exhibition and accompanying catalog to illustrate major milestones in the history of computers as architecture machines. Many others are awaiting further research and discovery. In addition we have started to unearth the history of architectural software and input devices, but this remains, even after this project, a desideratum.

Each case is associated with one of four chronologically arranged main themes that sum up major achievements: *Drawing Machines* explores early applications of computers to move beyond the drudgery of repetitive, time-consuming calculating and drawing tasks. It looks at how architects tried early on to subvert the prescriptive logic of software to automatically generate designs that seem almost random and that challenge the architect's claim to sole authorship ▶ Fig. III. *Computer-Aided Design* focuses on the evolution of architectural designs before and after commercial software became available in the 1980s and 1990s. From scripting to morphing and all the way to fractals and discrete design, it looks at how emerging technologies have shaped the way that architects conceive of structures based on the tools available ▶ Fig. IV. New forms such as the Blob or the Fold stand next to building systems based on biological or evolutionary approaches to form generation. They show how computerized design has broken free from Cartesian space to include new geometries that challenge the idea of architecture as a static object. *Storytelling* focuses on rendering and animation software such as Photoshop, Maya, or, more recently, Unreal Engine, which have created new ways of representing real and imagined spaces ▶ Fig. V. From early fly-throughs to photorealistic, fictional urban spaces, architectural designs come alive, borrowing from older story-based media such as film, photography, and painting. *Interactive Platforms* returns to early techno-utopian ideas by looking at the computer's potentials for interaction, democratization, and the creation of virtual realities ▶ Fig. VI. Since the introduction of the web 2.0 in 2004 a rise in online sharing and communication platforms has given unprecedented numbers of people access to freely available information and self-publishing. Virtual and augmented spaces make physically impossible designs accessible and challenge the gravitational forces of physical space and national boundaries alike.

Yet even with the history laid out in this book it remains hard to predict the architecture machine's future. Will robots take over the architect's job? Or will we, like Theodore Twombly in the movie *Her* (2013), become so enamored of the machines' intelligence that we happily relinquish control?

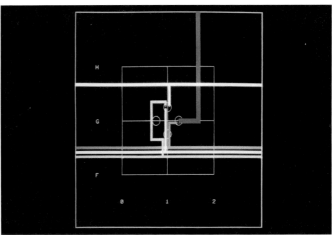

V Rendering of Munich airport building by Schmidt & Partner, mid-1980s

VI Screenshot of ARMILLA, an early BIM software by Fritz Haller

7 Joseph G. Herzberg, "Computer's Walk into Wall Averted by Hasty Doorway," *Commercial Appeal, Memphis, Tennessee*, August 28, 1968.
8 Georg Vrachliotis, "Architekturmaschine. Individualisierungssyteme," *Arch+*, December 2018, 36–43.
9 Malcolm McCullough, "20 Years of Scripted Space," *Architectural Design*, July–August 2006, 12–15.

Chapter 1
The Computer as a Drawing Machine

Essays

Case Studies

Paper(less) Architecture: Medial and Institutional Superimpositions

Anna-Maria Meister

The so-called digital revolution in architecture seemed to promise new forms, new lightness—a new, dematerialized complexity altogether. In the 1990s, Bernard Tschumi's so-called "paperless studio" in the Graduate School of Architecture, Planning and Preservation at Columbia University in New York appeared to show the way toward a purely computer-based future for architecture education, a liberation from the paper stacks and crumple. Architecture offices like that of Frank Gehry began to develop truly digital construction methods. It seemed as if the era of paper was finally over: data had left its status as zeroes and ones and had entered the aesthetic realm. Data could design and represent, and with mass customization and 3-D printing, now even a whole building could be built directly from the architectural digital plan to final materiality. Architecture started "being digital," as Nicholas Negroponte famously declared in 1995.[1] At least that is how the story of the discipline gets told.

But what does "digital" mean in an architecture practice, and where does digital architecture take place? And how is it taught? Is what makes architecture "algorithmic" programs such as Auto-CAD, Grasshopper, Rhinoceros, or Cinema 4D, or are the decision-making processes in design already an intuitive algorithm of sorts? To negotiate this question, I propose to read the digital alongside what Rebecca Uchill and Skylar Tibbits in the book *Being Material* (a corrective play on Negroponte's *Being Digital*) recently identified as the task of looking at "how the digital and the material are together brokering new scientific, physical, social, and political forms."[2] After all, the so-called digital is not the opposite of the material; rather, their mutual entanglements run deep and configure each other. Because if one looks into architecture offices today, one sees mostly one thing: paper. In fact, paper remains everywhere—in folders, on tables, on walls, and in trash cans. Paper that is stacked, stapled, folded, sorted, and thrown away. In a German office, paper takes up most of the archive. In fact, even in 2020, most architecture is commissioned, sketched, drawn, printed, sent, and judged—on paper.

In our current post-digital paradigm, where every aspect of life seems soaked through and changed by "the digital," it is this entanglement between matter and data that the space of this so-called

"digital" produces (and historically produced) which warrants a closer look. In this essay I investigate the materiality of digital production set in pedagogical institutions planning the future of architecture. Rather than rhetorics of a frictionless design process or arguments of rationality, these are histories of friction, of irrational excess, and of nonlinear trajectories; of institutional desires and delays on the one hand and material resistance on the other. This essay examines two attempts at digital processes at two very different architecture schools—the Ulm School of Design (HfG) in the late 1950s and the Technical University of Munich in the 1990s—and the material excess and institutional inertia that occurred in both. For this comparison it might be useful to keep these countercurrents in mind, as it seems that some attempts at a paperless architecture in fact happened mostly *on* and *through* paper.

Paper Trails at the Ulm School of Design: Designing Processes, Modeling Subjects

So let me set this up a bit. The Ulm School of Design, founded in 1953, was one of the institutions that brought technologies of what would become the digital turn into architecture education: cybernetics and process design. It is often credited as a beacon of digital design in a pre-digital era. The HfG was far from being a "technical school" in the sense of the TU Munich; the students there had as many (or more) classes in literature, politics, sociology, and other fields. Conventional representation techniques, however, were now subject to theorization and objectification, replacing a "good sense for form" through acts of programming: if one were to define the right parameters for education, one would be able to produce "good designers," who in turn would make "good design" in the world. The HfG was, if you will, a huge computer processing pedagogical information into a programmed curriculum.

Well known as the site of the advent of cybernetics in architecture pedagogy, the school (namely, Tomás Maldonado) brought new methods into architecture pedagogy through people such as the mathematician Horst Rittel, or Max Bense, a philosopher (and later Anthony Frøshaug and Abraham Moles), who were interested in

I   Horst Rittel teaching, 1958

II   Tomás Maldonado teaching semiotics, 1958

what we now call systems design ▶ Fig. I–II. As one of the most famous German architecture schools, the HfG shaped West Germany for decades after World War II. Songs by the Beatles and news about the economic miracle were heard from its famous Braun products, patients were served their food on HfG-designed stackable dishware for hospitals, anyone flying with Lufthansa was faced with its logos; and all of it was indebted to a neo-functionalist aesthetic combined with a neo-humanist belief held by the school's founders Max Bill, Otl Aicher, and Inge Aicher-Scholl. As Aicher stated, designers needed to go "back to matters, to things, to products, to the street, to the everyday, to people" to turn things around, as "the quality of the designs is the quality of the world."[3] This quality was to be implemented on all scales from, as Bill famously said, "spoon to city."[4] And when one looks at the HfG and its work, one can see that indeed there was not much difference between toys and buildings. The proto-digital method of the school had already obliterated scale.

To get to that point, the curriculum was programmed as much as design processes. When cybernetics entered the classroom through Maldonado's interest in semiotics, it seemed to promise the architectural dream of programmable design and objective beauty. As shared language of man and machine, cybernetics seemed to be the tool with which to finally remove the risk factor—"man"—from the design process altogether. But I would argue that this shift, which is often seen in the historiographies as the end of the "Good Form" phase at the HfG, was there *throughout* its history: programming had started much earlier.

And where did this programming happen, pre-computer? On paper. Hence one might look at paper as such a coding instrument, as the object that programs the process—not as punch cards carrying computer programs, but as a material object in the world. At the HfG, paper was a major material for the construction of both systems and processes, even models. It was the site where architecture's practice was transcribed into codified instructions.[5] As an institution built upon a circulation of carbon copies, transcripts, briefs, notes, and publications, the HfG used paper to constantly reconfigure its ideology, programs, and curricula, creating a pedagogical "paper architecture" through files.

The school's *one* unanimous opinion was that any opinion needed debate. Coding here was, supposedly, a coding of method, not of form (and we know these claims from more recent debates: Why is it that scripting produces a pseudo-organic, biomorph form? Why not script modernist housing blocks in Rhinoceros?). Even Horst Rittel, the mathematician, believed that the school's programmatic approach was formally (and ideologically!) open-ended: "It has to be this way and no other, because any *Gleichschaltung* of opinions would equal the loss of interior cross-examination and ability for

1   Nicholas Negroponte, *Being Digital* (New York: Knopf, 1995).

2   Marie-Pier Boucher et al., *Being Material* (Cambridge, MA: MIT Press, 2019).

3   Otl Aicher, "bauhaus und ulm," in *Die Welt als Entwurf* (Berlin: Ernst & Sohn, 1991), 90. "Vorwort" in *Die Welt als Entwurf*, 12. English translation in Otl Aicher, "bauhaus and ulm," in *World as Design* (Berlin: Ernst & Sohn, 1994), 13, 91.

4   German text: "Die ganze Welt, vom Löffel bis zur Stadt, muß mit den sozialen Notwendigkeiten in Einklang gebracht werden." Max Bill, *Die gute Form* (Zurich: Schweizerischer Werkbund, 1949); Max Bill, "Der Einfluss der zweiten industriellen Revolution auf die Kultur," in *funktion und funktionalismus: schriften 1945–1988*, ed. Jakob Bill (Bern: Benteli, 2008), 115–16.

5   Anna-Maria Meister, "Paper Constructions: Ethics & Aesthetics at the HfG Ulm," *Raddar: Design Annual Review*, no. 1 (2019): 70–100.

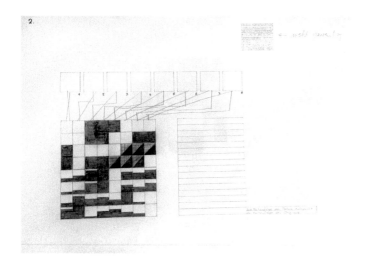

2.

III "Design of a Paper Management System," student work
     by Peter Schubert, Course Horst Rittel, 1961

correction. [...]"[6] And yet the formal output of the school was very consistent over the fifteen years of its existence, while its protagonists believed that they were not implementing a style but shaping opinions, a process that produced well-documented paper trails.[7]

The students emulated the bureaucratic system they saw, and responded in kind. They protested against some teachers or resisted certain methods, but they involved themselves in the school's numerous administrative schemes and committees. In an attempt to institutionalize a practice of perpetual self-critique, discussions were recorded, copied, and filed, composing official and private archives. Former student Frauke Koch-Weser remembers working on a new constitution with students and faculty in 1955, stressing the (perceived) importance of record keeping in diverse settings: "One needed to account for those [meetings]. Then the constitution for the student body needed to be written. I can type the fastest, hence this task always falls upon me."[8] There was no attempt to discriminate between the nature of those tasks once they were translated into their assumed stability of paper as a document: Koch-Weser typed the constitutional protocols alongside meal plans for the next week; paper became the grand equalizer of content. Students wrote reports about student protests and distributed the official records to administration and faculty using several carbon copies for more "transparency," while faculty disseminated multiple copies of responses to those protests back to students, creating a paper trail of institutional debate.[9] At points, the administration of oppositional debates was so embedded in the school that the debates themselves came to be seen as a bureaucratic chore.[10]

At a school of design, paper files were also subject to aesthetic judgments, and their handling became its own design subject. Peter Schubert's proposal for a course on "data organization, filing technique" (taught by Horst Rittel) aimed at the managing of sheets of paper in an open system, directly addressing their material quality ▶ Fig. III.[11] In October 1961, Schubert drew a self-programmed visual code (so paper *itself* was programmed here to behave a certain way) to address the requirements of the system, such as "personal color preference" or material denomination ("paper, plastic, metal"), following Rittel's claim (which

Schubert had noted on the same sheet) that "order is in the eye of the beholder" and depended on the respective user. The exercise was meant to grasp (*begreifen*) a system's ordering principles by reordering its elements, which reminds us of the early coding language of units, circuits, cycles, and feedback loops. Two months later, the system had evolved. Now Schubert designed a filing system for his own class notes, considering "the economy of means in color, form, and designation."[12] By doing so, Schubert gave form to the normed paper's ideology of filing as a means to order the world, while following Rittel's vision of a systematized, objectivized process of design and decision-making,[13] and the resulting pencil drawing resembled the aesthetic exercises and graphic studies from the basic course.[14] While the coding and its system claimed that it was not producing a specific form, the look and shape of the results were similar across the disciplines. So what was being programmed, and what was driving the programming? What was the institutional motivation, what the technology?

Finding ways to automate design in order to push the subject into the background must be read in the postwar situation of the school's founding: context was destroyed, and architecture (and architects) had made themselves guilty. So how was one to build in a guilty Germany after 1945? Trying to re-democratize society was the new

6   Horst Rittel in the student magazine *output* issue 1 (1961), 9 (translated by Anna-Maria Meister).

7   Martin Krampen, *Die Hochschule für Gestaltung Ulm* (Berlin: Ernst und Sohn, 2003), 36–37.

8   Frauke Koch-Weser's essay in Karl A. Czemper, ed., *hfg, ulm. Die Abteilung Produktgestaltung. 39 Rückblicke* (Dortmund, Germany: Dorothea Rohn, 2009), 30 (translated by Anna-Maria Meister).

9   René Spitz, *HfG Ulm: The View behind the Foreground* (Stuttgart, Germany: Achim Menges, 2002), 30, 164, 172.

10 Protocols of the pedagogical conference, July 1961, folder Se 049, HfG Ulm Archive, Ulm

11 Project was begun on November 28, 1961. See Folder Peter Schubert, HfG Ulm Archive.

12 Ibid.

13 Torsten Lange, "Rittel's Riddles: Design Education and 'Democratic' Planning in the Age of Information," in *Re-Scaling the Environment: New Landscapes of Design, 1960–1980*, ed. Ákos Moravánszky et al. (Berlin, Boston: Birkhäuser, 2016), 61–80.

14 Ibid.

IV   Photograph of CAD drawing on computer
     screen, collection Richard Junge

V   Photograph of CAD drawing on computer screen,
     collection Richard Junge

task, away from the bombed city of Ulm on the Kuhberg hill, in the "monastery of good design" as it was called—and the HfG attempted it through scripted, automatized processes, to ensure that the results would be more reliable than the subject had proven to be.

Virtues of the Virtual: Digital Models at the Technical University of Munich

Even an institution such as the HfG, famous for bringing cybernetics into architecture, worked, as discussed above, largely through paper and bureaucratic means. So what might one expect over four decades later in a different school located in a different Bavarian city, when someone brought the so-called digital into the classrooms—in a country well known for its love of files, bureaucracy, and (not least) the DIN A4 paper norm?[15]

When engineer and architect Richard Junge took over the chair for digital design at the Technical University of Munich (TUM) in 1999, he had already worked at the school for five years as commissary chair. Moreover, he had chaired committees at the International Organization for Standardization (ISO) in the early 1990s—the output of which was immensely influenced by the German DIN, which had provided more norms toward internationally valid standards than any other standardization agency. The committees that Junge was part of dealt largely with questions of computer-aided design (CAD); hence the translation of digital drawing tools was fixed and normed onto—indeed, paper. One year after Manfred Wolff-Plottegg (professor for CAD Drawing at the TUM in the academic year 1994–95) had purchased the first computers for the TUM, Junge took over Wolff-Plottegg's chair in an architecture school that was a truly modernist fortress of homogeneous convictions as to what constituted "good architecture." But what exactly happened in this Bavarian CAD space? Would a truly paperless architecture finally emerge? What role was played by the series of three-dimensional grid-volumes constructed with codes, sketched with light impulses on screens? ▶ Fig. IV

And yet—one might need to step back and reconsider what it is that this picture really shows ▶ Fig. V. Because it is not exactly

virtual space, and neither is it the seemingly scaleless 1:1 of CAD. Rather, we are looking at a documentation of institutional developments, resulting in (involuntary) translations across matter: a paper print of the digitization of an analogue photograph—a scanned slide, really, taken of a screen displaying the rendered line drawing of a CAD 3-D model. What we see here is a media archaeology, layers of materiality building up within pedagogical space. The slide collection is what its name conveys: a collection. It rendered the virtues of computational space demonstrable as a teaching tool, broken down into small snippets: a series of photographs, developed as slides, shown as enlightened projections in lectures about the potential of virtually designed architecture. And that collection almost immediately gained yet another material level: as archival files.

The work of German photographer Thomas Demand might offer clues to help decipher these layers ▶ Fig. VI. Demand developed a working method in the 1990s to early 2000s (the same period in which Junge built up his chair at the TUM) in which he oscillates between different medial constructions, translations, and representational scales. Taking publicly available images from newspapers, for example, he then builds full-scale paper models of the scenes depicted. After photographing those with a large-format camera and a telescopic lens, he destroys the model and displays the prints only, presenting an abstracted, strangely alienated and (timely and materially) removed image of a historical moment.[16] This process not only raises questions such as: What *is* the work, the model or the photograph? It also offers a way into the reading of complex material and medial layering of collective image production from documentary to spatial to representational that he deliberately constructs. The images Demand produces seem to be taken with a documentary intention. Producing photographs as "pieces of paper that show another piece of paper" (namely, the models), for Demand the medium of photography changed. As "just a record in the beginning," the resulting works became (if you will) a more truthful rendering of the original event than the journalistic pictures taken at the site, since "the image of something isn't necessarily a recognizable rendering of the object it shows."[17] Rather, what Demand produces—the photograph of the model

VI   Thomas Demand, *Drafting Room*, 1996,
C-Print/Diasec, 183.5 × 285 cm

of the photograph—is not an image but a truthful "proposition."[18] Demand awakens the *perception* of a familiar image in the public sphere—the understanding of a space, or an image as circulated in different media at a certain time, re-created from historical distance—only once it has become part of a collective visual memory. If we return to Junge's slide collection, questions of memory take on a different currency. Hard drives get overwritten with each production cycle, erasing the previous version in our imagination as well as in our hands. So when an architect looks at images of obsolete tools and technology today, she might feel alienated from what it meant to be "using a computer"—as she has adapted and relearned with every update along the way ▶ Fig. VII. The collective memory of political events distributed in newspaper prints, for example, as many of Demand's source materials were, does not carry over into the everyday of a beige computer screen with an apparatus called a mouse, even then. What is mapped in the slide carousel bears a different temporal quality: the layers of the slide films construct, almost as the spread-out frames of a film, an experienced project—not the singular event as in Demand's work. The overlay of historical "improvements" comes together in this collection to show a story of technological progress long over. Or rather, it shows the jump starts of a progress that elsewhere had long been happening, while the slides at the TUM collected dust in the archive, relics of a future that never fully came. What is it that these

slides really document: the temporal lagging of technology in the face of a robust practice or, against all odds, the vision of a new kind of space, slowly emerging from the flickering screen?

The space of pedagogy is often seen as a space of experimentation, one where a different future can be conceived and constructed. But in this case the pedagogical institution produced something very different: a paper space of inertia. The CAD drawings were collected by Junge at the TUM long before students would actually produce any designs on computers. In fact, in 1995 students at the TUM would draw with ink pen onto Mylar, construct perspectives with rulers and pencils, and still build models from gray cardboard (frequently cutting themselves). Rather than pushing the new, the different, the utopian vision, the architecture at the Technical University was glued to gray cardboard long after

15   Anna-Maria Meister, "From Form to Norm: Systems and Values in German Design circa 1922, 1936, 1953" (dissertation, Princeton University, 2018).

16   Roxana Marcoci, "Paper Moon," in *Thomas Demand*, ed. Roxana Marcoci and Jeffrey Eugenides (New York: Museum of Modern Art, 2005), 9–10.

17   Marigold Warner, "Q&A: Model Studies III by Thomas Demand," *British Journal of Photography*, October 22, 2018, accessed December 19, 2019, www.bjp-online.com/2018/10/qa-model-studies-iii-by-thomas-demand/.

18   "Thomas Demand in Conversation with Diana d'Arenberg," *ocula*, June 17, 2015, accessed December 19, 2019, ocula.com/magazine/conversations/thomas-demand/.

digital drawing had entered the profession. CAD drawings were deemed insubstantial, superficial even; the fear of the immaterial ran deep. And yet those concerned could have rested assured: the immaterial never came to bear on the design process in quite the way Tschumi had dreamed it up. It was not the *university* that had imagined paperless architecture, but the profession. Collaborations with engineers required schools in the polytechnic tradition to teach their students new skills—not new thinking.

Looking at these images, one might argue that the CAD software and its epistemologies never really entered architecture at the TUM—and neither did their (amazing) aesthetics. They were filed under the stuff of teaching: the slides did not show potential futures but became immediate archives. The Munich school of architecture had long been one where inertia ran strong; it remained (and maybe still remains) a deeply modernist design school. Looking at these schools and their digital developments, it seems that in the one linked to the larger TUM, an excellence cluster and one of the largest Technical Universities in Germany, ideas of change and paradigm shifts were outsourced to other departments, outside architecture—the ones that built machines and constructed labs. In architecture at the TUM, the flow of time was a different current.

What Is the Digital? Or, For Whom Is the Digital?

Programming has formal intentions, and forms have programmatic character. Political as much as technical histories have shown time and again that there is no such thing as "neutral technology"—just as there is no "neutral form." Both are driven by—and drive—political and aesthetic ideologies. But the seemingly converse currents invite the question of what brings algorithmic thinking into pedagogical institutions in architecture, and what prevents it. Is it technological enthusiasm, or the ongoing modern attempt to strip design, finally, of its subjective qualities? Or is it, instead, the weight of paper stacks, files, and folders that pushes one change forward and puts itself in the way of another?

Just like other technological turns before it (if one still wants to call them that), the so-called "digital turn" might be but one of a series of attempts to de-subjectivize design, which started long before computational methods. Coded design long had this dream: from proportions to norms, from standardization to Grasshopper, architects tried and try to find the "good design"—or rather, to let it be found. But at the same time, this is always the dream not just of aesthetic but of social and political control. We still find that promise in today's discussions around Artificial Intelligence, robotics, or computation. But rather than debate the "necessity" of certain technological innovations, we might look into the respective institutional settings that either desire or fear them. We might, indeed, more often look at the paper pushers, at institutional inertia and delays, the overlaps and hesitations, where material moves faster than architectural imagination—and vice versa. Because what these stories put forth is that a history of the digital, of modeling, or even of computation is not necessarily a history of computers; neither is it what we commonly understand as coding or scripting; and most definitely it is not a history of the virtual. It is, rather, a story of material-institutional practices.

If, as I have written elsewhere, institutions are modernity's time-saving machines, rendering bureaucratic acts repeatable in society, they might as well be understood as true sites of coding and modeling—of subjects, and through paper. Therefore, if we take this material quality seriously, we might take a stroll through architecture's paper modes as reconstructions of a collective moment. And maybe the subjective "first image" that Demand describes will then find another translation—into a collective imaginary.

VII Photograph of computer hardware,
collection Richard Junge

Architecture, Computer, and Technological Unrest: Toward an Architectural History of Anxiety

Georg Vrachliotis

"This cannot be left to a device that can make ifs and buts or yes/no decisions and nothing else!"[1] This sentence, which was clearly expressed in an interview in 1986, was written by Oswald Mathias Ungers, one of the most internationally successful German architects of the postwar period. The human activity at stake, which should never be left to a computer, was the act of drawing. Ungers based his criticism on the assumption that the digitization of drawing not only would have direct effects on the practice of designing but would also have an impact on how architecture would be thought of under these new technical conditions: "Architecture is graphically defined by the means it uses. CAD is a graphic means, two-dimensional. It would therefore be no surprise if architecture, which already appears flat today, became even flatter with the spread of CAD, a mere facade, two-dimensional like a drawing. [...] Today we think and design in miniatures. What we build is first made smaller by reducing scale. But this reduction in scale also changes what we have in mind as a concept. Space and material now only occur in the imagination, in simulation [...]."[2]

When Ungers tried to appeal to the collective conscience of architecture with the sentence quoted at the beginning, the first gray calculating machines were already on the drawing tables of architecture faculties and planning offices. Thin computer graphic lines flickered on small screens originally introduced by the military-industrial complex. The traditional idea of the coupling of drawing and seeing, but also of drawing as seeing, was exposed to scrutiny by a new kind of instrumental knowledge with the intrusion of the computer. The intuitive dialogue between the performing hand and the creative eye was thereby sensitively disturbed. But Ungers's exclamation was about more than uncertainty in the face of a new dimension of instrumental knowledge. It can be read as an attempt to prevent architecture from completely dissolving the productive contradictions of the human mind into the efficiency promises of the computer.

From Statistics to Machine Intelligence

Despite his critical attitude toward the computer, Ungers had early on explored its possible applications in architecture. Already at the end of the 1960s—while he was still withdrawing from the politically charged atmosphere of protest in the Berlin university landscape and answering the call of Cornell University—Ungers began experimenting with planning software. One of the earliest examples is a study on mass housing construction. In the interdisciplinary project entitled Optimal Residential Area Planning, Ungers and the economist Horst Albach investigated the density of the Märkisches Viertel, a district on the outskirts of Berlin.[3] After detailed analysis of statistics, Ungers concluded that facilities planned with high density are often less effective than those with low density. This was an enlightening and, for the housing association (Wohnungsbaugesellschaft), delicate result—not least because Ungers himself was involved in the gigantic housing project with a high-rise residential building.

Another example is the Series of Interactive Planning Programs (SIPP). Developed in 1972 with Tilman Heyde and Tom Dimock, the program was the result of a joint research project and was developed under the premise that in the future we will have to deal with a complexity of planning tasks that can hardly be managed anymore.[4] For an architect, this complexity is no longer conceivable, either mathematically or graphically. Ungers and his team of developers were confident that they had found an appropriate tool in the growing computing capacity of the computer and that they could thereby deal with this new situation appropriately. With SIPP it was possible to calculate large amounts of data and present the results in the form of schematic maps. The computer acted as a visualization engine of statistics.

For Ungers, therefore, the computer was nothing more than a powerful automaton with which statistical calculation processes could be optimized. He was critical of any idea that went beyond this in any way. The thesis that the computer could be characterized as possessing a form of design intelligence was therefore rigorously rejected. Ungers was worried that, precisely because drawing is closely linked to the design process and thus also to architectural thinking, the digitization of the one also means the digitization of the other.

I   Elevation on a screen

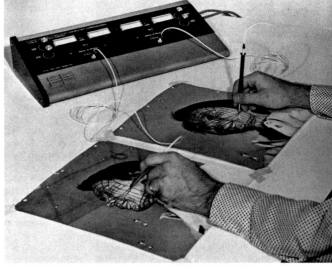

II   Free retracing by hand

Ungers was by no means alone in his strict attitude toward the computer. At the time when he was still working on statistics and digitally generated maps in Berlin, a similar but in some respects intellectually harder battle was raging on the US east coast over the interpretative sovereignty of human creativity. "What man makes, nature cannot make. What nature makes, man cannot make. How far can we entrust the machine to design?"[5] This is what Louis Kahn skeptically asked his listeners in the lecture hall at the Yale University Department of Architecture in April 1968. He was there for a panel discussion at the conference Computer Graphics in Architecture and Design, which promised to be a special event because of its topic as well as its participants. These included Frank Skinner from IBM, Nicholas Negroponte from the Architecture Machine Group, and Bruce Graham from Skidmore, Owings & Merrill. Kahn, certainly the most prominent member of the panel, was in distinguished company. The three other participants in the discussion were Charles Moore, dean of Yale's architecture department at the time, Steven A. Coons, the electrical engineer and pioneer of computer-aided design, and the cyberneticist Warren McCulloch, one of the founding fathers of neuroinformatics, head of the legendary Macy Conferences, and one of the most important intellectual minds in the postwar American scientific landscape.

The title of the discussion was "The Past and Future of Design by Computers." This was the first public debate on an issue that was very controversial. It challenged not only the traditional self-image of the architect as a creative genius but also the time-honored foundation of the discipline as a whole. Kahn made it clear from the start how little he thought of the computer: "The machine can communicate measure, but the machine cannot create, cannot judge, cannot design. This belongs to the mind. [...] If measure is accepted only when absolute, how could one measure realization, concept, truth, desire, silence?"[6] The idea that the individual handwriting of the architectural design process could be fundamentally influenced by the anonymous perfection of computers was something that Kahn was extremely critical of.

And by no means was he alone. The influential architectural historian Lewis Mumford also made it clear in his epic two-volume work *Myth of the Machine*—part one of which was published just

a few months before the conference—that he did not think much of the vision of the future resonating from the computer labs to the drawing tables of architects.[7] According to Mumford, computers could neither invent symbols nor "grasp thoughts that aren't already in their program."[8] Admittedly, it was conceivable that one might perform logical operations within these narrow bounds. But for Mumford, there was no way that a computer "could even dream of a different way of organizing itself than its own."[9]

The glorification of machine intelligence and computer graphics by Coons in particular must have irritated Kahn no end. So, during the panel discussion, Coons turned directly to Kahn with a plea: "I suppose that I am far away from all of you in spirit, and very close to the machine. But you bring to this task the viewpoint that I cannot furnish. You bring the viewpoint that no scientist, no engineer can fully fulfill. [...] You think of a machine, and computers are machines as rather rigid mechanisms like automobiles. [...] Computers are indeed machines, but they are not like automobiles, they are not like electric stoves, they are not like telephones that have specific functions. They are far more magic and general than that. [...] They are, perhaps, the most congenial mechanical device

This text is part of an ongoing book project on the architectural history of anxiety.

1   Oswald Mathias Ungers, "Das kann man nicht einem Maschinenprozess überlassen! Oswald Mathias Ungers im Gespräch mit Peter Neitzke," in *CAD—Architektur automatisch? (= Bauwelt Fundamente 76)*, ed. Walter Ehlers et al. (Braunschweig, Germany: Vieweg & Sohn, 1986), 249.
2   Ungers, *CAD—Architektur automatisch*, 251.
3   Horst Albach and Oswald Mathias Ungers, *Optimale Wohngebietsplanung, Band 1: Analyse, Optimierung und Vergleich der Kosten städtischer Wohngebiete* (Wiesbaden, Germany: Gabler, 1969).
4   Oswald Mathias Ungers et al., "Eine Serie von interaktiven Planungsprogrammen—SIPP," *Werk*, no. 6 (1972): 347–52.
5   "Panel Discussion: The Past and Future of Design by Computer," in *Computer Graphics in Architecture and Design: Proceedings of the Yale Conference on Graphics in Architecture*, ed. Murray Milne (New Haven, CT: Yale School of Art and Architecture, 1969), 98.
6   Ibid.
7   Lewis Mumford, *Mythos der Maschine: Kultur, Technik, Macht* (Vienna: Europa-Verlags AG, 1974).
8   Ibid., 537.
9   Ibid.

ever envisioned by human beings."[10] And as if he felt answerable to Kahn, Coons ended by pointing out that it was just the start of a computer culture that was still in the process of transformation: "Computers will be different tomorrow. They will be more capable, they will be cheaper, and they will be far more congenial to human beings than they are today. [...] We are only at the beginning."[11]

Kahn's harsh criticism was an immediate reaction to the rapid developments in digital architectural production. His statement "this belongs to the mind" makes it clear where the sore point was for him. Kahn saw the growing penetration of the digital into new areas of architectural work as nothing less than a menace to the meaning of thinking itself. To put it another way: it was the humanistic view of the world that Kahn wanted to save from the research on artificial intelligence. And at the time, he was not alone. Many skeptics feared (and do so even today) that, since drawing is closely tied to the design process and therefore also tied to thinking, the mechanization (or automation) of one must also mean the mechanization (and automation) of the other. Thus, from the very beginning, the idea of artificial intelligence was coupled with a twofold cultural devaluation: of the architect as the sole decision-maker and of the design process as a cultural technology.

Drawing as Gesture

Drawing has historically been considered a fundamental medium for architects and engineers. The architect uses drawing in the form of sketches, ground plans, and perspective views, and for presentation and design, so as to give form to the abstract contours in his or her imaginary world ▶ Fig. I. Yet, far more importantly, the act of drawing is also a means of intersubjectively visualizing the media-related traces of one's own thoughts. "Geometry and Line"[12] can articulate, communicate, and intensify knowledge contained inside the mind. In terms of an instrument, drawing is related to writing—regarding the free movement of the hand, the consolidation of one's own thought, or the individual character of one's handwriting ▶ Fig. II.

The act of drawing is a gesture according to the notions of Vilém Flusser, who conceptualizes writing as a gesture.[13] Flusser very roughly defines *gesture* as primarily "a movement of the body or of the tool connected to it, for which there is no satisfactory causal explanation."[14] Writing and drawing are closely related. They are both a "phenomenalization of the thought process."[15] First, the algorithmization of the drawing process triggered a ripple of conceptual and methodical uncertainty throughout the field of architecture, which then changed architectural drawing as a genre and, even more, architecture as a discipline. Ivan Sutherland, a doctoral student of Claude Shannon, was certainly aware of this when he developed his epochal Sketchpad.[16] It is well known that architects should be able to operate a machine not on a mathematical-logical level, as usual, but on a visual and descriptive level. The fact that, two years after Sutherland had completed his program, the "light pen" used until then to tap the screen was replaced by Douglas C. Engelbart's "optical mouse," which could be moved by hand, has not changed anything about the basic principle of visualization.[17] However, it turned out that the mouse was much more elegant and precise for creating and modifying a drawing than the somewhat unwieldy pen, which was attached to a cable and with which one had to tap on the glass of the screen ▶ Fig. III.

"If the use of computers by architects is inevitable, then, clearly the problem must be faced of how architects are to 'talk' to the computers": thus was articulated one of the key challenges of the Yale conference.[18] Coons tried to make it clear what the advantage of a graphical interface is: "No architect wants to become or should want to become an expert computer programmer. Architects want to do architecture. City planners want to do city planning. They don't want to have to invent and manufacture the pencils they use. They want to have them at hand. The computer is a tool. We want to arrange matters so that the computer can be used as naturally and easily as a pencil [...]."[19] So, Coons was about adapting the machine to the designing architect; architects should not have to change their technical understanding of their tools ▶ Fig. IV.

50th Anniversary Issue
A Celebration of Change

III   Cover of *Progressive Architecture* with light pen, 1970

Augmented Architect

Both Ungers and Kahn are part of the cultural history of industrialization, in which the anxiety of machines goes hand in hand with the anxiety of the supposed loss of certain humanistic values. The promises of rationality and efficiency of machines, together with the corresponding concepts of norms and standards, were perceived as a threat to creativity, craftsmanship, and individualism. In this sense, the development of the computer in the age of cybernetics could be understood as just another chapter in the cultural history of industrialization. However, such a theory would mean a reduced view of digital technologies, because it is no longer just about the industrialization of physical work but also of intellectual work.

So the early computer avant-garde understood that you had to focus on people's behavior and therefore also on their mental schematic. Influential figures such as Steven Coons laid the conceptual foundation for a machine world in which the mathematical control of abstract input and output variables rather than the mechanics of the physical object could be regarded as the characteristics of a machine. The boundaries between man and machine, nature and culture were to be overcome in order to arrive at a new kind of behaviorist machine thinking and finally at a superordinate method of algorithmic world analysis.

Exemplary for such a behaviorist view was Augmenting Human Intellect, a human–machine theory developed by the electrical engineer Douglas Engelbart. Similar to Coons, he held the view that computers could expand the cognitive abilities of humans. Engelbart designed a remarkable vision of the future for the architect. With the sentence "Let us consider an augmented architect at work,"[20] he began to describe the working process of a computer-aided architect. This "augmented architect"[21] was to have a screen and a small keyboard at his workplace, which he could use to communicate with the machine. "With a 'pointer', he [the architect] indicates two points of interest, moves his left hand rapidly over the keyboard, and the distance and elevation between the points indicated appear on the right-hand third of the screen."[22] It is possible to rotate a drawing constructed in this way. Using the keyboard, the architect can also enter metric data. After several

10   "Panel Discussion," 100.

11   Ibid.

12   Werner Oechslin, "Geometrie und Linie. Die Vitruvianische 'Wissenschaft' von der Architekturzeichnung," *Daidalos*, no. 1 (1981): 20ff.

13   Vilém Flusser, *Gesten. Versuch einer Phänomenologie* (Frankfurt: Fischer Taschenbuch, 1997), 32–41.

14   Ibid., 8.

15   Ibid., 35.

16   Ivan E. Sutherland, "Sketchpad: A Man-Machine Graphical Communication System," Lincoln Laboratory Technical Report No. 296, Massachusetts Institute of Technology, Cambridge, MA, January 1963.

17   David Evans, "Augmented Human Intellect," in *Computer Graphics in Architecture and Design: Proceedings of the Yale Conference on Graphics in Architecture*, ed. Murray Milne (New Haven, CT: Yale School of Art and Architecture, 1969), 62ff.

18   "Computer Graphics and Architecture. Program Statement: On the Relevance of Computer Processes, Specially Computer Graphics, to Architecture" (unpublished document, Warren McCulloch Archive, American Philosophical Society, 1968).

19   "Panel Discussion," 9.

20   Douglas C. Engelbart, "Augmenting Human Intellect: A Conceptual Framework," Summary Report AFOSR-3223 prepared for Air Force Office of Scientific Research, Stanford Research Institute, Menlo Park, CA, October 1962, 1.

21   Engelbart, "Augmenting Human Intellect," 4.

22   Ibid.

Measured & Drawn by
Frank Choukas,
Brown Auditor
1 9 3 2

Scale of Feet for Elevation
Scale of Inches for Details

·ONE·HALF·SIDE·ROB^T·KEAYNES·HALL·&·HALF·SIDE·IN·CIRCULAR·HALL·
·OLD·STATE·HOUSE·1657·1747·STATE·ST·BOSTON·MASS·

Classical detail from **Pencil Points** Oct. 1932.

URBAN 5, developed by MIT's Nicholas Negroponte and Leon Groisser, on an IBM 2250 console showing use of light pen.

From Pencil Points to Computer Graphics

By Murray Milne

As part of this anniversary issue, P/A has asked Murray Milne to examine the effect the computer has had on the evolution of the profession. Mr. Milne is an Associate Professor in the new Architecture Program at UCLA and is the editor of the book Computer Graphics in Architecture and Design.

For an architect in days past to lay down an ink line on linen or to float a watercolor wash was an act of considerable satisfaction.

Still today, it is pleasing to the senses to pull soft lead across clean vellum, to hear the squeak of a felt tip, to smell the dust of a pencil sharpener, or to tear off a nice square sheet of yellow tracing paper and feel it crackle as it is smoothed onto the board. The smell of ammonia, the feel of familiar triangles and scales, and the pain in the small of the back are all a

part of the architect's personal sensory environment. It is jarring and distasteful to realize that some day soon, almost all of this may be replaced by the clatter of teletypes, the hum of electronic equipment, and the blue penumbra of great blinking tubes.

Unfortunately, this is the price architects must pay for technological progress. But at least a few will be either too stubborn or too sensitive to accept it. To a lesser degree, the change from india ink to lead pencil probably caused the same nostalgic sense of loss. It seems inevitable that soon the architect's personal world will be strangely different. Undoubtedly, a new sensory aesthetic will develop in time, but still the joys of the present world will be gone forever.

Whatever its aesthetic satisfactions, drafting is at best a tedious and archaic process. Machines have

already demonstrated their superior skill at putting lines on paper. In 1893 the first recording pen oscillograph was developed. Eventually, X–Y plotters were hooked up to analog computers to trace out the performance of dynamic systems in real time. Today, high speed digital computers can turn out drawings of anything imaginable on flat bed and drum plotters with incredible speed in almost limitless quantities. Although the capability to produce automated drawings exists, the problem of making them more meaningful and useful will always be with us. The development of the digital computer has produced revolutionary changes in business, engineering, and the sciences, but up to now it has had very little affect on the design professions. And for good reason. Computers can grind up vast amounts of data and spit out huge quantities of numbers, but this is of little use to

168

JUNE 1970 P/A

JUNE 1970 P/A

169

IV "From Pencil Points to Computer Graphics" by Murray Milne, 1970

---

steps, the first outlines of the building would emerge. At the same time, the mechanical architecture assistant calculated possible effects of the designed building and tested them under different parameters. All the data produced in the course of such a working process—which, interestingly enough, Engelbart understood to mean not only "the building design" but also "its associated thought structure"—could ultimately be saved on a "tape" and retrieved at any time.

With Marshall McLuhan, we could say that Engelbart understood computers as a mechanical prosthesis, i.e., an extension by means of which the architect's cognitive and physical abilities can be extended and technically enhanced. The term "augmented architect" makes it clear that the architect should be woven into an information technology milieu and that the digital should be wrapped around him like a second skin. The architect's drawing table was transformed into an apparatus world of devices, surfaces, and databases.

A Machine as a Knowledge-Producing Object for Architecture?

Since "buildings without drawings"[23] and "programming culture in the design arts"[24] are popular topics today, it might be interesting to examine which of these forms has actually proven more effective, more useful, or, to put it bluntly, better in one way or another for architecture. Mathematician Frieder Nake shows us one productive way out of this comparison in his 1974 book *Ästhetik als Informationsverarbeitung* (Aesthetics as information processing).[25] There is a short section in the book where he speculates about the computer's potential influence on architecture. Nake makes an assumption that would interest any architect who contextualizes his or her actions or who constantly questions how the computer changes his or her ideas regarding architecture. He states that architects had an experience similar to that of linguists "when trying to solve problems with computers [...].

They discovered that their knowledge about their field of exper- tise was greatly limited. The infiltration of a new machine, a new production instrument, proved to be an inspirer and a motivator. It was a source of new insight, and an innovative means of gaining knowledge."[26] Nake presents us with a bouquet of metaphors in an attempt to illustrate both the computer's function and its relevance for architects. He also mentions linguistics, which is presumably a reference to the revolutionary wave of inspiration at the end of the 1950s brought on by the work of computer linguist Noam Chomsky, which caught the attention also of architects such as Christopher Alexander.[27] Nake goes on to speak of the "infiltration of a new machine" into architecture, of "production instruments," of "inspirer and a motivator," and of the "source," not only for "new knowledge" but—and Nake makes a fine differentiation—also as a "means of gaining knowledge."[28]

At first this use of metaphors might seem random, and perhaps even a bit excessive. But that is not the case at all. Nake is try- ing to describe something that is very difficult to visualize for the field of architecture and computers: he is producing conceptual images of research. Nake's term "production instrument" is based on an interesting premise. He claims that the computer led archi- tects to discover that "their knowledge about their field of exper- tise was greatly limited." Could this be a symbolic machine as a knowledge-producing object for architecture? Nake shifts the line of vision: architecture does not look to machines; machines look to architecture.

This might be an instructive point of departure for a new narra- tive of the architectural history of anxiety. It concerns the so-called technological condition of architecture, i.e., the fundamental ques- tion of the social and technological background against which architecture is designed, produced, and thought in the first place. The technological condition comprises both concrete innovations and applications as well as all the associated individual and social longings, hopes, and even anxieties. The difference from Kathryn Cramer and Peter Pautz's *The Architecture of Fear* or Anthony Vidler's groundbreaking *The Architectural Uncanny* is that since the age of cybernetics[29] it is not only about an anxiety of buildings but an anxiety of computational tools, algorithms, and data. It is

about showing that the search for a cultural manifestation of the computer was never a straightforward chronology of technological inventions, but one of social and even political controversies, dis- agreements, clashes, and heated debates—from the very begin- ning to the present.

23 Mike Silver, ed., "Programming Cultures," *Architectural Design*, no. 76 (July 2006): 46–56; "Computation Works: The Building of Algorithmic Thought March," *Architectural Design*, no. 83 (April 2013).
24 Silver, "Programming Cultures," 5–11.
25 Frieder Nake, *Ästhetik als Informationsverarbeitung. Grundlagen der Informatik im Bereich ästhetischer Produktion und Kritik* (Vienna: Springer Verlag, 1974).
26 Nake, *Ästhetik als Informationsverarbeitung*, 332.
27 Noam Chomsky, *Syntactic Structures* (The Hague: Mouton, 1957).
28 Nake, *Ästhetik als Informationsverarbeitung*, 332.
29 Georg Vrachliotis, *Geregelte Verhältnisse. Architektur und technisches Den- ken in der Epoche der Kybernetik* (Vienna: Springer Verlag, 2011).

Sketchpad/
Sketchpad Reconstruction

Ivan Sutherland/
Daniel Cardoso Llach,
Scott Donaldson

1963/2017

SOFTWARE
Sketchpad (1963, written in assembly language of
TX-2); Sketchpad (2017, Java, Android software
development kit (SDK))

HARDWARE
TX-2 terminal, switches, light pen, cathode-ray tube
display (1963); Android tablet, control knows, stylus,
keypad (2017)

PURPOSE OF SOFTWARE
drawing

Sketchpad was one of the first programs that allowed users to manipulate, operate, and activate categories of objects through a visual set of operations using a graphical user interface. MIT's Lincoln Laboratory's postwar directive was to develop software that enabled the hands-on use of computers without knowledge of programming languages. There, PhD candidate Ivan Sutherland proposed a graphical drawing software that relied on spatial and mechanical manipulation rather than the textual language of codes, scripts, and numbers. His dissertation "Sketchpad: A Man–Machine Graphical Communication System" presented an iterative drawing software that introduced some of the basic principles in use today. Drawings were produced through a set number of "constraints" rather than free-hand manipulation. The software ran on TX-2 computers, one of the earliest systems suitable for real-time control in which punch cards were no longer needed. Information was input through the Flexowriter, a console that resembled a typewriter, eliminating the division between operator and programmer. Sutherland integrated the TX-2 console but supplemented the Flexowriter with two new instruments: the light pen and a cathode-ray tube screen. To draw, the user pointed a light pen at the display and manipulated a console containing toggle switches to activate precoded operations, such as "start drawing" or "erase." The program then constructed a line segment or wireframe between the start and end points, ignoring all other manual divergences between the two points, thereby disciplining the errors of the hand through machine-corrected geometry. The direct interaction using the screen was a novel technological feat as the screen was transformed from a presentation space into a working surface. Steps toward a three-dimensional display were taken by Timothy Johnson's master's thesis, which extended the original 2-D into 3-D capabilities for Sketchpad III.

In 2017, Daniel Cardoso Llach with the Computational Design Laboratory at Carnegie Mellon University reconstructed the interface and functionalities of Sutherland's Sketchpad. The reconstruction replaces the light pen with a stylus, the TX-2 terminal with a custom station of control knobs and keypad, and an Android tablet in lieu of a CRT screen. By approximating the material and gestural conditions of the original Sketchpad console, the installation allows users to understand

I   Ivan Sutherland demonstrating Sketchpad on the TX-2, ca. 1963

the software by experiencing the ergonomic
framework of the man–machine interface—
by seeing, touching, pointing, gesturing, and
toggling.—*Jia Yi Gu*

Johnson, Timothy. "Sketchpad III, Three Dimensional Graphical Communication
with a Digital Computer." Thesis, Massachusetts Institute of Technology, 1963. ●
Sutherland, Ivan. "Sketchpad: A Man–Machine Graphical Communication System."
PhD dissertation, MIT, Lincoln Lab, 1963. ● Coons, Steven A. "Computer-Aided
Design." *Design Quarterly* 66/67 (January 1, 1966): 6–13. ● Cardoso Llach, Daniel, and
Scott Donaldson. "An Experimental Archaeology of CAD." In *Computer-Aided Archi-
tectural Design*, edited by Ji-Hyun Lee, 105–19. Singapore: Springer Nature, 2019.

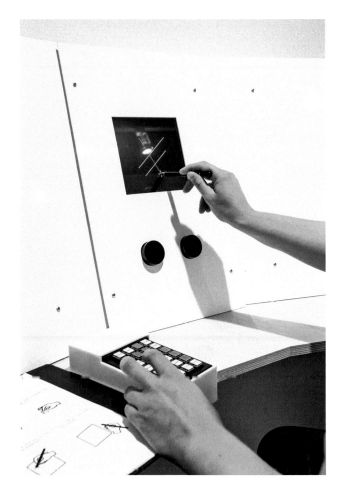

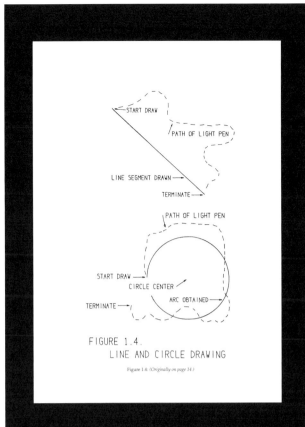

FIGURE 1.4.
LINE AND CIRCLE DRAWING

Figure 1.4: (Originally on page 14.)

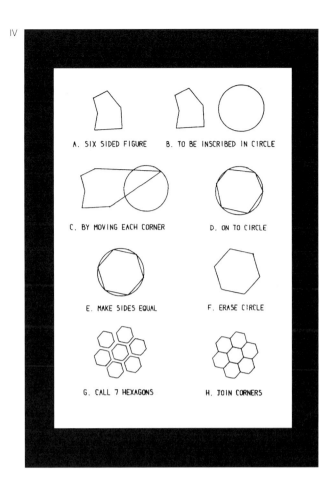

A. SIX SIDED FIGURE

B. TO BE INSCRIBED IN CIRCLE

C. BY MOVING EACH CORNER

D. ON TO CIRCLE

E. MAKE SIDES EQUAL

F. ERASE CIRCLE

G. CALL 7 HEXAGONS

H. JOIN CORNERS

II   Sketchpad reconstruction by Daniel Cardoso Llach
III Visual instructions for drawing a line and a circle
IV   Digitally constructing a circle in Sketchpad

Imaginary Architecture

*Otto Beckmann in collaboration
with Alfred Graßl (1968—1970)
and Oskar Beckmann (1970—1980)*

1968—1980

SOFTWARE
Markov chains (1968–1970), algorithms (1970–1980)

HARDWARE
Ateliercomputer, versions a.i./70–PI73 (1970–1980)

PURPOSE OF SOFTWARE
form generation

Otto Beckmann's *Imaginary Architecture* is a decade-long experiment with randomized form generation with the help of algorithms. Contrary to other early computer art, his work was based on real-time interaction between human and machine. Beckmann was an artist who worked in a variety of media, including drawings, metal, and enamel. He became interested in computer art in the 1950s through his contact with pioneers such as Herbert W. Franke, Frieder Nake, Georg Nees, and Hiroshi Kawano. In the fall of 1966 he founded *ars intermedia* together with scientists from Vienna University of Technology, focusing on computer and laser graphics, experimental film, and sound installations. Together with Alfred Graßl he experimented with creating lines on an oscilloscope connected to a stochastic Markov chain generator. From the summer of 1970 his imaginary architectures were generated by a bespoke computer called a.i./70 (a.i. stands for *ars intermedia*) that his son Oskar Beckmann built to his specifications. This computer was connected to a cathode-ray tube where results could be viewed but not saved. Thousands of these images survive as analogue screenshots that served as the basis for prints. In the early years the generated forms were of a two-dimensional nature, similar to facades or silhouettes. With later versions the computer could generate three-dimensional shapes displayed as elevations, perspectives, and floor plans. Originally, the images were black and white, but some include colors or measurements that were created with filters on the screen. In 1974, Beckmann began to montage these shapes into urban backgrounds of cities such as Linz or Vienna, many of which have become known under the title *Metropolis 2080*. He also used them as the basis for films such as *Imaginary Computer Architecture in Landscape*. Beckmann first started using the term *Imaginary Architecture* for his computer-generated work in 1970. To him these shapes were fictional architectural ideas that were detached from real buildings. In certain cases he preserved the parameters of a specific form with the image. For the 1971 exhibition *ars intermedia. Werkbeiträge zur Computerkunst* at Zentralsparkasse Vienna, Beckmann compiled boards that linked individual computer-generated forms and algorithms, suggesting a close relationship between the mathematical foundation and the shapes as part of the artwork.—*Teresa Fankhänel*

I   Architectural project, photomontage, 1977–80

Peer, Peter, et.al, eds. *Zwischen Mystik und Kalkül.* Cologne, Germany: Verlag der
Buchhandlung Walther König, 2008. ● Weibel, Peter. "Otto Beckmann: Pionier
der Computerkunst." *fair Zeitung für Kunst und Ästhetik,* no. 11 (2010): 9–11. ●
Beckmann, Oskar. "Otto Beckmann's Imaginäre Architektur." *Cserni Live,* no. 1
(2012): 22–27.

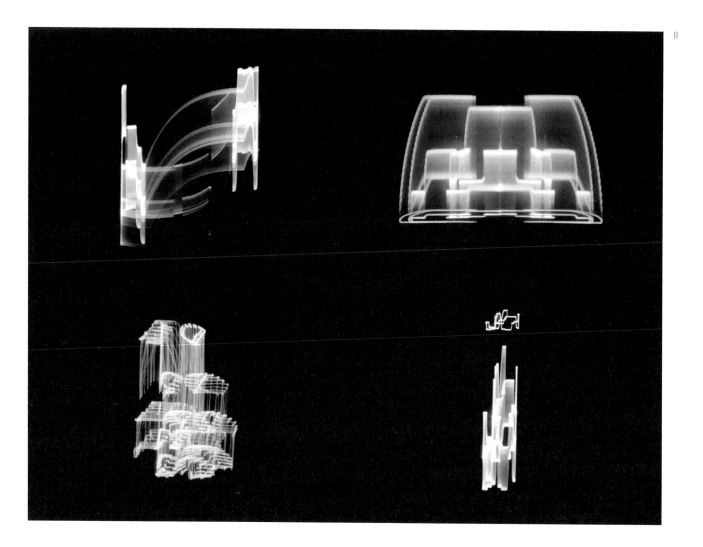

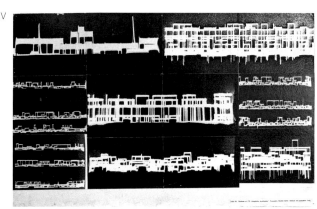

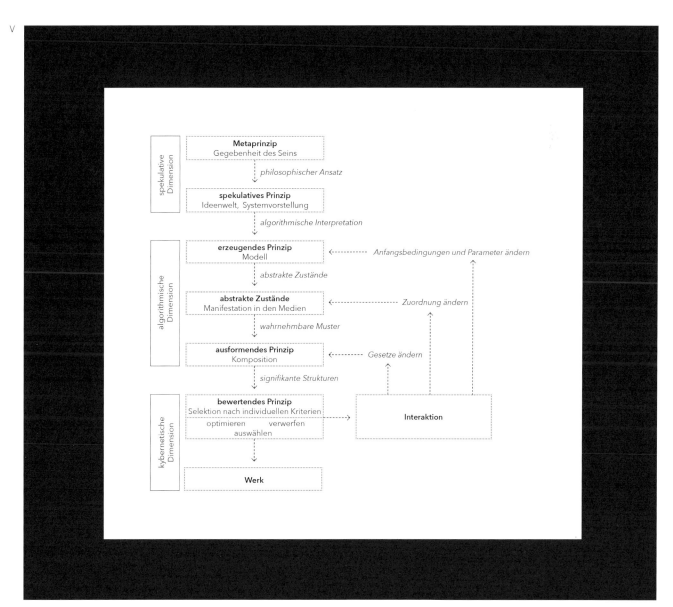

II Three-dimensional shapes generated by a.i./70
III Ateliercomputer PI73 with Otto Beckmann
IV Exhibition board with facade designs, ca. 1970
V Algorithmic flowchart

Federal Government Buildings Competition

Oswald Mathias Ungers, Werner Goehner

1971—1972

SOFTWARE
SIPP—Series of Interactive Planning Programs
(programmed in FORTRAN)

HARDWARE
IBM 360/65

PURPOSE OF SOFTWARE
statistical analysis

The competition entry for federal government buildings in Bonn used the computer as a statistical tool to analyze complex data sets for urban planning purposes. Oswald Mathias Ungers had become chairman of the Architecture Department at Cornell University in 1969, where he had gone to escape the student protests at TU Berlin and to learn more about American planners' work with computers. At Cornell he established a two-year design program focusing on urban planning and low-income housing systems in anticipation of future large-scale urban growth scenarios. To study existing communities, Ungers and his team worked on statistical approaches toward urban planning and mass housing. Students were involved in the research through seminars such as Data Transformation and Graphic Representation. A program called Series of Interactive Planning Programs (SIPP) was developed together with Tilman Heyde and Tom Dimock, which used statistical information for creating maps of cities like Ithaca, New York. The program was meant to visualize technical and statistical information and to show different variables, criteria, and solutions for decision-making during the design process. It was also used to visualize

spatial data for a competition entry for the Integration of Federal Government Buildings into the City of Bonn.

Since the city had become the West German capital in 1949, there had been several attempts to restructure Bonn's infrastructure, including long-distance train lines, local public transportation, and a new highway. In 1971 the government held a competition to find solutions for the integration of new federal government buildings and infrastructure into the city. Ungers's entry analyzed the existing and projected development of Bonn based on data regarding population density, building typology, and infrastructure, and proposed several options for reordering the city's infrastructure. Using a custom-designed notational grid, the entry did not present proposals for architectural forms but instead provided a zoning system for the new city. Statistical maps were created at Cornell by entering information into the computer with punch cards. The machine analyzed the relationship between the density of population, buildings, and types of employment and the size of available blocks within the city, and provided six different options that were included in the entry. Each solution was represented

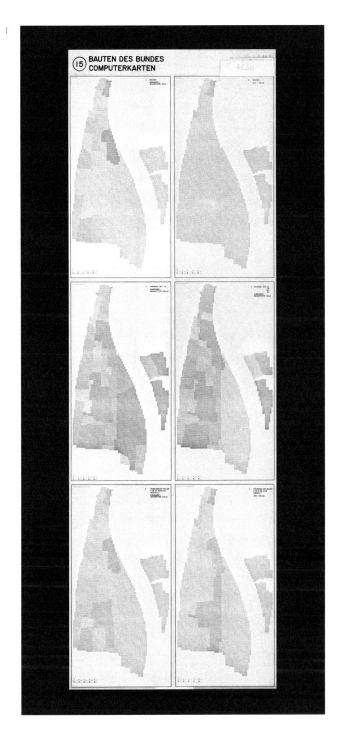
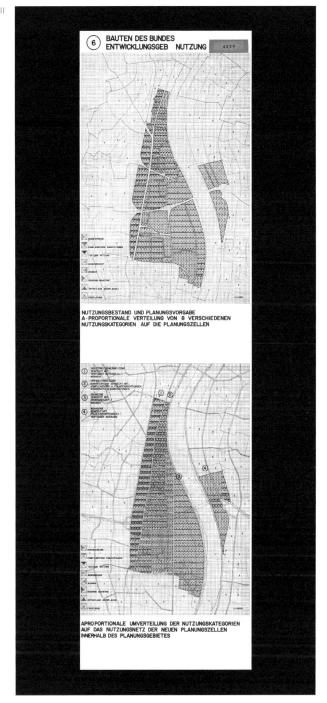

I Computer maps showing different solutions based on statistical information
II Notational system for outlining new zoning of the city

in shades of gray, using letters of the alphabet to indicate its variables. The ultimate design decision was left to the client.
—*Teresa Fankhänel*

Ungers, Oswald Mathias, et al. "Eine Serie von interaktiven Planungsprogrammen—SIPP." *Werk*, June 1972, 347–52. ● Goehner, Werner. "Ungers's Lost Project." In *Sichtweisen. Betrachtungen zum Werk vom O.M. Ungers*, edited by Anja Sieber-Albers and Oswald Mathias Ungers, 56–63. Braunschweig, Germany: Vieweg, 1999. ● Vrachliotis, Georg. *Geregelte Verhältnisse*. Vienna: Ambra Verlag, 2011. ● Cepl, Jasper. "Oswald Mathias Ungers und seine Schule." In *Architekturschulen*, edited by Klaus Jan Philipp and Kerstin Renz, 233–49. Berlin: Wasmuth & Zohlen, 2012.

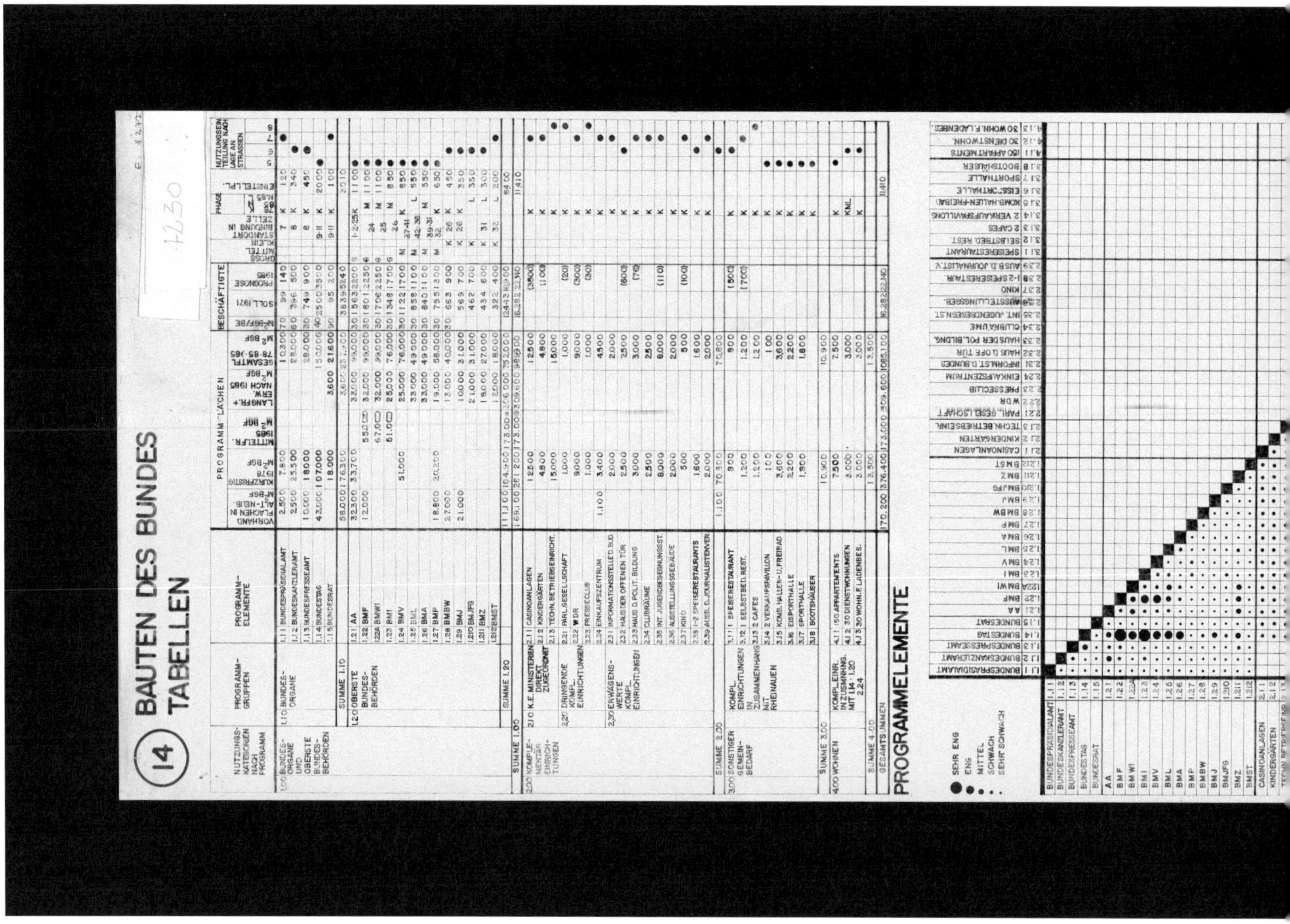

BAUTEN DES BUNDES TABELLEN

PROGRAMMELEMENTE

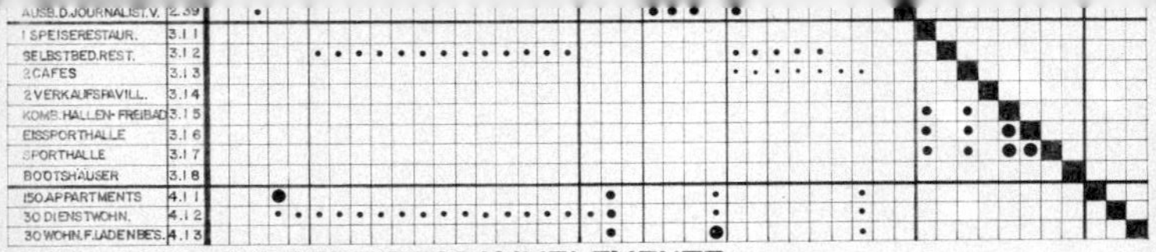
1 SPEISERESTAUR. 3.11
SELBSTBED.REST. 3.12
2 CAFES 3.13
2 VERKAUFSPAVILL. 3.14
KOMB. HALLEN- FREIBAD 3.15
EISSPORTHALLE 3.16
SPORTHALLE 3.17
BOOTSHAUSER 3.18
150 APPARTMENTS 4.11
30 DIENSTWOHN. 4.12
30 WOHN.F.LADENBES. 4.13

VERFLECHTUNG DER PROGRAMMELEMENTE

ZELLE NR	FLÄCHE HA	VERÄNDERBARKEIT KURZ	MITTEL	LANGFR.	BESCHÄFTIGUNGSDICHTE BESCH/HA	EINWOHNERDICHTE EW/HA	BESCHÄFTIGTE PRO ZELLE	EINWOHNER PRO ZELLE	GESAMTBEVÖLKERUNG PRO ZELLE	VORH. BGF PRO ZELLE = GES.BEV. x 30 M² BGF HA	DIFFERENZ ZW. VORH. BGF UND BGF BEI KONSTANT. GFZ = 1.0	VORH. GFZ
1	5.76			●	436	13	2500	59	2559	7.73	- 1.97	1.34
2	6.24			●	89	32	555	200	755	2.26	+ 3.94	0.36
3	4.86			●	151	93	731	461	1192	3.51	1.28	0.73
4	4.00			●	76	99	300	400	700	2.10	1.90	0.52
5	4.07			●	114	71	570	80	650	2.22	1.78	0.55
6	0.97	●			48	272	47	263	310	0.86	0.03	0.96
7	4.90	●			68	3	280	12	292	1.02	3.77	0.21
8	15.51	●			70	5	1090	70	1160	3.48	12.01	0.22
9	20.48	●			147	5	3000	760	3760	11.28	9.20	0.45
10	2.11			●	135	42	285	70	355	1.11	0.98	0.53
11	5.02		●		25	17	126	85	211	0.63	4.37	0.12
12	4.32				218	9	692	288	980	2.92	1.37	0.68
13	2.41			●	27	52	65	136	201	0.56	1.83	0.23
14	5.83		●		125	89	730	505	1235	3.40	1.89	0.64
15	9.10		●		34	35	309	316	625	1.88	7.22	0.21
16	1.15	—	—	—	4	16	5	18	23	0.07	1.03	0.06
17	5.36			●	11	57	59	305	364	1.08	4.22	0.20
18	5.00	—	—	—	39	16	195	80	275	0.83	4.18	0.17
19	25.00			●	9	21	225	525	750	2.25	22.75	0.09
20	3.00			●	259	3	772	14	786	2.35	0.64	0.79
21	13.85		●		92	4	1287	38	1325	3.37	9.83	0.28
22	10.96		●		56	2	612	20	632	1.90	9.00	0.17
23	4.30	—	—	—	0	0	0	0	0	0.00	4.30	0.00
24	3.50		●		173	0	605	0	605	1.82	1.68	0.51
25	26.00	●			0	0	0	0	0	0.00	26.00	0.00
26	5.70	—	—	—	24	11	136	67	203	0.60	5.10	0.10
27	12.80	●			21	7	115	29	144	1.08	11.73	0.08
28	2.80	●			24	10	67	28	95	0.27	2.51	0.10
29	17.28			●	8	52	138	902	1040	3.11	14.17	0.18
30	20.90			●	35	40	730	830	1560	4.70	16.18	0.22
31	9.30		●		78	27	722	253	975	2.93	6.37	0.31
32	6.87		●		4	40	27	278	305	0.91	5.99	0.13
33	24.25			●	0	11	0	266	266	0.80	23.50	0.03
34	3.80			●	2	0	8	0	8	0.02	3.77	0.00
35	9.67	—	—	—	0	0	0	0	0	0.00	9.67	0.00
36	5.30	—	—	—	72	82	381	434	815	2.50	2.85	0.46
37	37.28	—	—	—	8	1	298	37	335	1.00	36.20	0.03
38	58.48	●			1	1	58	58	116	0.35	58.10	0.00
39	32.01	●			1	1	32	32	64	0.19	31.81	0.00
40	8.88	—	—	—	0	0	0	0	0	0.00	8.88	0.00
41	7.33	●			0	0	0	0	0	0.00	7.33	0.00
42	27.83	●			0	3	0	83	83	0.25	27.55	0.00
43	30.74			●	0	2	0	61	61	0.18	30.52	0.00
	514.82				30	15	15.412	8.063	23.475	75.51	439.31	0.14

BESTAND

III Statistical information on population and employment density in Bonn

Multihalle in Mannheim

Frei Otto, Carlfried Mutschler

1972—1974

HARDWARE
CDC 6600 mainframe computer

PURPOSE OF SOFTWARE
calculation of three-dimensional angles,
creation of layout drawing

The Multihalle, also known as the "Wonder of Mannheim," was one of the first buildings in Germany to have layout drawings for components designed and drawn using a computer. The biomorphic, curved form of the large hall was originally planned to be a temporary structure, but it is still there after forty-five years. Entries were solicited from all over Germany for the competition to design the National Garden Show 1975. The winner was the team from architects Carlfried Mutschler + Partner and landscape gardener Heinz H. Eckebrecht. Mutschler initially envisaged an open structure made from disklike roof elements, that were supposed to be attached to oversized balloons. After some early enthusiasm, however, he had to discard his idea of a floating roof landscape in favor of a tentlike structure. To this end he enlisted the support of Frei Otto, who had already achieved fame with works such as the German pavilion for Expo 67 in Montreal and the tent roof at the Munich Olympics in 1972. The architects first built a free-form, wire-mesh model tor the preliminary design. Frei Otto suggested a lightweight structure that would minimize the amount of material used: a timber gridshell. This mesh consists of up to 35-meter-long timber laths, covers an area of 7,400 square meters, and is still the largest timber gridshell roof in the world. In the course of implementing the architects' design, the engineers built numerous models and carried out many tests. The University of Stuttgart used photogrammetry to capture the shape, which had been determined by a suspension model. The captured shape was then converted into a digital model so that the design of the timber lath grid could be verified. Engineers Ove Arup & Partners performed the analysis of the complex structure in London using conventional, analog methods. The findings indicated that especially the edges needed to be strengthened with additional vertices. The data sets created on the CDC 6600 mainframe computer at the University of Stuttgart were subsequently used for the construction planning. This was a new technique at the time and helped design and fabricate the complicated shape of the laths. Based on the information calculated by the computer, angles could be generated, and a digitally drawn layout plan of the gridshell was produced. Assembly of the wooden construction began in 1974. Despite all the computer calculations and numerous models, the Multihalle required a static load test after completion, in which 205 trash cans

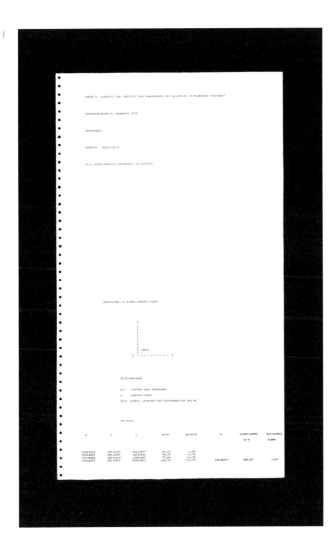

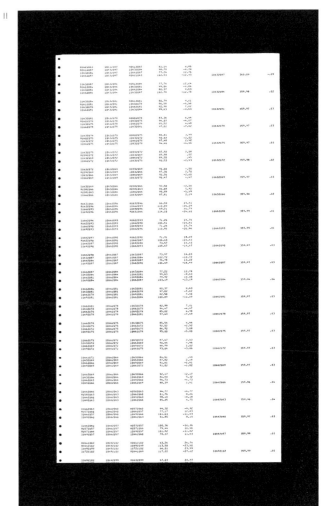

I Cover sheet of three-dimensional angle calculations for the Multihalle
II List of three-dimensional angle values for the Multihalle

filled with water were suspended from the gridshell. This snow load simulation showed a deflection of 79 mm—within 1 mm of the calculated value.—*Clara Frey*

Elser, Oliver, and Peter Cachola Schmal, eds. *Das Architekturmodell. Werkzeug, Fetisch, kleine Utopie*. Zurich: Scheidegger & Spiess, 2012. ● Vrachliotis, Georg. *Frei Otto, Carlfried Mutschler, Multihalle*. Leipzig: Spector Books, 2017.

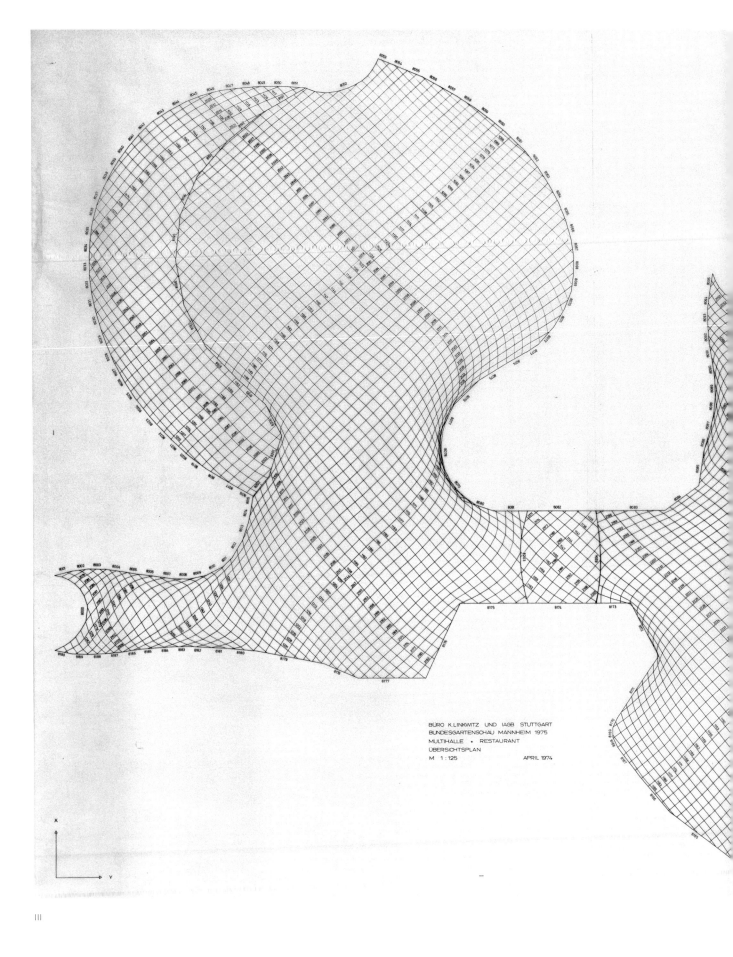

BÜRO K.LINKWITZ UND IAGB STUTTGART
BUNDESGARTENSCHAU MANNHEIM 1975
MULTIHALLE • RESTAURANT
ÜBERSICHTSPLAN
M 1 : 125   APRIL 1974

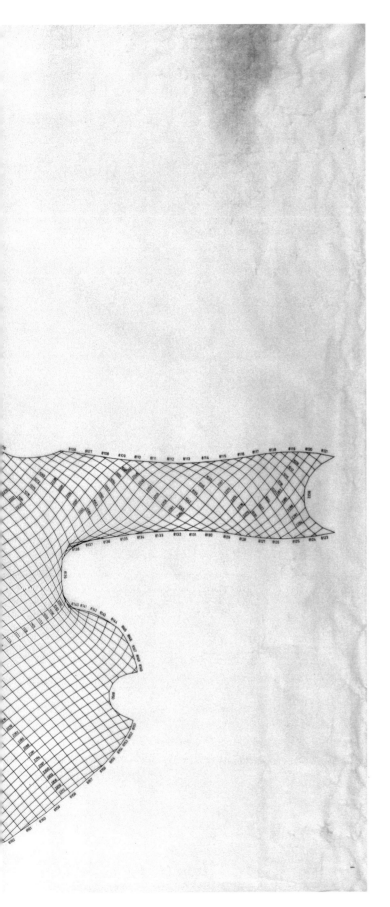

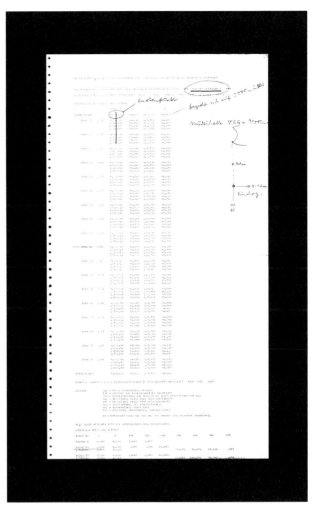

IV

III　Computer-generated layout plan of the gridshell, scale 1:125
IV　Edge development using equilibrium calculations in the restaurant area

Alternative Input Devices

John Frazer, Julia Frazer, Diploma Unit 11
(Architectural Association, 1989—1990)

1990

John Frazer's Intelligent Modeling Systems were designed to enable a computer-aided design process that replaced the then usual manual drawing methods and computer input devices such as the light pen or the computer mouse. Building on the experience of the Reptile Flexible Enclosure System, which Frazer developed during his studies at the Architectural Association School of Architecture in London (AA), regular adaptations of these systems followed to allow for a more universal application. Frazer's partner, the mathematician and architect Julia Frazer, and his son Peter Frazer were significantly involved in these developments. Together they designed Intelligent Beermats—a two-dimensional, individually configurable design method for evaluating floor plans based on square mats. The individual units were connected by cables to create data connections between them, and a computer detected and read their arrangement. The third design dimension was added with the development of the Intelligent Physical Modeling System. The method of self-inspection allowed each cube in this system to detect whether its adjacent surfaces were also occupied by cubes. Thus, when a unit was activated, an iterative process was initiated that inspected one cube after another and sent the results to the computer. The Universal Constructor, developed together with students of Diploma Unit 11 at the AA under the direction of John and Julia Frazer and Gordon Pask, was first presented to the public in 1990 and was the most elaborate version of these Intelligent Modeling Systems. It consisted of identical cubes linked by electrical connections. Up to twelve superimposed cubes were stacked on a base board with space in plan for 12 × 12 cells. This three-dimensional arrangement of programmable units was connected via the base board to a computer, through which the conditions required by the computer to calculate the organization of the cubes could be entered. Eight LEDs per cube communicated by means of light signals to show where the computer had calculated that units needed to be added or removed.

Parallel to Frazer's academic research, other input methods became established in practice. In the 1950s and 1960s the development of CAD programs awakened an inventive spirit that produced input devices such as the light pen, the tracking ball, or a cockpit-like arrangement of projectors and touchscreens as in the multimedia room at

I   Intelligent Physical Modeling System
II The first computer mouse, by Douglas Engelbart

MIT. In the long run, however, the computer mouse invented by Douglas Engelbart in 1963 became the best-known input device and the natural companion of almost every computer today.

John Frazer's spatial design methods did not gain acceptance in everyday architectural practice. Nevertheless, they were significant because they enabled a haptic interaction between designer and computer via mediating input devices that represented the architectural design in an abstract form at a time when CAD was little more than a pipe dream. They created an early form of virtual reality with which the architectural design could be evaluated.—*Philip Schneider*

Frazer, John. *An Evolutionary Architecture*. London: Architectural Association, 1995. ● Frazer, John. "Computing without Computers." *Architectural Design* 75 (2005): 34–43.

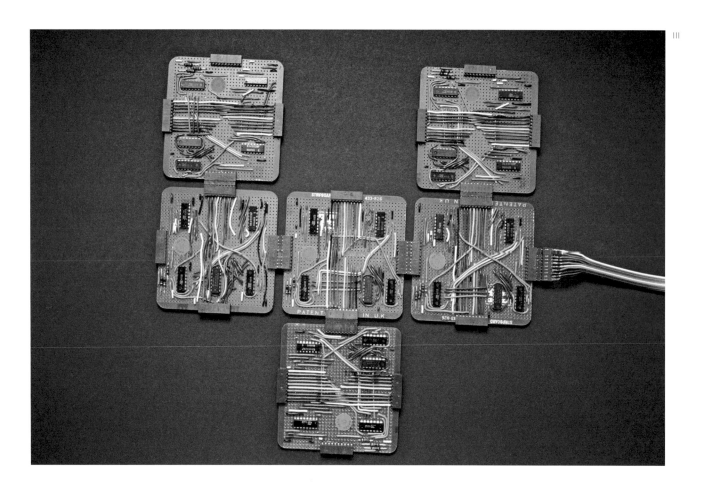

III Intelligent Beermats: two-dimensional forerunner of the Universal Constructor
IV Spatial configuration of Universal Constructor
V   Multimedia room at MIT

Plotter Drawings

Günter Günschel

1987—1991

SOFTWARE
Cubicomp PictureMaker 20, Softimage,
Alias|Wavefront, Photoshop

HARDWARE
Cubicomp PictureMaker 20 system
(computer 386/486, frame buffer, monitors),
HP 7475A pen plotter, Graphtec
pen plotter FP7100, NeXT laser printer

PURPOSE OF SOFTWARE
form-finding

Günter Günschel's plotter drawings are form-finding experiments that attempt to exploit the capacity of the computer as a drawing machine. With his architectural drawings he pursued "thought experiments on real objects targeting questions to the imagination."[1]

Günschel studied architecture at Burg Giebichenstein and at the Academy of Arts in Berlin. After initial experience in the offices of Max Taut and Hans Scharoun, he developed an interest in lightweight structures, including concrete shells, for which he applied for a patent in 1957. After obtaining his architecture diploma in 1955, Günschel was involved with lightweight and mobile architecture and in 1966 published, among other things, the three-part book series Große Konstrukteure. In his freehand sketches of the late 1960s, which he called Körper Fragmente, Netzkompositionen, or Metamorphosen (body fragments, mesh compositions, or metamorphoses), Günschel played with connections and networks, sometimes developed as architecture out of the landscape, sometimes as an abstract play with three-dimensional objects and lines in open space.

From 1987 he used the computer for free experiments without a set room program.

Günschel was inspired by the new possibilities of the computer: the way wireframes are visualized, and the rotation and accessibility of 3-D models on the monitor. The polygons of the vector drawings were drawn one after the other. Building up the image sometimes took several minutes on the computer. The architect himself described the comparison between drawing on the computer and painting on the easel as a dialog between the drawing surface and the artist. He created complex three-dimensional structures using the "cross section" function.

The architectural computer graphics in Günschel's late work are a consistent further development of his preoccupation with objects and mesh structures in the zone of interaction between the seemingly abstract ornamental and clear references to interior or exterior spaces. A further step in the development of these works took place in cooperation with his master student Bernhard Többen under the title Freigeregelte apparative Zeichnungen in 1990–91 at the Braunschweig University of Art (HBK), where Günschel taught as professor for experimental architecture from 1968. For his computer graphics there, Günschel worked with the 3-D and animation program

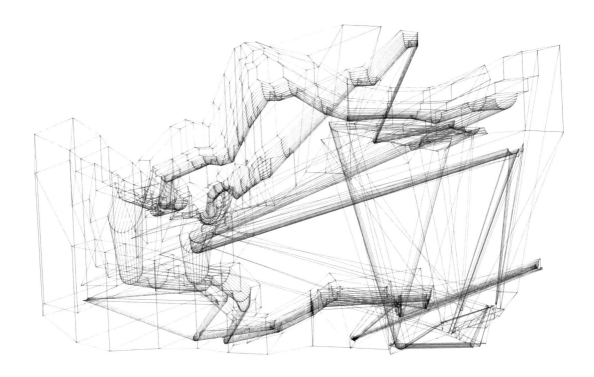

| Plotter drawing

PictureMaker. Mac and Silicon Graphics computers with software such as Softimage and Alias|Wavefront came into use later. He also did graphics work using the first graphics programs, such as Photoshop 1.0. He did not use a mouse to enter the information for the drawings. The plotter drawings were output directly on the printer from the CAD data.—*Laura Altmann*

1 Krawinkel 1988, 99. ● Krawinkel, Günter. "Dekompositorische Zeichnungen." *Daidalos* 29 (1988): 96ff. ● Fuchs-Belhamri, Elisabeth, ed. *Günter Günschel. Architektonische Denkspiele*. Braunschweig, Germany: 1999.

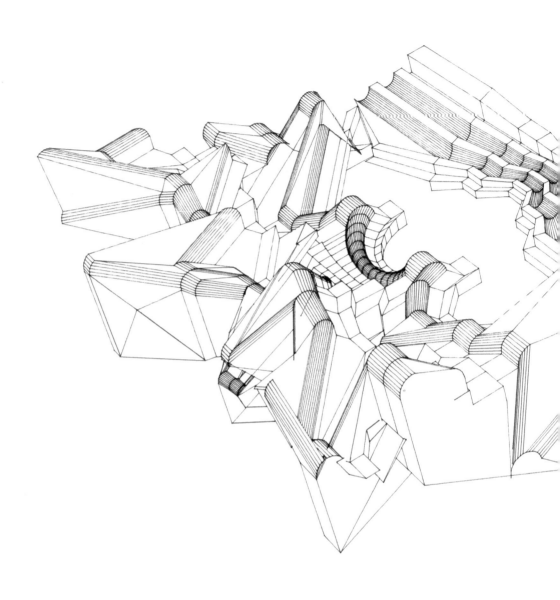

II

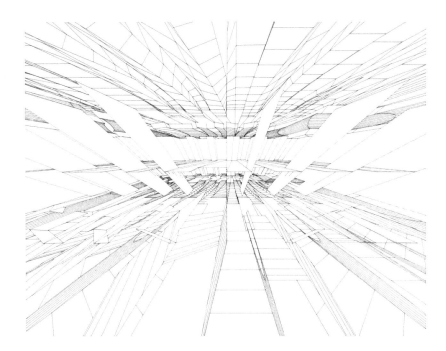

III

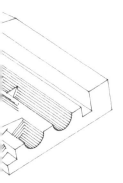

IV

Chapter 2
The Computer as a Design Tool

Essays

Case Studies

Architecture Goes Digital:
The Discrete

Mollie Claypool

This is an account of a broad narrative substantiating a contemporary architectural moment: that of the Discrete. The Discrete emphasizes part-to-part and part-to-whole relationships in the deployment and contextualization of architectural "wholes." As Daniel Köhler has written, the Discrete is derived from *mereology*[1] in philosophy, the theory of parthood, as well as discrete mathematical logics such as the use of numbers with distinct and separate values, which differs from the "smooth" mathematics of continuity such as calculus. The Discrete also utilizes a critique of matter, developed at the Massachusetts Institute of Technology by Professor Neil Gershenfeld, as having not yet been digital, as material is analog.[2]

The Discrete is inextricable to digital thinking, embedded in a discourse around the tools architects use, such as computer software and automated manufacturing technologies. Despite this connectedness to digital innovations, it has been argued by architect Gilles Retsin that it is via the Discrete that architecture is only now becoming digital[3]—almost eighty years after the invention of the first electronic computer. As this essay will show, core aspects of the Discrete that draw from computational developments such as notions of scalability, versatility, open-endedness, and distribution have existed within architectural production for decades. They are embedded within a history of architectural projects—both long past and very recent—that are disruptive of, but also contingent to, the changing relationships between people and capital, politics and space, domesticity and social practices fueled by ideology as well as innovation in computing and automated technologies.[4] To demonstrate how these relationships and concepts intertwined and contributed to the Discrete, I will situate the developments that have contributed to its emergence today between two distinct periods of time—the twentieth-century postwar period and the years after the 2008 financial crash—connected through dialogue around the role of computing technology with an economic and social project in architecture. I will articulate a history of Discrete part-to-whole relationships through the dissolving of architectural "wholes" into "frames," then "modules" and "surfaces," before reaching "parts." It is in "parts" that architecture goes digital.

A New Regime of Accumulation

The 1930s to 1950s was a period marked by social, economic, and political progress in relationship to the development of computing, associated mathematical and philosophical developments, and new manufacturing technologies. This moment cannot be extracted from the simultaneous invention and proliferation of new archetypical models for architectural production. These models were reliant on the articulation and provision of the "universal whole" as a mechanism for the provisioning of the welfare state within mid-twentieth-century capitalism. The Discrete has learned from this period of time, understanding that architecture can provide a platform for the expansion of a comprehensive social project.

The Discrete is also a response to, and critique of, the last two decades: a time of expanding computational power. Today, mere seconds of data processing equate to the labor of billions of human beings. This "end of modern science" outlined by architecture historian Mario Carpo, of understanding or truth enabled by observations of precedent and utilizing predictive modeling,[5] considers architectural production as an opportunity to completely rearticulate our current understandings of the relationship between labor and production in architecture and the built environment suitable for an age of automation.[6] This is, as one might imagine, a timely necessity. The asymmetrical hegemony of neoliberalism signified by the financial crash of 2008, and underpinned by the free market, deregulation, globalization, and corporatization since the 1970s and 1980s, is no longer sufficient. Accumulation for the sake of unlimited growth and productivity is inextricably bound to a continuation of capitalism, increasingly seen as creating financial instruments for the wealthy[7] and rapidly driving inequity through "top-down," "trickle-down" economics. This crisis of scarcity and abundance is ever more amplified by the ongoing climate emergency and our limitations in computing the consequences of this crisis in relationship to issues of social justice.[8] Architecture as a material hegemony has the opportunity—through catalyzing within its approach to design a social project that was lost in architecture utilizing mathematics and computational thinking in the late twentieth century and

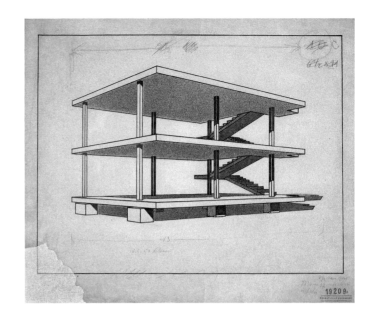

I   Maison Dom-ino, Le Corbusier, 1915

early twenty-first century—to be understood through positioning "emerging technologies as inaugurating a new regime of accumulation" rather than "continuing earlier regimes."[9]

Wholes

To contextualize this, a useful moment to go back to is over a hundred years ago. Oft presented as a disruptor of ideology, of history, and of precedent, the latency of Maison Dom-Ino (Le Corbusier, 1914) is contingent to technological innovation and discourse on the modernist ideological nature of a disciplinary social project. As a mechanism for the ordering and organizing of space and production, Maison Dom-Ino as a prototype was an embodiment of the rapid acceleration of technological progress due to twentieth-century militarization and symbolic of power relations within the production of the built environment ▶ Fig. I. The continued and undeniable presence of this archetype was enabled by changes in French governance that allowed its implementation at a large scale. Utilized across Europe and America, and later worldwide as a response to housing crises, it has formed much of the underlying rule set for the rationalization of relationships between architectural "parts" for mass-standardized production of architectural "wholes"—just six columns, three slabs, a staircase to make a "whole," which, combined, make larger wholes. Furthermore, the abstraction of architecture to the serialization of three different architectural parts that together constructed a prototypical, modular "whole" was made possible, as Pier Vittorio Aureli has written, "by a specific historical condition: the gradual transformation of life into economy and production."[10] As such, Maison Dom-Ino—a name derived either from the repeatable pattern-making game Domino or from a combination of *domus* (home) and *innovation*—embodied the techno-utopianism of industrial modernism in a time of postwar scarcity: efficient, universal, and abstract.

Frames

The inherent contradictions of this "whole" are apparent. Exposed in the section drawings are hollow tiles to be poured over with concrete on-site. The patent image, however, suggests an entirely prefabricated, mass-produced monolith.[11] In these images the new assembly line of the Taylorist factory had not yet entirely permeated architectural production. In fact, what Le Corbusier promised is no more than a "frame" through which architectural order of the postwar environment could be achieved on a mass scale. Nonetheless it is the visual description that has perpetuated a long-lasting image of an architectural archetype that is capable of becoming a tool of large-scale industrialization,[12] and thus automation—a totality, a "machine for living."[13] The mass standardization of building elements, and the possibility of prefabricating these elements in factories, recalibrated the production of architecture from the scale of the local or contextual to the precise, optimized

1   Daniel Köhler, *The Mereological City* (Bielefeld, Germany: transcript Verlag, 2016).
2   Neil Gershenfeld, "How to Make Almost Anything," *Foreign Affairs* 91, no. 6 (2012): 52.
3   Gilles Retsin, "Discrete and Digital," *TxA*, 2016.
4   Mollie Claypool, "Discrete Automation," *e-flux architecture*, 2019, accessed January 9, 2020, www.e-flux.com/architecture/becoming-digital/248060/discrete-automation/; Mollie Claypool, "From the Digital to the Discrete," *Proceedings of the 107th Annual Meeting of ACSpA*, 2019.
5   Mario Carpo, *The Second Digital Turn: Design beyond Intelligence* (Cambridge, MA: MIT Press, 2017), 33–40.
6   Mollie Claypool et. al., eds., *Robotic Building: Architecture in the Age of Automation* (Munich: Detail Edition, 2019).
7   Saskia Sassen, "Expanding the Terrain for Global Capital When Local Housing Becomes an Electronic Instrument," in *Subprime Cities: The Political Economy of Mortgage Markets*, ed. Manuel B. Aalbers (Oxford: Blackwell Publishing, 2012).
8   "Global Warming of 1.5°C," *IPCC Special Report*, 2019, accessed September 1, 2019, www.ipcc.ch/2019/.
9   Nick Srnicek, *Platform Capitalism* (Cambridge, UK: Polity Press, 2017), 7.
10 Pier Vittorio Aureli, "The Dom-ino Problem: Questioning the Architecture of Domestic Space," *Log*, no. 30 (Winter 2014): 155.
11 Le Corbusier, *Towards an Architecture*, 1923, 24.
12 Ibid., 236, 263.
13 Ibid., 4.

II   Maison Tropicale, Jean Prouvé, 1949–52

architectural coordination of a system for building able to be replicated across global contexts as a series of frames through which the world could be comprehended.

Le Corbusier was not alone in this search for an architecture that could bring together both the singularity of technological progress and the necessity of social unification at a time when the image of architecture that had existed previously was deemed wholly insufficient in the face of widespread postwar devastation. Hyper-rationalized architectural systems such as Walter Gropius and Adolf Meyer's "Big Construction Kit" (1923), Buckminster Fuller's notion of "doing more with less" most exemplified in *Nine Chains to the Moon* (1938) and the Dymaxion Deployment Unit exhibited at the Museum of Modern Art in 1941, the system of standardized steel component–based assembly of the Eames House (1949) by Charles and Ray Eames, or Jean Prouvé's three prototypes developed under the umbrella of Maison Tropicale (1949–51) were also created in the same period, with similar intentions of scalability and wide distribution across contexts ▶ Fig. II. In these moments the architect became the facilitator of the beginning of a process of reproduction, concerned with architecture's function as pure structure. Domestic space became a scaffold for projection, where the space for design was relegated to the "frame," to everything beyond the coordination of predetermined modular, structural "wholes." The total machine for living was a space of abstracted, ambiguous potential. This enabled the customization of the hung facade within the universal structural frame according to stylistic, aesthetic, or contextual concerns.[14] It was now the space for the reproduction of life itself—according to technological progress[15]—to be instantiated and imagined further into the domestic sphere, framed, or even gridded.

Modules

It is not by chance that the wide deployment of mass-produced and mass-standardized "modular" systems in the latter half of the twentieth century coincided with the development of early computing systems and automation technologies in the 1940s and 1950s.

Modular architectural syntax learned from the possibilities afforded by systematizing the organization of data and information during this period of expansion in early computing and cybernetic theory. This is found in the work of Claude Shannon ("A Mathematical Theory of Communication," 1948), John von Neumann ("The General and Logical Theory of Automata," 1948), William Grey Walter ("An Imitation of Life," 1950), and Norbert Wiener (*Cybernetics: Or Control and Communication in the Animal and the Machine*, 1948) as well as in earlier developments in manufacturing technologies in the 1900s, such as the linearity proposed by the assembly line.

Promising an optimized system of coordination of modules embedded in principles from early computing such as the notion of the "black-box" module masking internal processes, connectivity interfaces for the transposition of information, and "plug and play" systems, modularity proposed a solution to a modern scenario: the postwar crisis of architecture in an age of mass production. Each module is a complete whole, and is reliant on the supposition of a larger, more unifying whole, as a means of "confronting and managing complexity in a [...] systemic context."[16] Perhaps the most important example relating to the Discrete is the four-inch cubic standardized module outlined in *The Evolving House* (1936) by Alfred Bemis, which proposed a system of ideological management and coordination of parts at every scale of building ▶ Fig. III. Yet Bemis's argument existed in a period when methods of organizing architectural production were not as intelligent as the module itself. When scaled up, the module, like the frame, continues the redistribution of the function of structure to points rather than along a line. In this, modular architecture can become open-ended in terms of context, needing merely to "touch down" to be located. Its most important relationship is to the next module that it meets within the larger, economizing whole. The module must always have the same orientation in its repetition, and thus tends to have a relatively homogeneous distribution, as demonstrated in many projects throughout the twentieth century, including Yona Friedman's Spatial City (1959–60), Moshe Safdie's Habitat 67 (1967), or Kisho Kurokawa's Nakagin Capsule Tower (1972).

Aureli has written that "architecture became form devoid of any references outside itself at the moment it was fully conquered by the

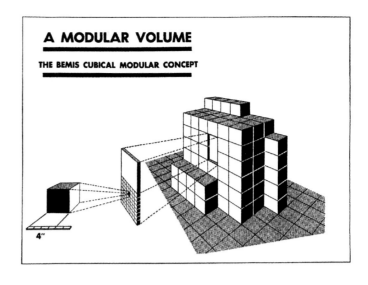

III Alfred Bemis's four-inch cubical modular concept
for housing, 1936

forces of industrialisation."[17] The utmost efficiency of the module set the seed for what came next: a well-publicized story of the questioning and downfall of modernist, standardized modular systems—of ideal and exact geometries—and indeed the eventual "death" of modern architecture delivered by the demolition of Pruitt–Igoe in St. Louis, Missouri, in 1972.[18] Parallel to the demise of the welfare state and rise of neoliberalism, its failure resulted in the projection of a transhistorical collective approach via analytical formalism[19] fading quickly from view. This happened just as the apolitical diversity inherent to the predominance of the "collage approach"[20] began to meet the potentialities presented by nonstandard digital mass customization. In its reduction of context, style, or aesthetics to the surface between points held in the frame of a larger whole, modularity must be seen as an actor in the rise of the contemporary surface of capital-driven "parametric design," where the exuberance of form relates to the maximum efficiency of available resources.

Surfaces

An antidote to modernism's failure, the "animation" of architectural form was made possible in the late 1980s and 1990s through engagement with new kinds of digital modeling and digital manufacturing technologies from aeronautical, naval, and automobile industries. The smoothing of the composite curve—composed of an array of circular segments—of industrial modernism was transformed into the Bézier, or spline, curve of calculus.[21] This was adopted by the architects of, as Mario Carpo designated, the "first digital turn," such as Greg Lynn, Frank Gehry, Reiser + Umemoto, Foreign Office Architects, and Bernard Cache.[22] The functionalism and structuralism of the previous "mathematics" of architecture found in the grids of Le Corbusier or Mies van der Rohe was abandoned for, as Lynn outlined in Animate Form (1998), the "free"[23] geometries found in continuous, calculus-based mathematics. In this model, the differentiation of points along a line constructs a smooth surface of "instanced" configurations, an "envelope of potential"[24] that was later referred to by architect and theorist Philippe Morel as a "logical figuration,"[25] one of an "inexact" tectonics.

This Big Data–based approach of infinite variability was suitable for the increasing degrees of computational power throughout the 1990s and 2000s, as computers were beginning to be able to "predict without understanding,"[26] thereby outperforming human capacity for calculating the best outcomes given inputted design parameters in the shortest period of time. Yet "digital design" and "parametric design" are bound to a mathematics of theoretical infiniteness, and, as Antoine Picon notes, "considering relations that can be far more abstract than what [...] design [...] usually entails."[27] Furthermore, as Lynn outlined in his essay "Architectural Curvilinearity" in 1993, this was a radical departure from the "conflict and contradiction" of earlier work around Deconstructivism, toward a "more fluid logic of connectivity."[28] Explored primarily through principles of "folding" inspired by the mathematics of Leibniz and the philosophy in Deleuze's work The Fold (1988), a logic of connectivity is a significant departure from the discreteness of the "whole" module and the Cartesian grid. Utilizing morphodynamic principles appropriated from topology, a

14 Antoine Picon, "Dom-ino: Archetype and Fiction," Log, no. 30 (Winter 2014): 169–75.
15 Beatriz Colomina, Domesticity at War (Cambridge, MA: MIT Press, 2006).
16 Andrew Russell, "Modularity: An Interdisciplinary History of an Ordering Concept," Information & Culture 47, no. 3 (Austin: University of Texas Press, 2012): 258.
17 Aureli, "The Dom-ino Problem," 154.
18 Charles Jencks, The Language of Post-Modern Architecture (New York: Rizzoli, 1977), 7.
19 Colin Rowe, "The Mathematics of the Ideal Villa," Architectural Review, March 1947, 101–4.
20 Colin Rowe and Fred Koetter, Collage City (Cambridge, MA: MIT Press, 1978).
21 Greg Lynn, Animate Form (New York: Princeton Architectural Press, 1999).
22 Mario Carpo, The Digital Turn in Architecture (Hoboken, NJ: John Wiley & Sons, 2012).
23 Greg Lynn, Folds, Bodies and Blobs: Collected Essays (Brussels: La Lettre volée, 1998), 202.
24 Lynn, Animate Form.
25 Philippe Morel, "Sense and Sensibilia," Architectural Design 81, no. 4 (2011): 125.
26 Carpo, The Second Digital Turn, 67
27 Antoine Picon, "Architecture and Mathematics: Between Hubris and Restraint," Architectural Design 81, no. 4 (2011): 35.
28 Greg Lynn, "Architectural Curvilinearity," Folding in Architecture (Hoboken, NJ: John Wiley & Sons, 1993).

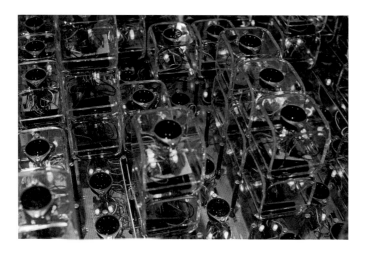

IV   Universal Constructor, John Frazer, 1990

branch of mathematics, the complex forms designed by architects using digital design tools during this period were conceptually, as Branko Kolarevic has highlighted, "less about spatial distinctions and more about spatial relations."[29] Yet the isolation of a building's structure and facade enabled by the development of the earlier steel frame and reinforced prefabricated concrete systems, as described above, meant that topological structures were often misinterpreted as curved surfaces, rather than a more holistic representation of "performative circumstances"[30] that included a design's material culture and production. And so the potential of the surface became a space of affect, perception, and the experiential, emphasizing the subjective appearance of form as a mediator between interior and exterior.

This misunderstanding by the architects of the early digital period resulted in the separation of architectural representation from forms of production. The complexity of a surface—typically a building's skin—existed in conflict with processes of materialization and was incompatible with mass production technologies that promised more efficient production chains. This is because automated mass production relied on the efficiencies of standardized, serialized repetitive actions, and here variant surfaces messily confronted physical reality. While some architects, such as Bernard Cache, attempted to resolve this dichotomy through direct engagement with the constraints of digital mass manufacturing technologies, such as the computer-numerical controlled (CNC) machine, to explore the potential of a digital continuum[31] or the relationship of manufacturing data to create nonstandard architectural objects—or objectiles,[32] as Cache and his partner Patrick Beaucé called these objects—these processes were not able to be easily scaled.

The construction industry has been slow to digitize its processes. This resistance to digitization required that the possibilities afforded by the surfaces of the 2000s were "post-rationalized"—sliced into panels, ribs, and waffles—in order to be realized using existing construction technologies. This extended production chains and vastly resulted in bespoke, "one-off," iconic pieces of architecture that required large amounts of capital to be realized, best exemplified by the Guggenheim Bilbao by Gehry Partners,

the Yokohama International Port Terminal by Foreign Office Architects, or the Mercedes Benz Museum by UN Studio. Postrationalization thus becomes about maintaining an efficiency of resources, of capital, in relation to an exuberance of form. The surface became an instrument of capital, symbolic of wealth and ideology[33] that supported the "trickle" of the top-down capitalist market, a centralizing regime of accumulation. The failure of the surface as a radical embodiment of the age of expanding computational power can be traced to the 2008 financial crash, when architecture and construction was brought almost to a standstill. It is here that the potential of the digital in architecture began to be rearticulated by a new generation of architects and designers.

Parts (Architecture Goes Digital)

The recession that followed the 2008 crash brought to the forefront of the architectural community the capacity for digital innovation to be completely subsumed by capital. In the public realm the "digital" in architecture began to be synonymous with asymmetries in power and the inequities that emerged from the failures of capitalism.[34] As has been pointed out by Peter Frase's[35] analysis of the relationship of computing, automation, and scientific progress, the way we construct society has traditionally seen these processes—and the inequities they produce[36]—as inevitabilities rather than choices a society makes. As such, the digital and automation are a design problem,[37] not just a technical solution to be commodified. The power of computation lies not just in the tools we use but in how and why and for what they are used. Architectural production, as it stands, is highly analog; new models for how architecture can come closer to the digital ubiquity of the contemporary world are necessary. To catalyze this "conceptual leap"[38] in architectural production, a radical departure from earlier approaches to the digital in architecture has begun, from the parts that make up architecture, up.

A parts-to-whole approach learns from the misunderstandings of topology embedded in earlier digital architecture. It looks back to the work of Julia and John Frazer (Universal Constructor,

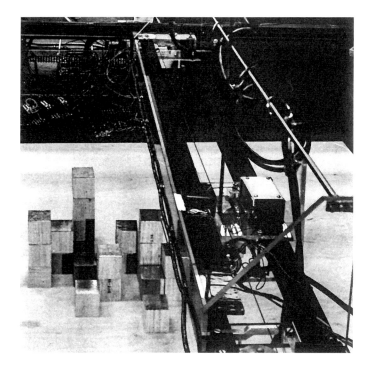

V   SEEK, Nicholas Negroponte, 1970

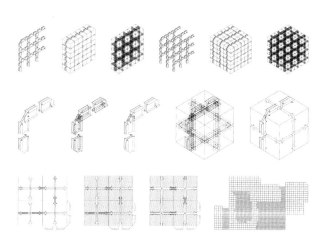

VI   Universal House, Philippe Morel, 2002

1990) ▶ Fig. IV and Nicholas Negroponte (SEEK, 1970) ▶ Fig. V, who understood spatial relations not through how they appear on curvilinear surfaces but through the relationships established between discrete volumes in assembly, described later as voxels, or three-dimensional pixels. Voxels can, just like pixels, be "coded" much like the 0s and 1s of computer code. "Based on [discrete] parts that are as accessible and versatile as digital data," Gilles Retsin has written that the Discrete "offers the greatest promise for a complex yet scalable open-ended and distributed architecture."[39] A "fully generic and voxel-based architecture," as demonstrated in early Discrete projects such as Universal House and Assembly Element (2004) ▶ Fig. VI and Computational Chair (2006) ▶ Fig. VII by Philippe Morel and EZCT Architecture & Design Research, utilizes a "constructive" approach, bringing parts, and their assembly, in line with available forms of automation for manufacturing—in this case the CNC machine. Similarly, François Roche's Olzweg (2006) embeds the way in which a building is constructed into the very center of the project, with industrial robotic arms on a gantry reorganizing voxelized space in real time.

Part-to-whole thinking was further supported by a critique of Lynn's spline curve as a space of potential animation of architecture. This was first done by Daniel Köhler in his Mereological Line (2016), and then by Gilles Retsin's Discrete Curve (2016) ▶ Fig. VIII. By imagining the line comprising "bits," like computer data or in discrete mathematics, rather than "weights" reliant on the entire figuration of a spline, a new negotiation between part-to-parts and parts-to-wholes in architecture was enabled. Furthermore, serialized mass production was reimagined not through creating variable nonstandard parts to compose differentiated surfaces, contributing to long production chains, but through designing self-similar parts using combinatoric principles. This enabled parts to combine in assembly and, as in the case of Bloom (2012) by Jose Sanchez and Alisa

29   Branko Kolarevic, *Architecture in the Digital Age: Design and Manufacturing* (London: Taylor & Francis, 2004), 8.

30   Ibid.

31   Ibid., 10.

32   Bernard Cache, *Earth Moves: The Furnishing of Territories* (Cambridge, MA: MIT Press, 1995).

33   Douglas Spencer, *The Architecture of Neoliberalism* (London: Bloomsbury, 2016).

34   Rowan Moore, "Zaha Hadid: Queen of the Curve," *Guardian*, September 8, 2013, www.theguardian.com/artanddesign/2013/sep/08/zaha-hadid-serpentine-sackler-profile.

35   Peter Frase, *Four Futures: Life after Capitalism* (London: Verso, 2016), 14–15.

36   Ruha Benjamin, *Race after Technology: Abolitionist Tools for the New Jim Code* (Cambridge, UK: Polity Press, 2019); Virginia Eubanks, *Automating Inequality: How High-Tech Tools Profile, Police, and Punish the Poor* (New York: St. Martin's Press, 2018).

37   Claypool, *Robotic Building*.

38   Philippe Morel, "Computation or Revolution," *Architectural Design* 84, no. 3 (2014): 76–87.

39   Gilles Retsin, "Bits and Pieces," *Architectural Design* 89, no. 2 (2019); Gilles Retsin, *Discrete: Reappraising the Digital in Architecture* (Hoboken, NJ: John Wiley & Sons, 2019).

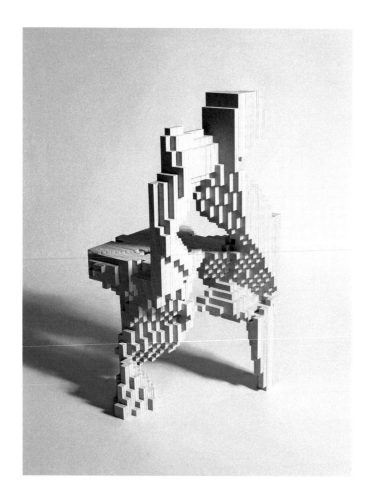

VII Computational Chair, EZCT Architecture & Design
Research, 2006

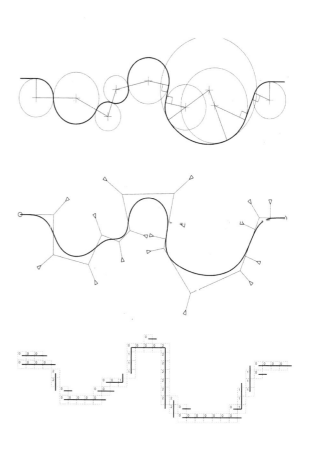

VIII Continuous versus Discrete Curve, Gilles Retsin, 2016

Andrasek, through processes of game play, rather than in strictly prescribed design outcomes.[40] A single part's geometry could be embedded with tectonic and spatial agency.

It has been argued by Sanchez, myself, and others[41] that, in its scalability and versatility, as a framework the Discrete can provide a model for architecture suitable for a postcapitalist economy that localizes and decentralizes production as a means of dealing with issues of scarcity and the resultant inequity. Part-to-whole relationships customized in assembly, or through their "composition" as Köhler has argued,[42] enable a rearticulation away from a modernist, deterministic, and hierarchical ontology that relies on the imposition of prescriptive totalities which conceal the larger economy of production that constructs them. In a Discrete ecology the meaning and value of the relationships between different agents emerges through their appearance rather than a top-down approach, as an accumulation of self-similar parts into heterogeneous assemblies, over time. This suggests a new understanding of the ecology between things, where the relationship between individuals, society, and nature[43] should not be fixed or predetermined through top-down universalism. It also distributes the potential of what form architecture takes into the process of making and unmaking, through social engagement and participation by users who impart their own understanding and values into how parts come together, informing and deforming possible outcomes.

Architectural "wholes" are accumulations of autonomous parts into heterogeneous assemblies, emerging through action, of appearance, in different contexts ▶ Fig. IX. The role of the architect becomes one of facilitation of a framework of production, linking the digital tools for design and fabrication in a way that makes them accessible. In this "new regime of accumulation" the Discrete presents a notion of how a new understanding of part relations—tectonic, spatial, social, economic, material—in architecture can catalyze production away from the failures presented by the deterministic and hierarchical architectural ontology that persisted well into the twenty-first century. In its attention to part-to-part and part-to-whole relationships rather than "whole-to-part" or "top-down" frameworks, the Discrete is prospective, open-ended, and anticipatory rather than prescriptive and closed.

40 Jose Sanchez and Alisa Andrasek, "Bloom—The Game," FABRICATE 2014, 2014.
41 Jose Sanchez, "Post-Capitalist Design: Design in the Age of Access," in Parametric Tendencies & Design Agencies, ed. David Gerber, 2014; Mollie Claypool, "Our Automated Future: A Discrete Framework for the Production of Housing," Jose Sanchez, "Architecture for the Commons: Participatory Systems in the Age of Platforms," and Gilles Retsin, "Bits and Pieces," Architectural Design 89, no. 2 (2019).
42 Köhler, 2010.
43 Ibid.

IX INT (Zoey Tan, Claudia Tanskanen, Qianyi Li, Xiaolin
Yin), Research Cluster 4, Design Computation Lab,
The Bartlett School of Architecture, UCL, 2016

Creativity and Problem-Solving: Tracing the Stakes of Computer-Aided Design

Molly Wright Steenson

Creative means "inventive, imaginative; of, relating to, displaying, using, or involving imagination or original ideas," according to the *Oxford English Dictionary*.[1] From the mid-1950s to the 1970s, the question of creativity—through inventiveness, imagination, or originality—was at the center of debates about architecture and computation. As computers developed into machines capable of representing and generating design solutions, architects questioned the ramifications for the design process and what it might mean for the human aspects of creativity. At the same time, working with a computer required the architect to conceive of design problems in the computer's terms. The design process was predicated on problem-solving, on the notion that design could be viewed as a problem to set up and solve. What would happen to the very notion of design if it were relegated to a computer's problem-solving methods? If a computer could produce novel, creative solutions, would it detract from the ingenuity of its human user? What were the stakes of computational creativity in architecture?

My aim in this essay is to trace the contours of creativity and problem-solving in architecture, drawing a broad path around the development of computer-aided design from the 1950s to the 1970s. My argument will touch on debates emerging from the work of Douglas Ross and Steven Coons in the CAD Project at MIT, methods of problem statements through heuristic reasoning used by architects and computational researchers alike, and Stanford Anderson's notion of "problem-worrying," a challenge to the predominant uses of problem-solving. These questions were of interest not only to architects but also to researchers in computation and artificial intelligence who thought that design and architecture might unlock promising and demanding uses for computation. In the mid-1970s architects including Cedric Price and John and Julia Frazer used the computer as a means of provoking the architect and suggesting new approaches to design, turning the previous framing of computer aids to design on its head. Rather than obviating the creativity of the architect, Price and the Frazers offered a new way of conceiving of the designer and user—and perhaps of creativity in general, with implications for the contemporary moment.

Nouns, Verbs, and Problems

In the late 1950s and early 1960s, computers were rare and very expensive, sometimes as costly as commercial airliners. Few architects had access to computers and the ones who did first used them for quantitative purposes that were easily adaptable to architecture. Until computers were designed to accommodate multiple, simultaneous users in a relatively responsive fashion in the early 1960s, they could not be widely used outside engineering or large-scale corporate contexts, which meant that more creative uses for computers were not on the table until computer systems offered representational capabilities at a lower cost to more users. In these early days, architectural and engineering firms and academic researchers turned their attention to areas in which computing would provide the greatest return, such as computer programs that defined functional requirements, analyzed data, performed engineering calculations, provided metadata for projects, and calculated costs.[2] Examples here include Skidmore, Owings & Merrill's computerized specification system, engineering calculations for the John Hancock Tower in Chicago, and Bolt, Beranek and Newman's programming of hospital space using a computer, as well as the concept of "automatic data processing" (ADP).[3]

The Computer-Aided Design (CAD) Project at MIT, led by Douglas Ross and Steven Coons between 1959 and 1970, explored systems that could carry out design processes ▶ Fig. I. Their perspectives on automation and augmentation represented sides of a philosophical debate about what creativity was, what was human about creativity, and what the computer could enable.[4] CAD Project researchers outfitted time-shared computers with input/output devices such as oscilloscopes, cathode-ray tubes, and light pens that allowed a user to "draw" and perform transformations of these drawings. Coons served as an adviser (along with Claude Shannon and Marvin Minsky) on Ivan Sutherland's dissertation, Sketchpad, the first interactive graphics system. The next version, Sketchpad 3, which could calculate and render three-dimensional shapes, was developed in the CAD Project by Timothy Johnson. The CAD Project itself grew out of several initiatives at MIT, including Project MAC and the Semi-Automatic Ground Environment Program (SAGE),

I   Steven Coons and Douglas Ross in a CAD Project
    meeting at MIT, 1962

and the Servomechanism Lab.[5] Ross came from the Servo Lab, which developed tools for automated milling of engineered metal shapes (such as for aircraft parts). The system for numerical control was encoded on punched paper tape; the milling machine read this and then followed the instructions in order to mill these geometries. The production of these instructions on tape was arduous, however, and Ross developed the Automated Programming Tool (APT) computer language in 1956 that automated this process (carrying forward the research at the Electronic Systems Lab, or ESL, as the Servo Lab was renamed in 1959). The APT used a conceptual representation called the "plex" that referred to variables such as x, y coordinates for lines. Plexes could potentially be used for many design problems. "Beyond its partial implementation into an operable software system, the *plex* construct synthesized a fledgling philosophy of design and manufacturing linked to software construction. This philosophy sought to take problems from the messy worlds of materials in the machine shop into the clean worlds of symbolic abstraction in computer code," writes Daniel Cardoso Llach.[6] For Ross, the computer code became the symbolic representation of design; he envisioned computers as "universal tools able to fully automate design."[7]

Coons, a mechanical engineer, was interested in practical use cases and applications for computers in design. He saw computers as augmenting the capabilities of their users in the design process—not automating design, but working in conjunction with users and taking over the drudgery. When a designer approaches a design problem, he or she does not yet know the particulars of what will be designed, and begins a process of discovery that is "interspersed with long periods of rote behavior—sheer unadulterated dull work—noncreative but necessary," Coons wrote in 1966.[8] Why not relegate this work to a computer? In the early 1960s, he called this a master–slave relationship (a troubling term). By 1966, he instead highlighted how a time-shared computer would interact with the user: "the designer can sit with the computer, 'holding its hand' [...] and talk to it, while the computer will seem to pay attention only to him," although it would nearly simultaneously be able to perform other tasks for users while it "held hands" with the user in question.[9]

1   "creative, adj." OED Online (Oxford University Press, September 2019), accessed November 3, 2019, oed-com.proxy.library.cmu.edu/view/Entry/44072.
2   Boston Architectural Center, *Architecture and the Computer: First Boston Architectural Center Conference* (Boston, MA: Boston Architectural Center, 1964), 2.
3   Ibid.
4   Daniel Cardoso Llach, *Builders of the Vision: Software and the Imagination of Design* (London: Routledge, 2015), 54.
5   Karl Wildes and Nilo Lindgren, *A Century of Electrical Engineering and Computer Science at MIT, 1882–1982* (Cambridge, MA: MIT Press, 1985), 348.
6   Cardoso Llach, *Builders of the Vision*, 44.
7   Ibid., 53.
8   Steven A. Coons, "Computer-Aided Design," *Design Quarterly* 66/67 (1966): 7.
9   Ibid., 8.

Computers required architects to format what they wanted to do in terms of a problem to solve. Coons used the language of problem-solving and heuristic reasoning, as did many of his contemporaries, echoing George Pólya's *How to Solve It*, an elegant book about teaching students to solve math problems that had far-reaching consequences on operations research, cognitive psychology, the foundations of artificial intelligence, and evidently Coons's thoughts on the design process.[10] Problems are about discovery, or "heuristics," as Pólya writes, which means "serving to discover."[11] As rules of thumb that scaffold a problem, heuristic reasoning invokes "provisional and plausible" approaches to problems.[12] This reasoning unfolded over four key steps to solving a problem: "Understanding the Problem," "Devising a Plan," "Carrying Out the Plan," and "Looking Back"—the first two steps of which were the most involved and correlated to the design process.[13]

For Coons, heuristic reasoning became a foundational approach to solving problems that could then be augmented by a computer to take up the repetitive tasks. Coons echoed Pólya's terminology in his description of common design processes. "This design process unfolds something like this: at the beginning, in the design of a device or system (be it a motion picture projector, an airplane, an automobile, or a battleship), the designer does not have a very clear notion of what he wants to do," Coons wrote. "He has only a vague concept, or none at all, of how he will go about accomplishing his task. In this sense, the design process is a learning process during which the designer must learn what the problem is and how to solve it."[14] The curious perspective that engages a problem-solver in the process of discovery, of moving from unknowns to knowns, and in seeking applications to other kinds of problems, is at the heart of heuristic reasoning. For Coons, this is where design is born. "The typically human aspect of the design process is invention: the grasping of schemes that are at the beginning vague, tenuous, dream-like, and solidifying them into something tangible that can be looked at, explored qualitatively, and evaluated quantitatively," he wrote.[15] The difference between Ross's and Coons's approaches could be likened to whether design was viewed as a "noun" or a "verb." As Cardoso Llach writes, in Ross's ESL team, "design was understood as a noun: a geometric specification that

could be calculated and in fact manufactured if the design problem was adequately represented in a formal [...] language. In contrast, for the experienced designers from the Design and Graphics Division, design was more of a verb: an open-ended and essentially human activity."[16] The noun makes the work of the computer the completed object, whereas the verb opens up the computer to broader possibilities of creativity.

Architecture and the Computer

The fault lines of the debate about architects and computer creativity were fully on display at the 1964 Architecture and the Computer conference, whose speakers grappled with the effects of computing on architecture, engineering, and their related fields ▶ Fig. II. The computer could be creative, architects claimed, but only to a point. Engineers and scientists argued that the computer could play a sizable creative role, and it needn't render the architect obsolete. The stakes were evident: architects didn't want to lose their claim on their expertise, and engineers argued that computers would soon be able to do more creative work than they were doing at the time. The speakers included Steven Coons, Ivan Sutherland, Serge Chermayeff, Marvin Minsky, Christopher Alexander, and a statement read on behalf of Walter Gropius, who was too infirm to attend.

What was unique to the architect in an age of computers? Architects provided an "expression of cultural experience" in the ways that they set up problems and exercised judgment. They explored "visual relationships and phenomena," which they expressed in formal terms. "The architect is an artist whose brain serves as the ultimate computer, programmed by years of experience and sensitivity to visual phenomena," said conference chair Sanford Greenfield in his introduction to the conference. This acuity led to the eventual forms that an architect would define, and the architect's carefully honed intuition would determine "the aesthetically correct solution."[17] Intrinsic to architectural expertise was intuition, sensitivity, sensory engagement, societal and cultural situatedness, aesthetic sense, tradition, and sophistication, gained through education,

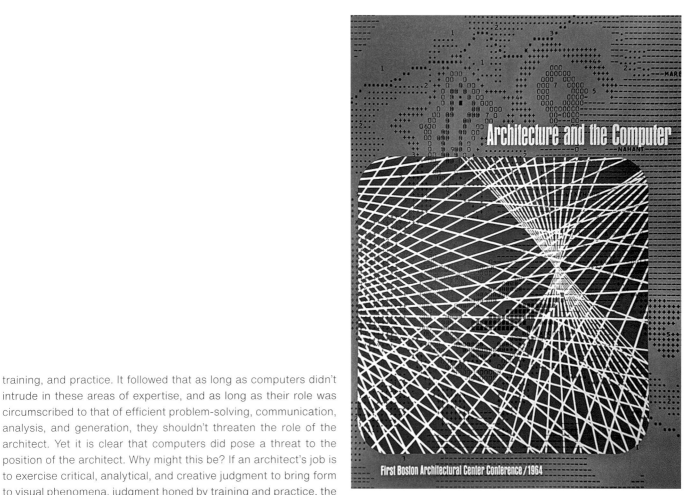

II Cover of Architecture and the Computer proceedings from the 1964 conference hosted by the Boston Architectural Center

training, and practice. It followed that as long as computers didn't intrude in these areas of expertise, and as long as their role was circumscribed to that of efficient problem-solving, communication, analysis, and generation, they shouldn't threaten the role of the architect. Yet it is clear that computers did pose a threat to the position of the architect. Why might this be? If an architect's job is to exercise critical, analytical, and creative judgment to bring form to visual phenomena, judgment honed by training and practice, the computer had its place. But if the role of the architect was defined by tools and practices such as drawing and modeling, then the computer certainly called into question the architect's expertise.

The computer required a stock-taking of what architectural expertise was. Walter Gropius's opening statement situated computing within a history of mechanization, in the sense that Sigfried Giedion had conceived of it in *Mechanization Takes Command*. "It will certainly be up to us architects to make use of them intelligently as means of superior mechanical control which might provide us with ever-greater freedom for the creative process of design," he wrote.[18] What Gropius couldn't envision was the daily applicability of the tool. Would it require a new kind of architectural education, based on the formulation of problems for a computer? (Maybe it would.) As Chermayeff said in a panel that followed his lunchtime presentation, "It is not in the least interesting to put this marvelous machinery to use in order to find out how to do things. It is infinitely more significant to find out why we should do anything at all."[19]

Coons poked fun at the stereotypes of how designers and engineers viewed design; one can imagine him teasing his colleague Douglas Ross. "Engineers tend to like to think that the design process is entirely rational, and they tend to minimize and ignore the creative process as though it were something slightly immoral. Engineers prefer to replace all black arts, necromancy, and art itself with science and scientific method," he said. "On the contrary, many architects, and the archetypical members of their coterie, artists, use the word 'design' to mean only the innovative, generative, intuitive acts of conception," leaving out other concerns such as structures, heat flow, and the like.[20]

Minsky, on the other hand, saw new kinds of opportunities for architecture and computing in the long term that could reframe the questions before the Architecture and the Computer audience. "[...] In no more than 30 years, computers may be as intelligent, or more intelligent, than people," he said. Machines would be able to do the full assembly (as we now see in robotics) of objects if not buildings, computers would employ scanners for reading drawings, and all of this would happen at great speed and low cost, he predicted. "Contractors will have to face automation in construction just as the architects will have to face automation of design. Eventually, I believe computers will evolve formidable creative capacity."[21] That last sentence might explain why Minsky found architecture productive and useful for problems of artificial intelligence.

10 AI luminaries such as Allen Newell and Marvin Minsky cited the importance of *How to Solve It* for their work. Pólya's book still proves influential today.
11 George Pólya, *How to Solve It: A New Aspect of Mathematical Method* (Princeton, NJ: Princeton University Press, 1945), 113.
12 Ibid.
13 Ibid., xvi–xvii.
14 Coons, "Computer-Aided Design," 7.
15 Ibid.
16 Cardoso Llach, *Builders of the Vision*, 58.
17 Boston Architectural Center, *Architecture and the Computer*, xi.
18 Ibid., 41.
19 Ibid., 48.
20 Ibid., 26.
21 Ibid., 45.

When creativity met communication and analysis, new modes of interacting with computers would emerge—what J.C.R. Licklider called "man-computer symbiosis" in 1960, nearly five years prior to the Architecture and the Computer conference. Licklider wrote, "The hope is that, in not too many years, human brains and computing machines will be coupled together very tightly, and that the resulting partnership will think as no human brain has ever thought and process data in a way not approached by the information-handling machines we know today."[22] These were the very ideas that Coons wanted to build into computer-aided design systems as well—namely, that humans and computers might come together to produce new ways of creating. And for the purposes of engineering researchers in burgeoning fields such as artificial intelligence, the creative use of computers by architects and designers would necessitate more computing power—which people including Minsky and Licklider were very eager to develop.

Problem-Worrying and Other Subversions

Architecture in computing presumed that it could be framed as a problem to solve. There is, of course, a question of whether problem-*solving* at all is the proper approach. Should an architect or designer go looking for problems? Do they run the risk of the "if you have a hammer, everything looks like a nail" bias? Stanford Anderson, professor of architectural history at MIT, warned in 1966 that architects' interest in problem-solving might be an attempt to evade criticism and instead offer ways for architects to justify their work *post facto*. "The ideas of problem-solving which have recently interested architects are involved with either problems of achieving definite goals or else with problems of synthesizing from a body of established facts," he told an audience at Cranbrook. "Because of these characteristics of either definite goal orientation or inductivism, these notions of problem-solving are neither descriptive of the traditional behavior of the best architects nor applicable to the current problem situation of architecture."[23] Rather than problem-solve, why not "problem-worry," as Anderson called it? The problems of designing for humans in the built environment do

not fit readily into predetermined goal orientations. "If this interpretation of the architectural problem situation is correct, any problem-solving technique that relies on explicit problem definitions or distinct goal-orientation will distort the human purposes involved," he said.[24] The work of the architect is much different from that of an engineer and thus doesn't fit into most methods in computer-related problem-solving. To fit design into such a mold would be to cut it off from what an architect learns throughout the design process. Induction doesn't provide adequate data, Anderson argued, and "the process of creative design is artificially simplified in order that it may be viewed more systematically," he said.[25] Anderson's problem-worrying might be closer to the second step in *How to Solve It*, "Devising a Plan"—because, as Anderson puts it, "the strongest and most flexible rational system available is to give the creative person free reign subject only to responsible, reasonable, and sensitive self-criticism and the public tests of performance and criticism [...]. Growth of architectural learning and practice calls for a relentless rational and sensible criticism that 'worries' the problem, striving for a better problem—especially a better problem—and then also for a relation of problem and form that is resistant to criticism."[26] Could problem-worrying open up a role for critique in architecture in the design processes that Coons and others were investigating? Perhaps it would incorporate possibilities for architectural expertise and reflection that might otherwise go missing within computer-aided design systems. It would still be necessary to use problem-solving framing for design problems, but problem-worrying opened design problems up to other kinds of teasing, even if worrying didn't solve them.
Cedric Price and John and Julia Frazer, inspired by and in collaboration with cybernetician Gordon Pask, subverted the questions of what computer-aided design was meant to do.[27] They issued a different challenge: How could a computer alter the relationship between the designer/architect and the design process? How could the subversions be useful for changing not only what could be designed but what the design process could be altogether? Price believed that architecture should be contingent, adaptive, unfixed. While he didn't use computer-aided design programs, he incorporated ideas from cybernetics and information systems in his

projects to support possibilities for continual change in architecture and learning for his users. As Royston Landau wrote, Price used technology to provoke: the purpose of technology was "to take part in the architectural debate, perhaps through contribution, disputation, or the ability to shock."[28] These themes were steady throughout Price's career across a wide variety of projects, among them the Fun Palace, a massive cybernetic frame for leisure and theater that he designed with director Joan Littlewood; Oxford Corner House, a four-story news and information hub with hydraulic floors in central London; Generator, which was touted as the first intelligent building; and the Inter-Action Centre, which was built starting in 1973 and demolished in 2003. Price's fax machine allegedly never worked, but his incorporation of information technology served to expand the possibilities for architecture and interaction.

Price's Generator project (1976–79) put this notion to the test. In 1976, Price was hired by paper executive and arts patron Howard Gilman to design an art retreat center in northern Florida. Composed of a set of twelve-foot-by-twelve-foot cubes on a grid that could be moved by mobile cranes, and a kit of parts that included barriers and walkways for movement and encounters ▶ Fig. III–IV, Generator was a recombinable architectural project that allowed its users to change their minds to suit whatever activities they desired. But how to encourage Generator's users to make changes to it?

Two years into the project, in 1978, Price recruited John and Julia Frazer, programmer/architects, to take up this challenge. They proposed a suite of computer programs and microcontrollers that would be attached to Generator's components to support the design of new plans: an inventory program and architect program, which together knew the status of Generator's elements and how they could be combined, and a physical modeling kit that plotted and rendered onscreen the plan in action (what the Frazers referred to as the "intelligent beermat"). "The computer program is not merely a passive computer-aided design program nor is it just being used to assist with the organization of the site, but is being used to actively encourage continual change and adaptation to changing requirements […]. In a sense the building can be described as being literally 'intelligent,'" the Frazers wrote.[29]

To this end, they proposed the "Boredom Program." In the event that Generator's users had not requested adequate changes, Generator would learn from its previous successful programs and come up with "unsolicited plans and improvements," in an early architectural application of machine learning. The Boredom Program tips its hat to Pask's Musicolour Machine, which responded with movement and light to a musician playing with it. If the music got too repetitive, the sculpture got bored and stopped responding. Similarly, if Generator's users became too complacent, Generator would redesign itself. Boredom, something that might typically be considered the most passive of all responses, became the impetus for change, and the fact that Generator's boredom could spur change demonstrated its intelligence. "It was felt that Generator should not be dependent entirely on the users for instigating the reorganization of the site but should have a mind of its own," the Frazers wrote.

Generator presents a challenge in a world of programs that do their users' bidding. "If you kick a system, the very least you would expect is that it would kick you back," the Frazers wrote to Price.[30] Not only does intelligence mean boredom, it means attitude, responsiveness, countermeasure. John Frazer wrote a postscript by hand on a letter to Price about the aim of the project: "You

22 J.C.R. Licklider, "Man-Computer Symbiosis," *IRE Transactions on Human Factors in Electronics* HFE-1 (1960): 4.

23 Stanford Anderson, "Problem-Solving and Problem-Worrying" (lecture, Architectural Association, London, March 1966, and at the ACSA, Cranbrook, Bloomfield Hills, MI, June 5, 1966), 1.

24 Ibid., 2.

25 Ibid., 6.

26 Ibid., 14.

27 A longer treatment of Cedric Price's Generator and his interest in technology can be found in Molly Wright Steenson, *Architectural Intelligence: How Designers and Architects Created the Digital Landscape* (Cambridge, MA: MIT Press, 2017).

28 Royston Landau, "A Philosophy of Enabling," in *The Square Book*, ed. Cedric Price (London: Architectural Association, 1984), 11.

29 John Frazer to Cedric Price, January 11, 1979, Generator document folio, DR1995:0280:65 5/5, Cedric Price Fonds, Montreal, Canadian Centre for Architecture.

30 Ibid.

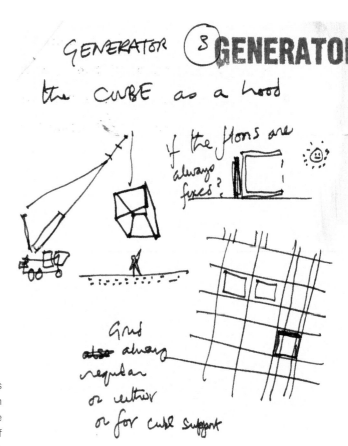

GENERATOR 8 GENERATOR

the CUBE as a hood

if the Mons are
always
fixed?

Grid
also always
regular
or neither
or for cube support

III   Cedric Price's sketch of Generator's grid and the mobile
       crane that would move its cubes, 1976–80

seemed to imply that we were only useful if we produced results
that you did not expect [...]. I think this leads to some definition
of computer aids in general. I am thinking about this but in the
meantime at least one thing that you would expect from any half
decent program is that it should produce at least one plan which
you did not expect."[31] Intelligence and creativity means producing
the unexpected and the surprising—what neither human nor computer might have foreseen.

Conclusion

How would the computer affect creativity, and what is intrinsic to
the role of the architect? Should the computer be kept in a con-
venient package? Would it destroy the uniqueness of a human
creator?
I find myself thinking about Masahiro Mori, who coined the term
"uncanny valley" in 1970 in an article about what happens when
robots or other figures are too eerily close to humans. We like
these figures to a certain point, but when they're too similar, we
find ourselves in the uncanny valley. The point of his argument was
not only that we should learn to design robots for which people
have affinity, but also that robots are a mirror on ourselves. "We
should begin to build an accurate map of the uncanny valley, so
that through robotics research we can come to understand what
makes us human," he wrote.[32] I return to this idea when I consider
the role of creativity and computers in architecture. If we want to
unlock what's at the core of creative interaction in computation,
we need to consider what surprises and challenges us—then, in
1959, as now, in 2020. It is at this intersection of the uncanny and
the eerie—the system that kicks us back—that the questions of
intelligence lie. Who are we when we interact with a computer?
What questions do our design systems raise about who we are,
about our creativity? These are the sparks of intelligence that
endure long past production cycles for hardware and software, or
commercial releases and upgrades. It's a question of what makes
us architects and designers—and what makes us human.

31 John Frazer to Cedric Price, January 11, 1979, Generator document folio,
   DR1995:0280:65 5/5, Cedric Price Fonds, Montreal, Canadian Centre for
   Architecture.
32 Masahiro Mori, "The Uncanny Valley: The Original Essay by Masahiro Mori,"
   IEEE Spectrum, June 12, 2012, spectrum.ieee.org/automaton/robotics/
   humanoids/the-uncanny-valley.

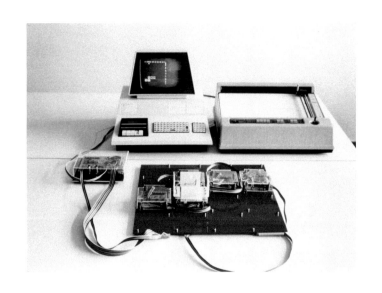

IV John & Julia Frazer, working electronic model of
Generator that ran its four program prototypes, 1979

Reptile Flexible Enclosure System

John Frazer, Richard Parkins (programmer), Francisco Guerra (assistance and programming)

1966—1973

SOFTWARE
programmed in FORTRAN with Atlas machine code subroutines, Autographics Autoplan

HARDWARE
Cambridge Atlas Titan computer, PDP7 minicomputer, pen plotter

PURPOSE OF SOFTWARE
automated design

The Reptile Flexible Enclosure System was an early attempt at creating a parametric and biologically inspired evolutionary design system for architecture. John Frazer had been educated as an architect at the Architectural Association in London. During this time, in 1966, he began experimenting with alternative design methodologies that involved the use of computers. His intent in exploring novel design methods was to transform the then common process of design evolution on drawing boards and through physical model making into a process that allowed for more freedom in finding architectural forms. This, he thought, could be achieved by means of computer modeling and simulation. The methods he conceived can be seen as a computational translation of natural selection—an iterative process of design creation and alteration whose outcome is subject to selection and improvement through multiple repetitions of the same process. Frazer published a monograph on his work, *An Evolutionary Architecture*, in 1995 that summarized his ideas and could be regarded as a predecessor for what later became subsumed under terms such as *parametric* or *algorithmic* design.

The Reptile Flexible Enclosure System (*rep-tile*, from "repeated tile") was an early version of such an exploration of computational design methods. The basis for this method was a versatile architectural concept consisting of an initial geometry, a structural unit, which was arranged in such a way that it formed an initial spatial form called a seed. On this seed, a computer program performed geometrical operations to grow the structure by adding new units of the geometry or deleting existing ones. The program organized and modified the initial geometry in a virtual three-dimensional environment. The organizing operations were commands that consisted of five integer numbers that the computer interpreted in order to define their position in relation to structures that already existed. Each unit could be rotated in eighteen different ways. For a process that would now take less than a second for a computer to calculate, Cambridge University's Atlas Titan computer was needed to compute the Reptile Flexible Enclosure System in the 1960s. To visualize the design, the final drawings were printed by pen plotters at Glen Computing in London.—*Philip Schneider*

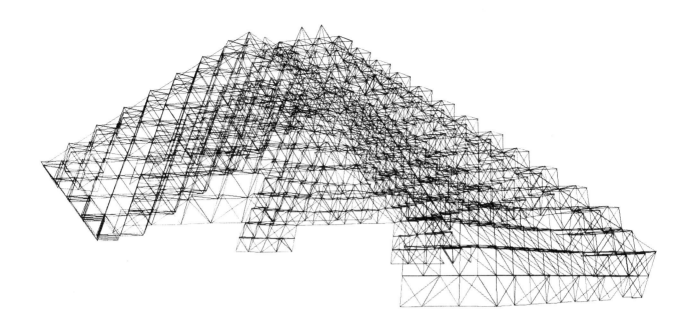

| Perspective view of a gymnasium design created with the Reptile Flexible
Enclosure System, 1970

Frazer, John. *An Evolutionary Architecture*. London: Architectural Association, 1995. ●
Pisca, Nicholas. "Forget Parametricism." In *Computational Design*, edited by Neil Leach
and Philip Yuan, 43–48. Shanghai: Tongji University Press, 2018.

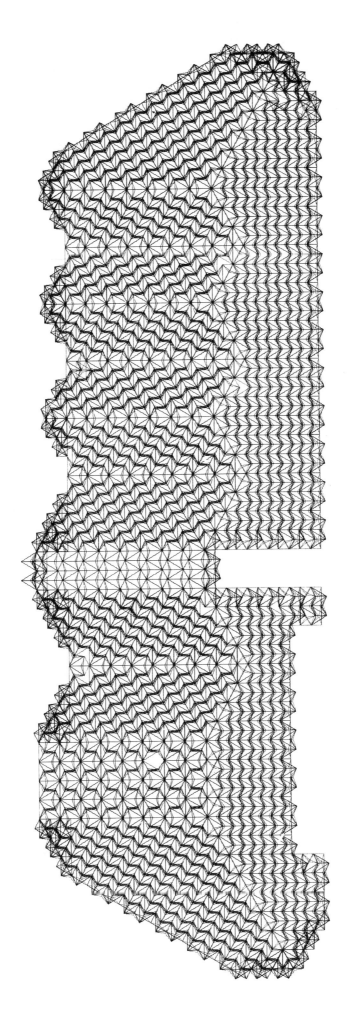

II   Roof structure usin g Reptile Flexible Enclosure System

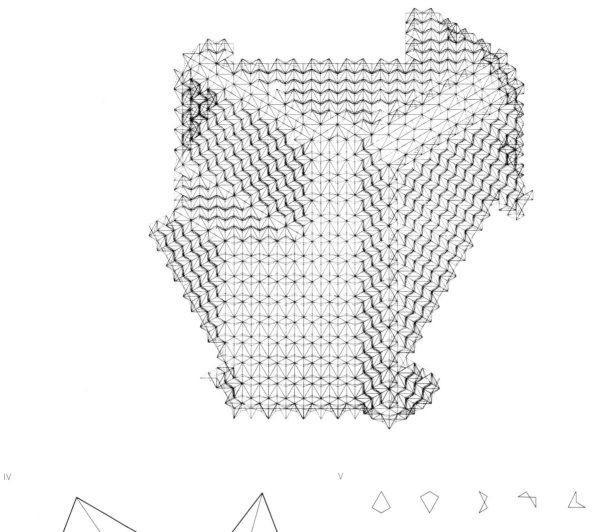

IV

V

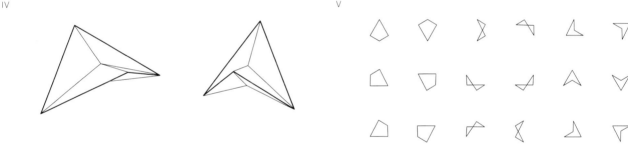

III Plan of a gymnasium design created with the Reptile Flexible Enclosure System
IV Two structural units of the Reptile Flexible Enclosure System
V Possible orientations of the structural units

Siemens CeBIT-Pavillon

Ludwig Rase and Georg Nees
(Siemens Design Department),
Jost Clement (structural analysis)

1969—1970

SOFTWARE
project-related software, written in ALGOL
(Siemens AG)

HARDWARE
Siemens 4004 mainframe computer (BS1000),
Graphomat Z90

PURPOSE OF SOFTWARE
form-finding, drawing

The Siemens CeBIT Pavilion for the Hannover Messe 1970 was Germany's first completed building designed using a computer. The mainframe computer involved was marketed under the banner *"Siemens 4004 entwirft Messestand"* (Siemens 4004 designs trade-fair stand). This was the first time, according to the somewhat exaggerated claim, that an electronic brain had generated an architectural design and performed a creative feat previously reserved for humans. The real creative brains behind the pavilion were Ludwig Rase, exhibition architect at Siemens, and Georg Nees, who headed the Siemens computer center in Erlangen and was a computer pioneer. The overall concept of the pavilion follows Ludwig Rase's credo of making the complex world of technology easier to understand. A computer in those days was an enclosed cabinet and kept its capabilities hidden from the observer. To make computers more comprehensible, the exhibition was intended to adapt its overall construction and interior architecture to the technical character of the exhibits.[1]

The main architectural requirements of the pavilion were to provide a floor area of 1,100 square meters, an upper level for meetings, a stairwell core, and a flexible, reusable structure; to use prefabricated construction elements; and to have a basic shape that could accommodate two seated groups. Rase opted for a modular construction with steel columns and ceiling elements and a basically hexagonal shape in plan, since the pavilion was expected to have a large number of variants. Georg Nees wrote the computer program to fulfill these requirements. The computer was used in several phases of the design. The first was to determine the ideal layout in plan, a phase often referred to as the "structure design." The computer created several variants, which Rase then examined. This method led to the optimal dimensions, shape, and arrangement of the elements. The computer assisted in the second phase, the structural design. The program could draw perspectives of individual elements or even the whole structure. Rase checked the design with the aid of these representations. The third stage was visualization. The computer-generated perspectives demonstrated the machine's usefulness in product marketing through printed artwork and posters. The effect of the posters was strengthened by adopting an extreme viewing angle. The structure appeared more slender and higher than it was in reality due to the "greater height

| Constructed elements

factor" used in the generation. At the end of the project, Rase said that the trade-fair stand could have been designed equally well without a computer, but he saw it as a test run for the future of the design of complex structures. In the following years the Rase–Nees team completed other modular construction projects with computer-aided design and visualization techniques, including an exhibition pavilion in São Paulo.—*Heike Werner*

1 Ernst Margonday and Ludwig Rase, "Von der Produktdarbietung zur Multimedia-Schau—Messen und Ausstellungen im Dienste der Technik" (From Product Presentation to Multimedia Show: Trade Fairs and Exhibitions in the Service of Technology), in *So wirbt Siemens*, ed. Dankwart Rost (Düsseldorf/Vienna, 1971), 192. ● Rase, Ludwig. "Konstruieren mit Hilfe des Computers" (Designing with the help of computers). *Deutsche Bauzeitung*, October 1970, 848–49. ● Rase, Ludwig, and Georg Nees. "4004 entwirft Messestand" (4004 designs trade-fair stand). *Siemens Data Report* 5 (1970): 2–7. ● Rase, Ludwig. "Computerdesign für Raum und Fläche" (Computer design of volumes and surfaces). *NOVUM Gebrauchsgraphik*, August 1972, 48–56. ● Rase, Ludwig. "Künstliche Kunst. Computer-Grafik—Plastik—Architektur—Lasergrafik" (Artificial art. Computer graphics—sculpture—architecture—laser graphics). In *Jahrbuch 1975*, edited by Jürgen Blumenberg, 76–92. Munich: Technische Universität München, 1976.

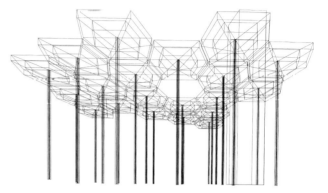

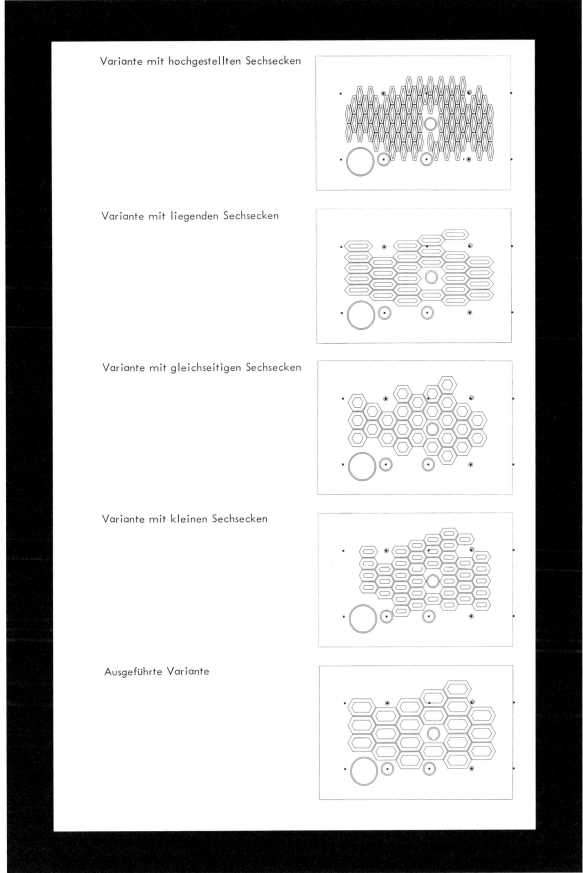

Variante mit hochgestellten Sechsecken

Variante mit liegenden Sechsecken

Variante mit gleichseitigen Sechsecken

Variante mit kleinen Sechsecken

Ausgeführte Variante

II   Structure of the pavilion in São Paulo
III Perspective of the whole structure of Siemens CeBIT-Pavillon
IV   Layout plan variants for the pavilion; the bottom one was built

RESOWI Center

Manfred Wolff-Plottegg

1985

SOFTWARE
script in FORTRAN

HARDWARE
VAX computer

PURPOSE OF SOFTWARE
design

Manfred Wolff-Plottegg's design for the RESOWI Center in Graz, Austria, is an early attempt to have a computer generate floor plans automatically. Wolff-Plottegg has been the head of an architectural office in Graz since 1983 and was the first professor for CAD at TU Munich in 1994–95. In 1985, when hardly anyone was speaking of generative design, Wolff-Plottegg experimented on a VAX computer at the University of Graz with algorithms to autonomously generate a design for a new faculty building. The project was a forward-looking initiative in the computer-aided design of a complete competition drawing. Wolff-Plottegg continued with computer-generated architecture in later texts and projects, including the *Binary House*. The algorithms for the RESOWI Center were based on rectangles with randomly selected proportions, angle of rotation, and location within the maximum volume. They were created, inserted, and extruded as rooms using a random generator. Where rooms overlapped, they were combined and enlarged by the overlapping area. The views, axonometric projections, and perspectives were created as 2½-D drawings and adopted the aesthetics of the then prevailing wireframes. The hardware at that time limited the project to a thousand lines. Countless variations of the planned layout were printed on continuous rolls of paper and further developed. Since these algorithms could not consider the access and circulation system, lighting, spatial quality, and synchronization of the floors, the human architect was still responsible for the final selection and further processing of the design. For this reason the algorithms represent an important ideal, but not a direct technical basis for current approaches to generative floor layout design. Wolff-Plottegg's design received a commendation in the competition. Even before this design he had been experimenting with morphing techniques, including for *Hybrid Architecture* (1981). Further experiments with randomly generated designs were the basis for his competition entry for the urn cemetery in Graz (1985), in which a script generated variants of the distribution of gravestones on the available space at a pixel-based scale.—*Julian Trummer*

Wolff-Plottegg, Manfred. *Architektur Algorithmen*. Vienna: Passagen Verlag, 1996. ● Wolff-Plottegg, Manfred. *Plottegg: Architecture beyond Inclusion and Identity Is Exclusion and Difference from Art*. Basel: Birkhäuser Verlag, 2015.

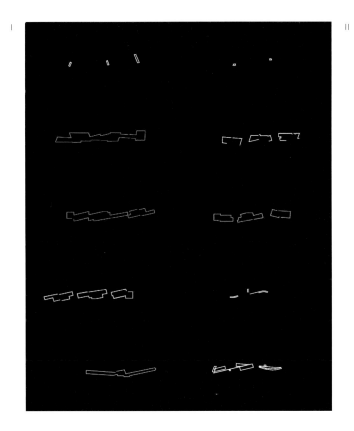

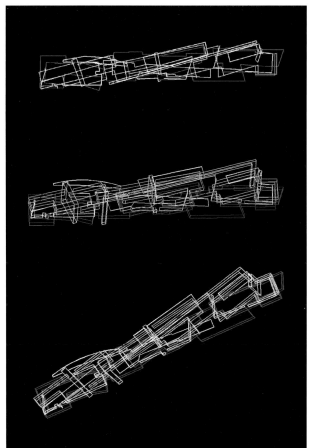

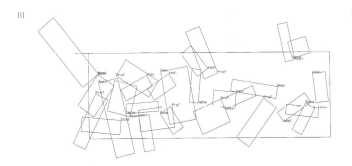

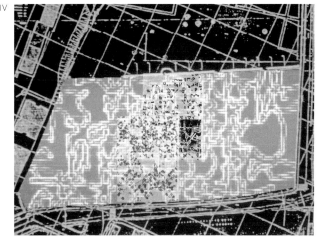

I   Individual floors of the building
II Extruded elevation of the RESOWI Center
III Final generated layout
IV Random distribution of gravestones for the urn cemetery in Graz

BMW Bubble

*Bernhard Franken with ABB Architekten,
Bollinger + Grohmann Ingenieure
(engineers)*

1991—1999

SOFTWARE
Wavefront Explorer, Rhinoceros, Maya, CATIA,
AutoCAD, RSTAB

HARDWARE
Silicon Graphics O2 Computer (Irix 6.5 / Unix)

PURPOSE OF SOFTWARE
form-finding

BMW Bubble was one of the first digitally designed architectural blobs, and was realized in full scale at the 1999 IAA Frankfurt Motor Show. Bernhard Franken had studied architecture between 1988 and 1996 at Technische Universität Darmstadt, where he began experimenting with digital tools for design purposes. In 1995 he was artist in residence at Institut für Neue Medien, a part of the Städelschule in Frankfurt, which gave him access to animation software that had originally been created for use in filmmaking. Since then, Franken no longer uses traditional design approaches such as sketches or models but works exclusively on the computer. BMW Bubble is his first design of a parametrically designed building, and was realized in collaboration with ABB Architekten.

The design was based on the simulation of two drops of water moving toward one another to create a shape that would become subsumed under the iconic term *blob*. An algorithm in Explorer simulated the behavior of water to determine the final master geometry, which served as the reference for all further tests on the digital model. Explorer, made by Wavefront Technologies, and PowerAnimator, made by Alias, became the basis for the well-known animation program Maya, which launched in 1998 and allows the user to modify and morph shapes according to a predefined set of rules. After the master geometry was finalized, an analysis of the curvature of the BMW Bubble was done in Rhinoceros and renderings were created in Maya. 2-D drawings were made with AutoCAD and skin shop drawings were done in CATIA. The engineers Bollinger + Grohmann Ingenieure used RSTAB to visualize the momentum of the curves and for a finite element analysis. A small 3-D printed model—one of the first made for an architectural project—was produced in-house by BMW, as stereolithography remained too costly for architectural offices in the 1990s. A larger structural model was CNC-milled directly from the digital model.

The temporary pavilion was assembled from 305 unique Plexiglas panes and 3,200 milled structural parts that were machined using the digital model. After its first installation in Frankfurt, it was rebuilt as a dance club at Expo 2000 in Munich. The disassembled parts were destroyed in 2005.
—*Teresa Fankhänel*

Franken, Bernhard. "Pavillon auf der IAA." *Arch+*, no. 148 (October 1999): 72–75. ● Franken, Bernhard. "Parametrischer Entwurf und digitale Kontinuität." *Baumeister*, April 2001, 36–37. ● Michel, Matthias. "Bubble. BMW setzt auf Wasserstoff." *CAD News*, no. 6 (2000): 8–10. ● Lloyd Morgan, Conway. *Franken Architekten. Spatial Narratives*. Ludwigsburg, Germany: avedition, 2008, 8–21.

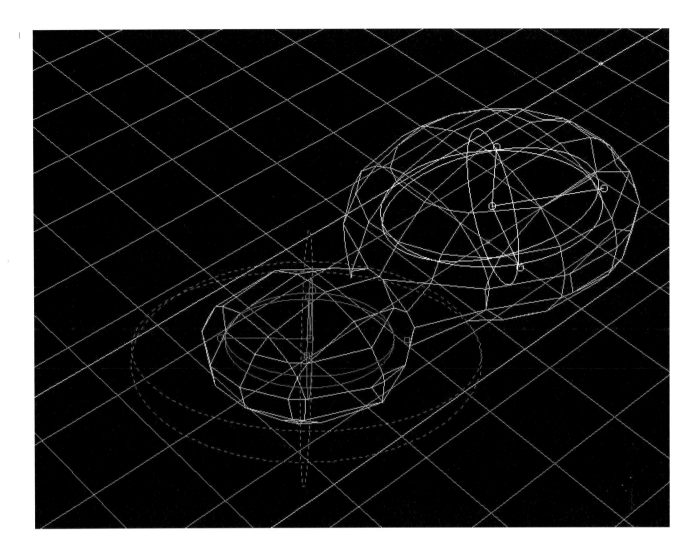

| Final master geometry in Wavefront Explorer

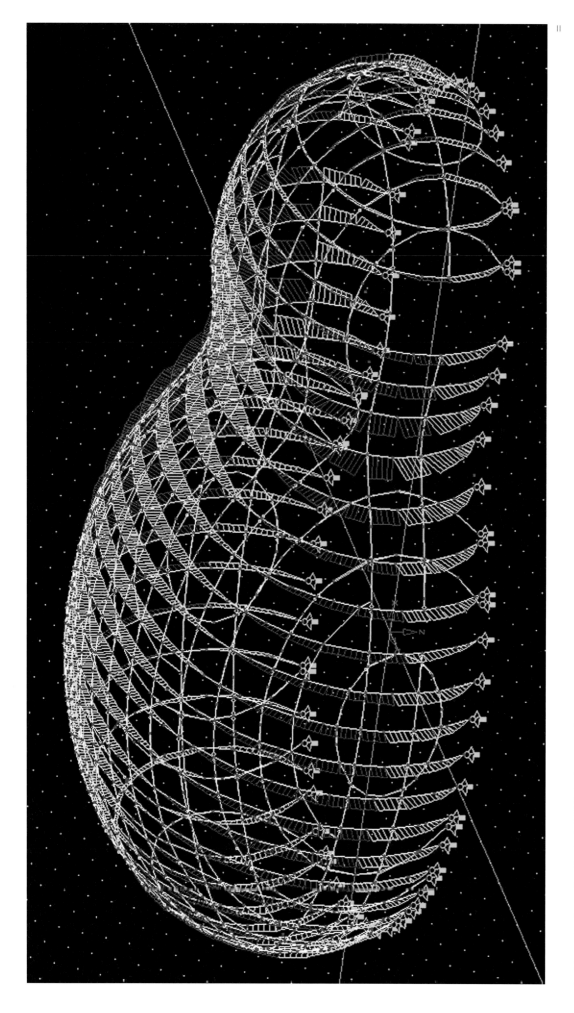

I   Momentum Curve Visualization in RSTAB by Bollinger + Grohmann Ingenieure

Chapter 2 — The Computer as a Design Tool

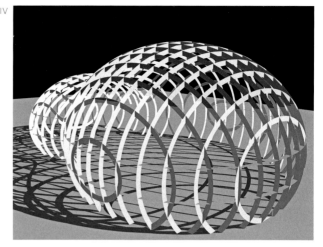

III Sintered model made by BMW
IV Rendering of structural grid in Maya
V Pavilion at the IAA in Frankfurt

Victoria and Albert Museum Spiral Extension

*Daniel Libeskind, Cecil Balmond,
Francis Archer, Daniel Bosia,
Arup Advanced Geometry Unit*

1996—2004

SOFTWARE
Vectorworks, form·Z

HARDWARE
Dell Personal Computer

PURPOSE OF SOFTWARE
form-finding

The fold has been fashionable in architecture since the appearance of Gilles Deleuze's *Le pli* (published in English as *The Fold: Leibniz and the Baroque*) in 1988, influencing architects such as Daniel Libeskind, Peter Eisenman, and Greg Lynn, who often used new architectural software for their designs. In his oeuvre Libeskind deals with order and disorder in architecture. Valid visual habits are disrupted by intervening in the facade, displacing parts of the building, and erecting fragments. These ideas are reflected in the design of the extension building for London's Victoria and Albert Museum, consisting of a continuous, spiraling, and self-supporting exterior wall. The building, with its smooth, spiraling outer skin, dispenses with traditional facade divisions, and functions structurally by rotating around a repeatedly interrupted central axis. The facade is covered with "fractiles"—a conflation of the mathematical term *fractal* and *tile*. The complex facade surface consists of the constant repetition of three tile types and is based on the idea of fractals, which are composed of self-similar shapes reproduced at various scales. The design was developed using many hand drawings and folded paper models in close collaboration with the engineer and artist Cecil Balmond. The analog preliminary work served as a basis for further development using the computer in Balmond's search for an underlying mathematical principle for a nonlinear spiral without a fixed center. The design also required that all the walls should intersect at different points to permit a column-free interior. With the help of the computer, the kinked spiral was created by the rotation of a long, three-dimensional wall segment, which is compressed or stretched at various angles. At the end of this process, the result was a digital model that came very close to the original analog model. However, both the basic idea and the recognition of the result required the intervention of a human architect, since the computer could not decide when the work was finished: "How would the computer know when to stop, and what does that have to do with what we like?" The computer model was later used for structural engineering calculations, which were printed out and glued to the analog model to illustrate the close connection between the digital and analog designs.—*Laura Altmann*

I

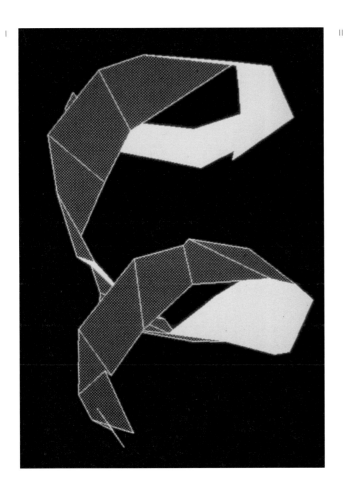

II

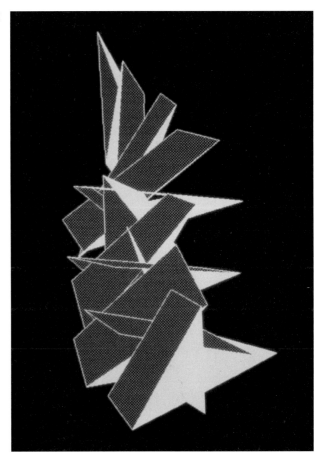

I–II Rotation of the wall segment at various angles

1 Balmond and Smith 2007, 214. ● Forster, Kurt. *Daniel Libeskind: radix–matrix*.
Munich: Prestel, 1997. ● Nerdinger, Winfried, et al., eds. *Konstruktion und Raum in
der Architektur des 20. Jahrhunderts*. Munich: Prestel, 2002. ● Balmond, Cecil,
and Jannuzzi Smith. *informal*. Munich: Prestel, 2007. ● Goldberger, Paul. *Coun-
terpoint Daniel Libeskind*. Basel: Birkhäuser Verlag, 2008.

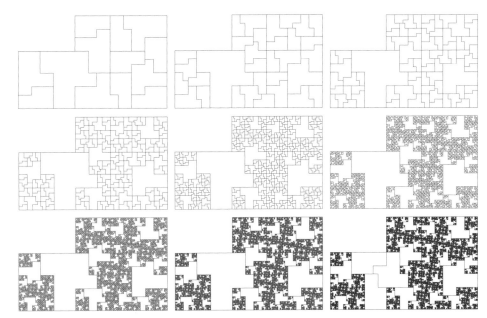

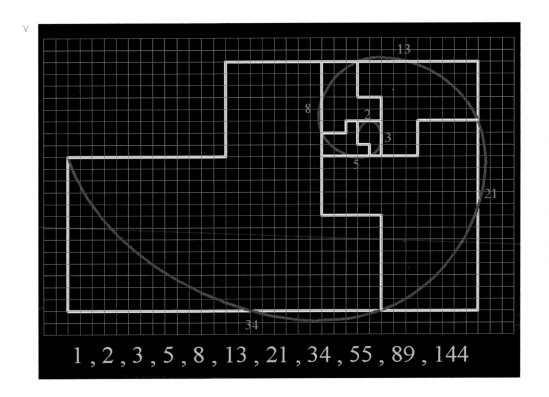

1 , 2 , 3 , 5 , 8 , 13 , 21 , 34 , 55 , 89 , 144

III Model of the extension
IV Fractiles on the facade
V   Underlying golden ratio of the fractiles

Dunescape

SHoP Architects

2000

SOFTWARE
Rhinoceros

HARDWARE
PC, Microsoft Windows

PURPOSE OF SOFTWARE
form generation, construction drawings

Dunescape, the winner of the inaugural iteration of the MoMA/PS1 Young Architects Program (YAP), was a temporary installation designed by SHoP Architects. Its main structure comprised six thousand unique 2 x 2 cedarwood elements, which ranged from 2.44 to 3.66 meters. While the architects pitched the design as an "urban beach" intended to shake off the heat of Y2K summer in New York, early sketches indicate that the project was largely conceived as an opportunity to experiment with topological operations and mass customization. By shifting the vertices of a notional mesh that covered the ground of PS1's sculpture courtyard on the computer, SHoP arrived at a geometry of overlapping surfaces, the modulation of which produced an artificial landscape for slipping into one's swimsuit, wading, lounging, climbing, and tanning. As Gregg Pasquarelli explained: "We wanted to show how a single surface can mutate into each of the functions."[1]

Three of SHoP's four partners had met while studying architecture in the early 1990s at Columbia University's Graduate School of Architecture, Planning and Preservation, then a hotbed of experimentation in the use of computers through its "paperless studios." Faced with YAP's small budget and limited resources, in 2000 SHoP had to devise an ad hoc protocol to transform their frictionless digital design into a physical artifact. In doing so, the architects discretized the continuous surfaces of the 3-D model into a series of cross sections, each of which could be reduced to a few linear elements. Soon nicknamed "CAT scans," these sections were then blown up to full-scale printouts that would be laid down on the site as construction templates. Thus, minimally trained workers could trim down standardized wood boards to the appropriate length in PS1's workshop, and assemble them with 0.9-meter wood screws into the bays of the slotted structure. Dunescape's largely handcrafted fabrication was far from a seamless digital-to-analog transition. It was SHoP's invention of a low-tech yet streamlined translation from drawing to building, however, that enabled eight students hired by the architects to assemble the 12,000-square-foot (1,115-square-meter) installation in merely four weeks. — *Evangelos Kotsioris*

1 Clifford A. Pearson, "Never Swim Alone," *Architectural Record* 188, no. 8 (August 2000): 59. ● Goldberger, Paul. "Dept. of Recreation Surf's Up at P.S. 1." *New Yorker*, July 10, 2000, 22. ● Pearson, Clifford. "Never Swim Alone." *Architectural Record* 188, no. 8 (August 2000): 59–61. ● Cramer, Ned, and Anne Guiney. "The Computer School." *Architecture*, September 2000, 93–107. ● ShoP. "Eroding the Barriers." *Architectural Design* 72, no. 5 (September 2002): 90–100.

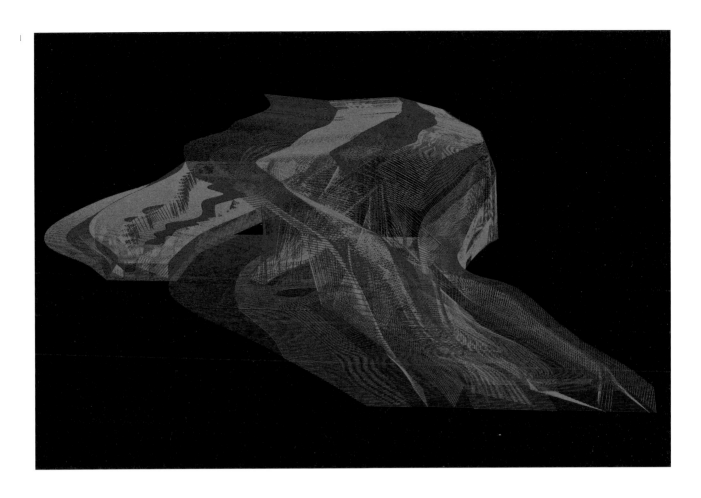

I   Axonometrics of a "CAT scan" describing the surfaces of the main structure

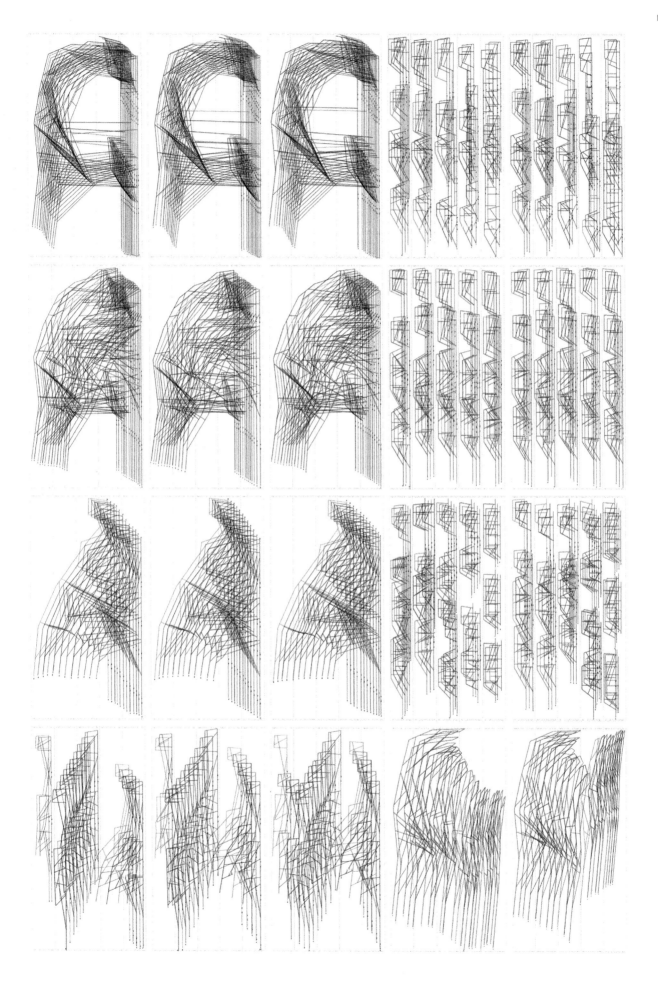

II Full-scale construction document templates

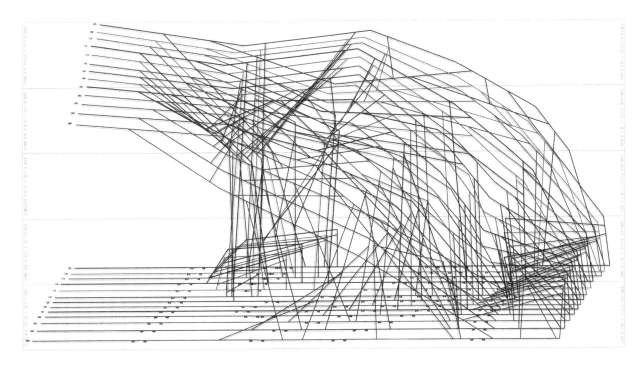

III Full-scale construction document templates of the "cabana" area
IV Full-scale templates used in construction on-site
V The Dunescape installation occupied

Ark of the World Museum

Greg Lynn

2002—2003

SOFTWARE
Maya

HARDWARE
PC

PURPOSE OF SOFTWARE
3-D modeling, form generation

Greg Lynn, known for his biomorphic architectural designs, was a pioneer in the field of computer-aided design through his use of animation software in the 1990s. After studying both architecture and philosophy at Miami University in Oxford, Ohio, Lynn graduated from Princeton University with a graduate degree in architecture. While establishing his office Greg Lynn FORM in 1994, he wrote and published extensively on the subject of CAD and calculus, the study of ever-changing mathematical forms, in architecture. The Ark of the World Museum is a commissioned work initiated by architect Walter Hidalgo Xirinachs, who wanted to create a center for ecotourism, natural history, and contemporary art in the rain forest of Costa Rica. A plan and exhibition concept already existed. The building was imagined in the jungle on the Tárcoles River, right where it flows into the Pacific Ocean.

The design shows an axisymmetric, mushroom-like building that is topped with a billowy roof of petal shapes. To one side the walls melt down into curved tubes, which form a low-rise exit from the center. On the opposite side a forecourt lined by biomorphic parasols frames the entry. The structure is placed on a water basin whose shape is reminiscent of the Mandelbrot set, a reference to the building's algorithmic foundation. Designed in Maya, a software for three-dimensional modeling and animation usually used in film production, a plane long rectangle was the starting point for form development. Rolled up into a tube, mathematical commands compressed and stretched it using a tool in Maya called "blend shape," then quadrupled it to form a circle. The tubes were inflated and bent continuously until the main structure was outlined, then folded onto one another. There, the tubes open up again to a plane surface to form the roof, a shape that, looking back on the design, Greg Lynn and Sanford Kwinter likened to a "cobra snake head." After the final form was found, Lynn created an animation that sums up the modeling process, which took a month and a half to show the major design decisions. Here, the algorithmic design evolves seemingly between pause and play, stopping and changing direction. The experiment ends in the coloration and texturization of the digital model. Inspiration is again drawn from the jungle environment and its inhabitants: the crocodile-skin surface is dyed in parrot-feather colors to represent the gradual upward fold of the structure. — *Sina Brückner-Amin*

I   Bird's-eye view of the surroundings and the Ark of the World Museum's back
    entrance
II View into the open ground floor and main entrance

Lynn, Greg, and Mark Rappolt, eds. *Greg Lynn Form*. New York: Rizzoli, 2008. ●
Ednie-Brown, Pia. "On a Fine Line." *Architectural Design*, January 2013, 44–49.

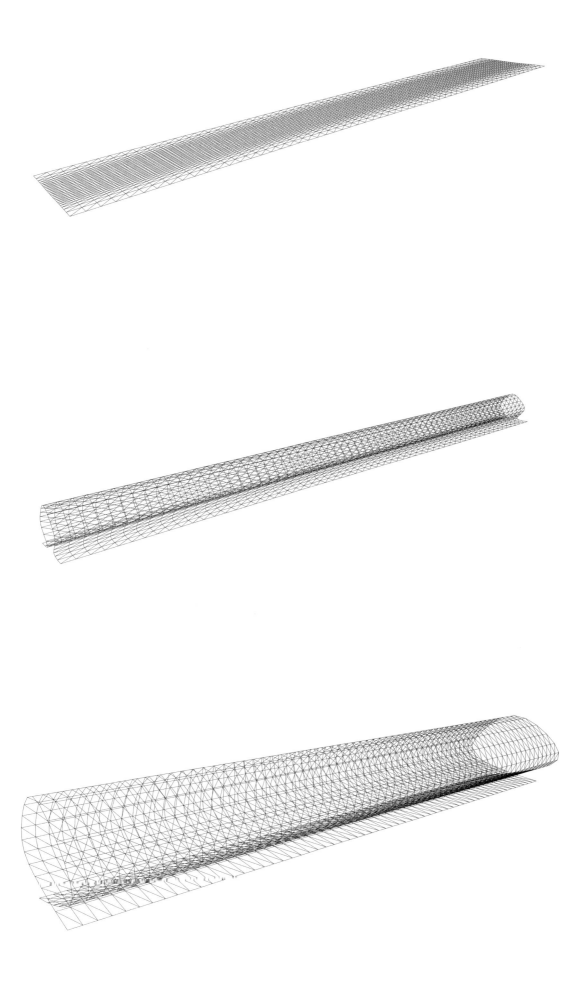

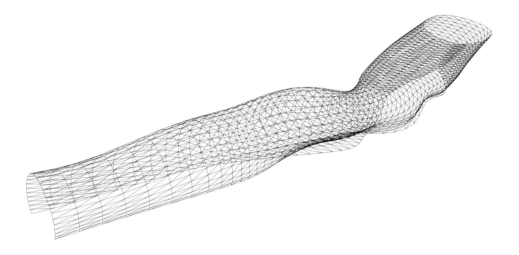

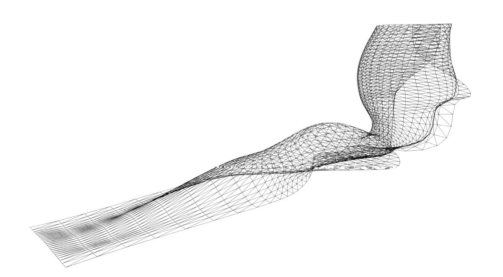

III–IV Stages of deformation of the wireframe model

TRUTEC Building

Frank Barkow, Regine Leibinger (architects), Martina Bauer, Matthias Graf von Ballestrem, Michael Schmidt, Elke Sparmann, Jan-Oliver Kunze (project architects), Chang-Jo Architects, Seoul, Kim Byung-hyun (architects, Seoul), Schlaich Bergermann und Partner, Stuttgart, Jeon and Lee Partners, Seoul (engineers), Arup, Hong Kong, Berlin, Alutek Ltd., Seoul (facade)

2005—2006

SOFTWARE
Vectorworks, form·Z

HARDWARE
Apple PowerMac G5, NVIDIA GeForce 6800 Ultra
DDL graphics card

PURPOSE OF SOFTWARE
form-finding (architects), construction details,
programming of the CNC milling machine (Alutek)

Since the early 2000s, Barkow Leibinger has been interested in "discrete" elements in design and experimenting with designs incorporating shapes inspired by biology, such as honeycomb or tube structures. In this context, the objective of the design for the TRUTEC building was to achieve the greatest variability and complexity with the least possible number of elements. Barkow Leibinger designed the building in the middle of the construction boom that the city of Seoul, population 20 million, experienced due to the explosive growth of the high-tech industry. The 20,000-square-meter structure was intended to allow small and medium-sized enterprises from Europe to have a presence in the South Korean capital. Five levels of underground parking and twelve aboveground stories were erected in only eighteen months in the new Digital Media City office district. Because the business park was not built at the time, Barkow Leibinger could not analyze the surrounding architecture. The building's design, with its crystalline surface, would nevertheless challenge the many faceless office buildings already to be seen in Seoul.

The reflective glass facade functions as a projection surface that decomposes the visual impression of the surroundings into pixels and recomposes them in a kaleidoscopic manner at intervals and in different lighting conditions. The many manually produced drawings and models confirm that the preliminary design of the building took place conventionally. The facade reflections, for example, were tried out on physical models. A key issue was the search for a suitable "prototype" of the facade module. Working closely with the facade manufacturer Alutek, the architects were able to include the option of computer-controlled production of the facade frames using CNC at an early stage in their considerations. The result was a 3-D facade element measuring 4.2 × 2.7 m with a relief and depth of 20 cm, to which was added a flat 2-D element. The architects arranged the elements according to geometric rules of rhythm and alternation. The apparently arbitrary distribution of oblique lines on the facade module was also based on its width and height. The basic element, which had been determined by analog methods, was duplicated on the computer for the drawings in order to simulate the effect on the whole facade of their placement by rule and to check the performance of different versions. The objective was to merge the repeating facade modules into an infinite, complex pat-

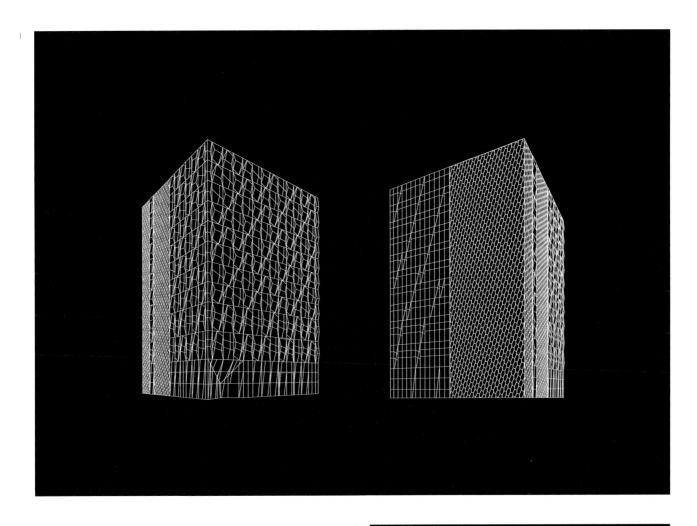

I

II

I 3-D model of the facade
II Model of a window element

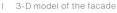

tern. The linearity of the basic self-contained element is transferred through the apparent irregularity of the glass units. The diagonal lines influence areas way beyond the quadrilateral frames, extending over the complete building and simulating a type of continuous growth that makes reference to the biological form-finding processes of evolutionary architecture.—*Stefan Gruhne*

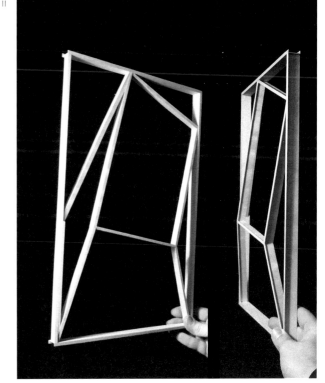

Lepik, Andres, ed. Reflect: *Building in the Digital Media City, Seoul, Korea.* Ostfildern, Germany: Hatje Cantz, 2007. ● Brensing, Christian. "Kritisch betrachtet: Trutec Building in Seoul." *Detail*, issue 5 (2007): 472–73. ● Brensing, Christian. "Trutec Building." *Bauwelt* 14 (2007): 26–31 ● "Trutec Building." *Architectural Design*, April 2010, 18–19.

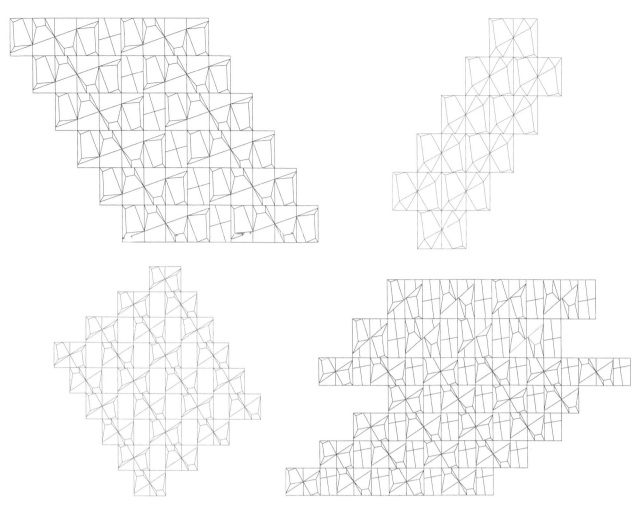

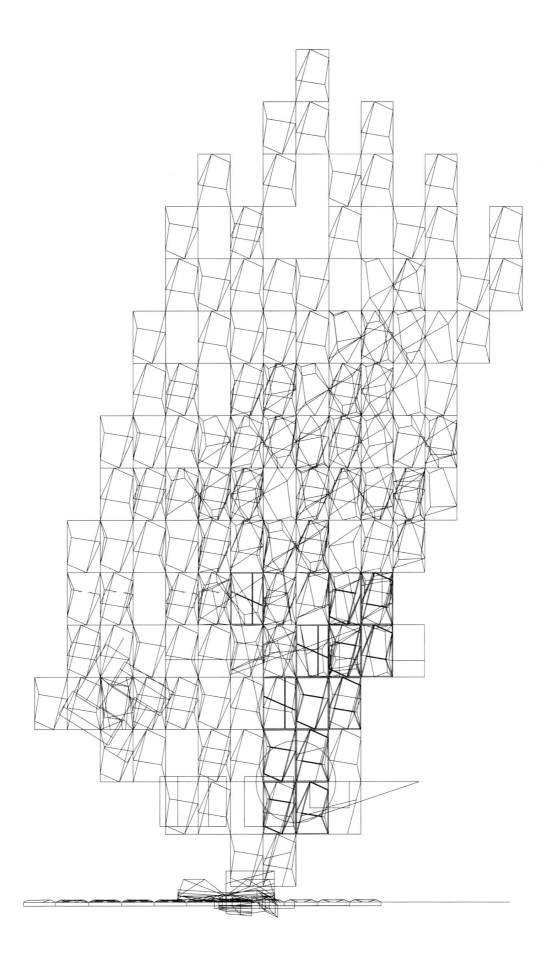

III Simulation of different facade patterns
IV Exploded drawing of the facade grid

O-14

Reiser + Umemoto RUR Architecture, ERGA Progress (architect of record), Ysrael A. Seinuk PC (structural engineers)

2006—2011

SOFTWARE
Rhinoceros, AutoCAD, Rhinoscript

HARDWARE
PC

PURPOSE OF SOFTWARE
3-D modeling, 2-D design, drawing set production

Digital and analog randomization was the main design interest for the O-14 building's unique facade. It resulted in the creation of a white concrete exoskeleton as the most important eye-catching element of the skyscraper, functioning both as the facade and the main structure. The exoskeleton provides a free and wide core as well as column-free open spaces. It is also the primary vertical and lateral structure for the building, allowing the open-space office slabs to span between it and the minimal core. Seeking to create a unique building to sit among iconic structures by noted architects on Dubai Creek, Jesse Reiser and Nanako Umemoto intended to disregard the design's urban context by constructing a perforated concrete shell on an elevated podium that functions as a gate for passersby. The facade design process started with the creation of a symmetrical diagrid of holes on which the location of the floor levels can be easily discerned. The architects used Rhinoceros and AutoCAD to randomize a set of neatly arranged perforations in the facade. However, the scripted program produced versions that appeared too perfect. Only with manual interference were the architects able to create variations that appeared arbitrary.

The architects deliberately shifted the connection points between the floor levels and the facade and changed the diagrid to an out-of-phase one. By shaking the initial diagrid and by changing the size of the holes, Reiser and Umemoto created "a turbulence field" and provided viewers with "an extreme amount of redundancy" so that people would get different impressions of the building while moving around it.—*Sina Zarei*

Steele, Brett. *O-14: Projection and Reception: Reiser + Umemoto.* London: Architectural Association, 2012. ●"O-14/Reiser + Umemoto." *ArchDaily,* September 18, 2012. Accessed December 13, 2019. www.archdaily.com/273404/o-14-reiser-umemoto.

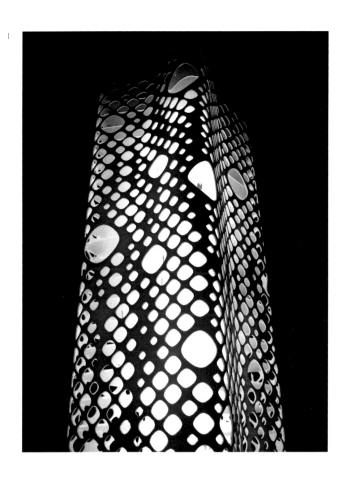

I Concrete exoskeleton at night
II Unrolled layout of the perforations

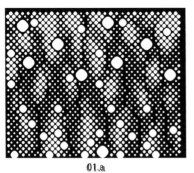

01.a

large hexgrid yields boring patches of uniform opacity and overly simplistic gradient

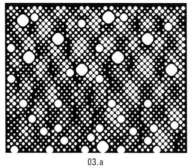

03.a

made the hexgrid smaller, still overly simplistic gradient and it looks kind of patchy

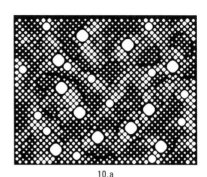

10.a

with a greater weighting placed upon the turbulence pattern the grain becomes coarse and frankly, too swirly - needs more directionality

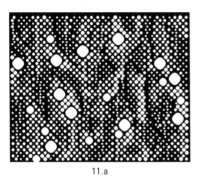

11.a

made the turbulence pattern larger gaining greater detail, lost the swirls but still too loose

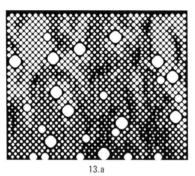

13.a

in attempting to make the pattern more transparent it lost specificity , detail and direction

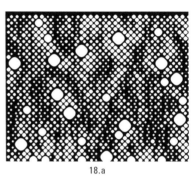

18.a

placed more attraction/repulsion lines in attempt to regain lost detail, but it doesn't seem to advance much since iteration 11a.

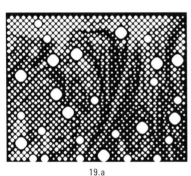

19.a

the much maligned 19a. became too figural, a mutation which we quickly suppressed

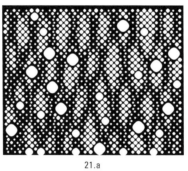

21.a

in an attempt towards a structural optimum, the attraction/repulsion lines were used to reinforce the hexgrid transferring load to the columns, works well looks bad

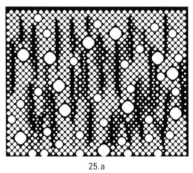

25.a

a shift away from the hexgrid in favor of vertical pattern yielded greater contrast at the expense of subtly

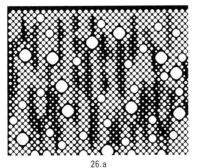

26.a

more or less the same as 25.a but became a bit fuzzier, still not so subtle

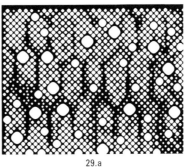

29.a

hexgrid is back at work which brought about a more refined pattern with greater detail, feeling sort of hopeful

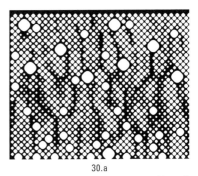

30.a

a break in the symmetry and regularity of the grid generated a more heterogeneous pattern, previous effect is maintained with greater transparency

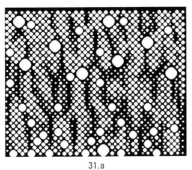

31.a

an evolved iteration of 30a. with greater contrast and opacity, this iteration reinstated the transfer of load to the columns

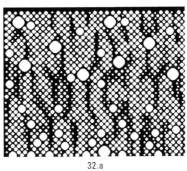

32.a

hybridized 31.a and 30a., the right amount of heterogeneirty is achieved, looking good

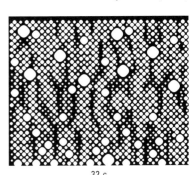

32.c

minor revisions which at the time of publication we were unable to detect

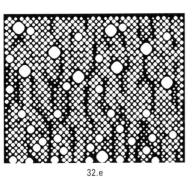

32.e

a subtle blurring of the veins reduced individual intesities

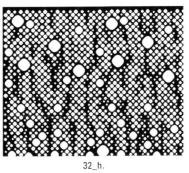

32_h.

a further break in symmetry of the underlying pattern refining the asymmetrical balance

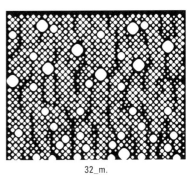

32_m.

final refinement involved a thinning of the veins and a subtle increase in transparency

III–IV Iterations of the facade design

Geno Matrix

Tang & Yang
(Ming Tang, Dihua Yang)

2007

Geno Matrix is a voxel-based design by Tang & Yang and received a special mention at the high-rise competition of the online architecture magazine *eVolo* in 2007. The competition, which has received hundreds of entries every year since 2006, looks for speculative, future-oriented ideas that question the architectural form of the high-rise building in the light of current technical, social, and ecological challenges. The design is based on a modular system with cuboid blocks, which takes its inspiration from genetic evolution in biology. It is a critique of the generally static nature of architecture, which cannot change its construction in reaction to changes in the environment. As an alternative, the Chinese-American architects suggest high-rises with a mobile structure, similar to a living organism. The Geno Matrix takes its name from the biological term *genotype*, which describes the genetic makeup—i.e., the genetic basis—of a living being. Various phenotypes, different expressions of a genotype, may develop. Tang & Yang also examined biological analogies between architecture, urban planning, and paleontology in their book *Urban Paleontology: Evolution of Urban Forms* (2008).

The design uses "discrete" cuboid objects, also known as voxels, which can be arranged as desired within a gigantic 3-D framework. Individual cubes can be moved like molecules into different locations in the system, allowing an almost infinite number of arrangements. Units can also be combined to form larger voxels. More refined generations of a specific design can be created based on a genetic selection process to further develop the design's positive features. As well as biology, the design is inspired by modular systems such as Lego, which can be used in a similar way to assemble a whole from many identical individual parts. In recent years computer games such as *Minecraft or Block'hood* have transferred this idea of 3-D construction kits into the digital realm. This rearrangement of individual units of the Geno Matrix changes the appearance of the entire skyscraper, illustrating the social structure and the relationships between the units. These organizational patterns can also be used to communicate with the environment collectively and symbolically via the facade.—*Teresa Fankhänel*

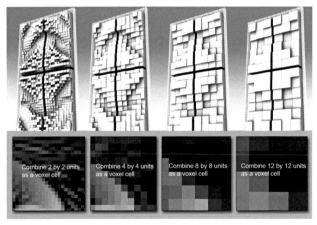

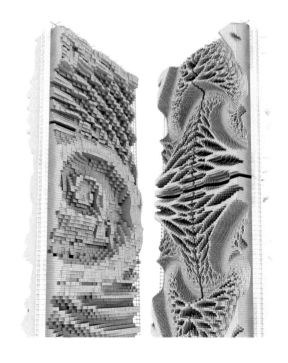

I   Rendering of a fictitious high-rise
II Voxel growth
III Two different solutions for the arrangement of individual elements

Tang, Ming, and Dihua Yang. "Geno Matrix," competition entry, 2007. ● "Geno Matrix." *eVolo*, December 15, 2009. evolo.us/geno-matrix/.

Chapter 3
The Computer as a Medium for Storytelling

Seeing by Numbers:
A Short History of
Computer Renderings

Roberto Bottazzi

The history of the relation between representational techniques and digital design is a complex, slightly deceptive one as, superficially, it lends itself to a rather linear account. Artificial Intelligence or digital simulations, on the one hand, mark a clear break with pre-digital approaches. The digitization of spatial representation, on the other hand, appears as a straightforward absorption of prior knowledge. The mathematics of perspectival construction are still largely those codified since the beginning of the fifteenth century, with one substantial transformation: digital tools have made all these operations much easier. Speed, however, is an essential characteristic of the digital, and quantitative changes are the preconditions for qualitative leaps. Easily constructed perspectival views allow designers to work directly in three-dimensional space, bypassing the traditional design process that moves from simpler orthographic representations to three-dimensional ones.

Underpinning this process of removal of orthographic representations in favor of 3-D representations is the underlying logic of the digital, the base code of (binary) numbers with which data and algorithms comply. The possibilities for image manipulation therefore massively expand as users can play with both a vast array of editing tools and a wealth of metadata embedded or generated by digital images. In discussing the status of digital images, German artist Hito Steyerl perspicaciously noticed that in the digital age *how* we see is more important than *what* we see; the power of the digital apparatus can no longer be considered as "neutral" but rather is fully participating in the construction of digital images. The thick and often inaccessible layer of algorithms separates user and machine and the very space in which architectural ideas and design narratives can be injected because of the numerical, systematic, and ultimately abstract logic of the digital.[1] This layer is not neutral, as it implicitly frames the domain of what can be imagined. These initial remarks already suggest that to recapitulate the history of computer-generated images (CGI)—the objective of this paper—we ought to engage the very architecture of computation as its logic has been propelling changes in this field. To chart how technical transformations have impacted designers' ideas, we must also acknowledge that this is not a task we can leave to technical literature. The effect of CGI on architecture can only be observed by recognizing that design is complex and a hybrid, juggling technical, historical, intellectual, and material concerns. There is in fact a gap between the expectations of CGI, in which the quest for realism and concerns of commercial profitability drive development, and the conceptual and aesthetic instances that informed the construction of digital tools. The former obscures the latter: not only do CGI form a clear field of research, they also constitute one of the sources of creativity for digital designers.

As for many other aspects of CAD, drafting tools draw inspiration from nature; rendering tools, for instance, are modeled after the physiology of sight. Such a mechanism broadly divides between sensing spatial information (the equivalent of the eye) and elaborating it through algorithms to form the final image (the brain). The history of digital sight is a long attempt to perfect these two complementary activities based upon speculations on how the eye–brain pair functions. The language of mathematics modeled advancements in the science of vision (mathematization of reality), which gave rise to techniques and processes that form both the tool sets of the digital designer and, in this discussion, the very place from which to critically examine the relation between CGI and design. What is of interest here are the possibilities these processes engender, such as the ability for artists and architects to capture aspects of reality not accessible to the human eye.

This is the case for wireframe visualizations or voxel rendering, which not only generate images by diverging from the natural model of the eye but also elicit new forms of representation and design. CAD, therefore, is entangled in a complex, dynamic web that different techniques, concepts, and disciplines have been morphing. As the mathematics of image construction changes, so does the range of things we can represent. It is from such a vantage point that we can assess with greater precision the impact of CGI on architecture, from Leon Battista Alberti's *Prospectiva artificialis* to volumetric representations based on voxels. Whether these innovations were merely absorbed by CAD or were born-digital, they only acquire relevance if they are able to dislodge assumptions on the nature of design and its process. The formalization of sight passed through two successive inventions: mathematical tools and physical machines that literally reified mathematical principles into contraptions. These two lines of development have been conflated by digital computers, engendering the unification of two problems: that of geometry, by finding precise rules to reconstruct surveyed objects, buildings, and even landscapes, and that of the treatment of light, shadows, and colors through ray casting.

Invariants and Variables: Numbers and Geometry

The genealogy of computer rendering finds its ultimate foundation in the invention of mathematical perspective in the first half of the fifteenth century. If the techniques introduced by Alberti's *De Pictura* (1435) were to be interpreted according to contemporary CAD culture, we could speak of devices to store and compute spatial data to construct perspectival views. In many instances such techniques were actual machines that would physically translate geometrical principles into various contraptions. In the case of Jacopo Barozzi da Vignola (1583), the machine consists of two distinct parts that neatly map the eye–brain divide; through this clear break between observation and computation, Vignola's perspective machine could survey entire landscapes ▶ Fig. I. New images, such as orthographic drawings, could be derived from views by applying mathematical principles to recompute the initial data. This technique had immediate application for military purposes as it allowed plans of fortresses to be obtained through simple observation.

More conceptually relevant are Alberti's observations on the power of mathematics in synthesizing reality, as it allows the generation of abstract views that are inaccessible to the human senses by showing the profiles of objects not directly visible. In today's digital parlance we refer to such images as wireframe visualizations, a common feature of any CAD software. In the first book of the *De Pictura*, Alberti warned the reader that his approach to the subject of painting was that of an artist rather than a mathematician, as "mathematicians measure with their minds alone the form of things separated from all matter."[2] It is nevertheless this very ability to see things beyond their perceptual reality as intellectual constructions that enables the production of drawings of objects

I   Engraving of Vignola's perspective machine published in Jacopo Barozzi da Vignola, *Le Due Regole della Prospettiva*, edited by E. Danti, 1583

in which all edges are represented. This is the case for drawings of the *mazzocchio*—an accessory to the hat usually worn in the Renaissance—which was often the object of choice for virtuoso perspectival constructions ▶ Fig. II.

Wireframe views are intellectual constructions resting on rigorous mathematics that endow drawings with the ability to exceed reality and become instruments for speculation and invention. Among the many examples of creative use of wireframe visualizations in design, OMA has been employing this mode since the 1980s, first for the competition entry for Parc de la Villette in Paris (1982), in which the technique enhanced the design concept based on overlaying different programmatic layers. These techniques were

1   Aden Evens, *Logic of the Digital* (New York, London: Bloomsbury Academic, 2015), 5–30.
2   Leon Battista Alberti, *On Painting*, trans. C. Grayson (London: Penguin Classics, 1991), 5.

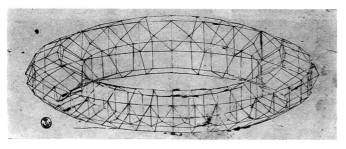

II   Paolo Uccello, Perspectival study of *mazzocchio*,
       15th century

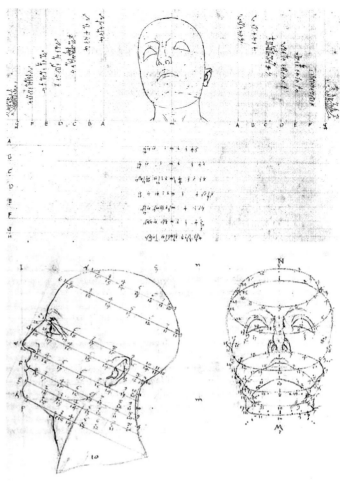

III   View of a human head from below by Piero della Francesca,
       published in *De Prospectiva pingendi*, 15th century

explored with greater emphasis in the design of the concert hall Casa da Música in Porto (1999–2005), in which the Rotterdam-based office produced dazzling and beautiful wireframe views of the final building by superimposing all the plans.

The technical ability to hide objects sitting in the background also represents one of the cornerstones of computer graphics. The invention of the "hidden lines" algorithm by Lawrence G. Roberts in 1963 not only was able to remove parts of covered objects but also marked the moment in which mathematics could automatically draw things "as they are seen," removing Alberti's major criticism of the mathematician's view of reality.

Alberti's polemics also open up two separate strands of research that ran in parallel for a long time before being united under the abstract logic of binary computation of digital computers. The first is concerned with mathematical and geometrical notions to reproduce, or better recompute, the data sets surveyed to generate new drawings. Alberti himself had developed some of these techniques for his survey of the city of Rome captured in the *Descriptio Urbis Romae* (1450). It is, however, with Piero della Francesca's *Other Method* (ca. 1470–80) that we fully appreciate the creative use of mathematics in drawings. Whether ever employed by Piero, his method proposed a proto-version of Gaspard Monge's descriptive geometry to recast a set of points taken from objects that were no longer bound to their original measurements. Piero gives several examples of this method, but the most compelling is its application to the depiction of the human head surveyed in 128 points. By experimenting with his method, Piero was eventually able to create the first view of a human head seen from below ▶ Fig. III. Here mathematics allowed a complete separation between the perceptual experience of the object and drawing, which, again, became a mental re-elaboration of the data.

Furthermore, we can see how mathematics allows a division between data gathered, which become invariants, and their apprehension through mathematics (algorithms), which acts as a variable. This is still how CAD operates: for instance, whenever we rotate the viewing angle in a perspective, the original coordinates describing the vertexes of objects are passed through a matrix that outputs the new positions of the points onscreen, still playing with invariants and variables. CAD software also appropriated these techniques for modeling operations such as scaling, moving, or rotating, demonstrating how the basic numerical logic of the digital encouraged transfers, generalizations, and conflations of tools (in this instance, by merging representational and editing commands) ▶ Fig. IV. We can see not only how numerical, quantitative transformations eventually became qualitative ones, but how the mere quest for realism in CGI offers opportunities for richer conversations involving disciplinary, narrative, and aesthetic considerations. Alberti's work on mathematical perspective also implied the possibility of automating the operation of survey and adding mathematical knowledge to surveying techniques. Albrecht Dürer's engraving of the process of surveying a lute shows a process that almost automatically draws perspectival views of objects without human intervention ▶ Fig. V. This etching not only explicitly takes advantage of some of the principles already illustrated by Alberti but opens up a long series of inventions and machines to automate drawing that drastically changed with the arrival of photography in the nineteenth century. The digital reunites these two lines of experimentation through the development of scanners and the automation of photogrammetry.

$$R_x(\theta) = \begin{bmatrix} 1 & 0 & 0 \\ 0 & \cos\theta & -\sin\theta \\ 0 & \sin\theta & \cos\theta \end{bmatrix}$$

$$R_y(\theta) = \begin{bmatrix} \cos\theta & 0 & \sin\theta \\ 0 & 1 & 0 \\ -\sin\theta & 0 & \cos\theta \end{bmatrix}$$

$$R_z(\theta) = \begin{bmatrix} \cos\theta & -\sin\theta & 0 \\ \sin\theta & \cos\theta & 0 \\ 0 & 0 & 1 \end{bmatrix}$$

Beyond Perspective: Numbers and Light

The development of techniques to compute light and shadows is equally long and complex. As for our considerations on geometry, we will only foreground how the digital has triggered qualitative changes out of quantitative ones. The smooth, elegant plateau of binary computation allowed the translation of any medium into numbers and the possibility of editing them via logical operations. If, on the one hand, the digital lowered the skill level required to interact with images, on the other hand it opened up profound questions about the legitimacy and legibility of images that impacted society well beyond architecture.

IV   Mathematical matrixes for view rotation in CAD

This complex story finds a first major transformation with Roberts's "hidden line" algorithms, which inaugurated a long period of discoveries driven by academic research that first impacted the movie industry and only later entered other design disciplines. The 1960s was the decade in which the formula "computer graphics" was coined by William Fetter at Boeing while developing the first software for flight simulation. In parallel, new types of software packages took full advantage of the transformation of the image from a chemical trace on a photo to a numerical field on a screen: first SuperPaint, designed by Richard Shoup with a team of experts that included Alvy Ray Smith (who later cofounded PIXAR), and then, much later, the omnipresent Photoshop introduced by Thomas and John Knoll in 1987. The University of Utah under the guidance of Ivan Sutherland led the research on algorithms to calculate the reflection and refraction of light on objects; most of these algorithms are still in use and named after their inventors. French computer scientist Henri Gouraud devised the first algorithm to smoothen the faces of curved surfaces, which was subsequently improved by Edwin Catmull, James Blinn, and finally Bui-Tuong Phong. Blinn is also credited for the invention of "bump mapping," which inaugurated a series of tools that extended the possibilities of image-editing tools (introduced in software such as Photoshop) to three-dimensional modelers. Architects would only enter this domain in the 1990s, when a young generation of designers began to work with workstations that could run software able to model and render complex geometries. In about a decade, architectural representation moved from wireframe visualizations of SOM's proposal for 875 Third Avenue in Manhattan (1981) to fully colored renderings of Frank Gehry's Villa Olímpica (1989–92) in Barcelona ▶ Fig. VI.

In the case of "bump mapping" we begin to observe the combination of properties generally belonging to image-editing software and surface modelers. Again, the unifying abstraction of binary computation allows recombining elements and, perhaps more importantly here, exploitation through algorithms. These have their own rules that determine what will be computed and how. Algorithms are therefore active components that can extract radically different images from the same data set. This new condition is a consequence of Turing's architecture, one in which hardware, software, and data are all handled through a single logic, that of binary numeration. The complex interplay between invariants and variables can therefore take place, and with it the possibility of radically challenging not only the status of images and objects but also the notion of creativity itself.

When Carlo Sini examined such automatic processes, he turned to Nietzsche's account of how knowledge emerges by moving something from the domain of the unknown or stranger into that of the known or familiar.[3] Such a process has similarities with

3   Friedrich Nietzsche, *Frammenti Postumi 1885–1887*, Italian translation, *Opere*, vol. 8 (Milan: Adelphi, 1975). Cited in Carlo Sini, *L'Uomo, La Macchina, L'Automa: Lavoro e conoscenza tra future prossimo e passato remoto* (Turin: Bollati Boringhieri, 2009), 48.

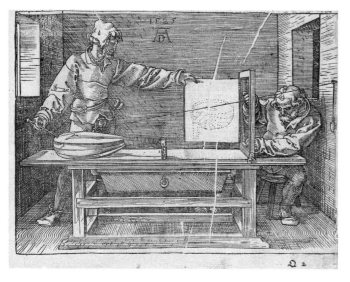

V   Albrecht Dürer, *Underweysung der Messung, mit dem Zirckel un Richtscheyt*, 1525

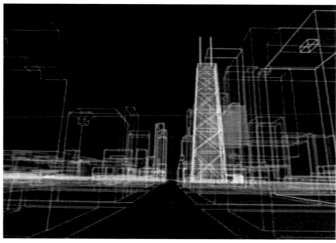

VI   Still frame from Skidmore, Owings & Merrill's *9 Cities* animation, 1984

algorithmic apprehension and is of use in framing how digital images and design interact. Two steps characterize it: "exteriorization" of data and individuation of a unit of measurement. With the first step, Sini identifies the extraction of a particular data set from the totality or flow of data, a process of discrimination between what will be computed and what will not. The second operation pertains to algorithms as they apprehend a data set according to the instructions scripted in them. This process eventually returns a new image of the initial data set. In Piero's example 128 points are selected from the totality of possible points surveyed, and these are then algorithmically recalculated to generate infinite new drawings of the human head from the data rather than the original model.

Despite the massive distance in time, similar conversations took place at the US National Bureau of Standards, where Russell A. Kirsch developed the first digital scanner in 1957. While working on the project, the team led by Kirsch confronted the new numerical nature of digital images when they had to script an adequate algorithmic process that acknowledged the non-perspectival nature of an image generated by a scanner. The image (a picture of Kirsch's son) emerged not from geometry but from the bounce of a beam of light. The model of reference was still human sight, except that rather than concentrating on the "eye," it was the "brain" (i.e., the algorithm) that focused the team's efforts. Kirsch looked at the cognitive sciences for his algorithm and came up with a model that equated neuronal activities to binary inputs. The result could only be composed of a series of black-and-white pixels that immediately appeared to be excessively oversimplified. Rather than being purely technical, the issue was also intellectual. The algorithm was not sufficiently advanced in setting adequate processes of "exteriorization" and measuring.[4]

The rewriting of data by algorithms also affects CGI. Among the many excellent examples are the renderings produced by Richard Voss in the early 1980s of different mountainous landscapes generated through fractals. Incremental tweaks in the algorithm's parameters gave rise to substantially different landscapes despite the fact that they were all based on the same data set ▶ Fig. VII.

Computer Renderings: Designing in a Field of Numbers

The cumulative effect of these developments merging pre-computer and born-digital innovations brings us to the role of CGI in contemporary design discourses and an examination of what this affords designers. Though these effects may influence different and possibly unrelated areas of design, they are held together by the common ability to affect more than just technical developments and provide designers with opportunities to rethink both output and working methods.

As already mentioned, the computational architecture of CAD has provided a platform whereby techniques that had been running on parallel trajectories for several centuries were able to merge. Computer renderings combine scientific technologies such as surveying, optics, and descriptive geometry, which played a key role between the fifteenth and eighteenth centuries, with photography, and its ability to record light and color, as well as cinema, which enabled the introduction of time. Today most CAD packages provide tools that seamlessly merge techniques coming from all these fields, while adding tools for manipulation based on algorithms. This is a new aesthetic condition in which designers can easily interact with at least four different artistic disciplines, borrow from them, and apply them to their work.

This also extends to the mode of consumption of such artifacts that are no longer bound to the screen: Virtual and Augmented Reality allow volumetric and real-time interactions with the objects modeled. Such a technological convergence allows designers to work simultaneously with data, algorithms, and space, and to venture once again into the representation of elusive qualities of space, including architectural elements such as lighting effects, transparencies and translucencies, and ephemeral elements that

VII Richard Voss, *Changing Fractal Dimension*, 1983

may only appear under certain scripted conditions. Similarly, AR and VR move the designer's point of view (and, later, the user's) in the digital space, which can be read as either a simulation of actual space or an end product in its own right.

This technological convergence constitutes a distinct feature of the digital age, and of our contemporary culture in general: not only can synesthetic properties of spaces be conjured up, but they can find in the plasticity of algorithmic thinking a fertile infrastructure for expression. The ease with which designers manipulate a complex three-dimensional space has changed the way they interpret their role in the city. Many parameters can be altered in the settings menus of rendering engines to test different lighting conditions and to simulate different environments an object or a building might encounter in its future life. More radically, these engines provide an ideal testing ground for capturing the ephemeral and perceptual qualities of architecture that may both exceed and add to the formal qualities of the architecture. A case in point are the rendering techniques employed by Jean Nouvel, who deliberately deployed these tools to deviate from the codes of architectural representation. For instance, orthographic drawings of his buildings are situated in more extreme, subtler, and, in other words, less normative conditions such as nighttime to emphasize the ephemeral, complex interaction between buildings and cities. In his words, "[...] We should be able to take advantage of the emerging poetic dimension of technology. It is ridiculous to see that schools still study the buildings through the production of 45 degree shadows [...] For me it is also important to study a building as it will appear in the fog, under the rain, or at night [...] I think that the coloured red lights and signs of a commercial street are one of the most astonishing architectural spectacles."[5] What computer renderings are challenging here is the solidity and permanence of architecture, which is progressively eroded by portraying buildings as dynamic objects in dynamic environments affected by various lighting conditions or by mutating technological and socioeconomic qualities of their context.

From a strictly technical point of view, CGI take place in two distinct digital spaces: objects are modeled in the vector space of CAD, whereas renderings materialize as collections of pixels arrayed in a grid in the raster space of the screen. Vector space is by definition a scaleless environment: objects are described by coordinates and transformations are governed by mathematical operations such as addition or multiplication of vectors. The collection of objects populating such a space are an invariant in regards to the choices users make to visualize them; operations of zooming or rotating the point of view do not alter the objects in the space, but simply recompute their position onscreen. On the other hand, the space of the screen is bound to its resolution and therefore to issues of scale; altering a resolution has tangible effects on what is produced or visible.

In their work Michael Hansmeyer and Marjan Colletti have been able to entangle both spaces to create formal compositions that explore and bypass the limitations of raster space by working on the vectorial (formal) resolution of their designs. In Colletti's work, these possibilities are explored in 2-D drawings, 3-D compositions, and animated space. The spatial complexity of the final composition is such that the fragment no longer appears as a simplification of the whole ▶ Fig. VIII. By taking advantage of the properties of vector space, his design aesthetic no longer seeks reduction as it does not need to confront the potential loss of resolution imposed by raster display. When observed in its totality, the composition can subsequently reach stunning levels of complexity by exploiting such abundance of information unencumbered by preoccupations of top-down order and legibility ▶ Fig. IX.

In order to better appreciate the innovative qualities that raster manipulation of space has brought to architecture, it is useful to compare Colletti's work to Richard Voss's, which was based on fractal algorithms. The ability to maintain unaltered levels of resolution when moving from the whole to a part evokes ideas of fractals and self-similarity. The comparison, however, does not go

4 Roberto Bottazzi, *Digital Architecture beyond Computers: Fragments of a Cultural History of Computational Design* (New York, London: Bloomsbury Academic, 2018), 112.
5 Alejandro Zaera-Polo, "Incorporating: Interview with Jean Nouvel," *El Croquis: Jean Nouvel 1987–1994*, no. 65–66 (1994): 35.

VIII Marjan Colletti, Zooming (3.13%–6.40% without loss of resolution) into the vectorial field of a 2½-D drawing, 2000–2004

further as, equipped with exponentially more powerful machines, Colletti conjures up spaces that are no longer bound by predetermined notions of order, not even self-similarity. The technological possibilities of CAD's vectorial space allows designers to morphologically articulate objects ad infinitum by closing the gap between data and form to establish connections and mutual transformations between the two.

One novel aspect of this line of research is its ability to blend the rigor of computation with perceptual effects that are born-digital. The most immediate reference for such an approach would be baroque architecture, but this would also be limiting: if baroque architects often expressed similar cultural concerns by employing spirals in their buildings—an open, disorienting geometrical figure without beginning or end—here it is the exploitation of the properties of software modelers and renderers that allows contemporary designers to overcome inherited models of order.

Finally, the digitization of images prompted by their numerical translation supersedes the visual paradigm of modern perspective and the lenticular culture behind it, Computer vision finds a key turning point with the invention of the digital scanner, developed at the US National Bureau of Standards by Russell A. Kirsch in 1957. This invention, which came at the end of almost a century of research, moved the image acquisition process beyond both mechanical (perspective machines) and chemical (photography) paradigms, as it utilized electrical signals to both scan and transmit data. We saw how this differs from, for instance, Piero's *Other Method* and the new role algorithms acquired in this process. As we pointed out in the introduction, "seeing by numbers" constitutes a new paradigm in which how we see increasingly coincides with what we see—a decisive difference from historical precedents. Kirsch's team experienced firsthand a condition that we all confront now. The centrality of algorithms is all the more obvious today and completely redefines what seeing means: Military drones using computer vision "see" humans not as geometries but as warmer areas (through heat maps), bypassing visual semantics. Architects increasingly survey cities or landscapes through LIDAR scanners that "see" through a laser beam. There are no lenses, and therefore there is no need for light to act as a conduit of information to be recorded on a medium.

As perspective is abandoned as a "symbolic form," another mathematics takes care of the synthetic apprehension of reality, no longer directly accessible to humans but rather interpreted by algorithms. Because of its pervasive application, computer vision represents the frontier of digitally generated images, the liquefaction of medium into numerical fields apprehended by algorithms. It is on this level that architects and designers in general will have to develop a new form of digital literacy, one that may broadly look like the historical overview provided here—that is, the performance of a complex dance between history and technology in order to tease out and exploit creative opportunities.

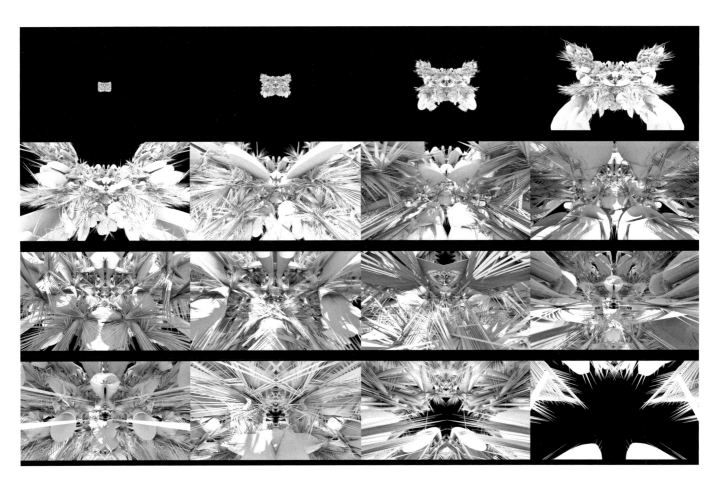

IX   Marjan Colletti, Screenshots of a fly-through into the
     vectorial field of a 3½-D model, 2014–19

Movement, Time, and Architecture

Teresa Fankhänel

"Computer graphics is growing very rapidly; only computer animation grows faster."[1] So began the second edition of the book *Computer Animation: Theory and Practice* by Nadia Magnenat Thalmann and Daniel Thalmann, which was the first comprehensive guide for computer animation when it first appeared in 1985. When the updated and expanded edition came out five years later, animated films were just about to make their commercial breakthrough. Two films that premiered in cinemas in 1991 became milestones in the history of digital film: *Terminator II* and Disney's *Beauty and the Beast*. Both used pioneering methods: *Terminator II* made the public familiar with morphing and texture mapping, while *Beauty and the Beast* was the first feature film to have computer-created, three-dimensional color images.[2] *Toy Story* (1995), the first completely digitally created feature film, came out four years later. The techniques, which were invented in the research laboratories of North American universities and by subcontractors to the film industry, not only displaced traditional film and animation techniques from their dominant position but also considerably influenced design professions such as those related to architecture.

Much happened between 1957, the year in which Russell Kirsch scanned the first computer-generated raster image with only 176 × 176 pixels, and the premiere of *Toy Story*. In the 1960s it became possible for the first time to create two- and later three-dimensional drawings with computers and eventually to model solid objects. Almost at the same time there were new programs to color, texture, and illuminate these objects with natural lighting effects in order to achieve a more realistic appearance. In architecture the computer made it possible for the first time to depict time and motion digitally—in design, for presentations, and for experiencing architectural spaces. Virtual objects began to move and deform according to specified parameters. Today, users can walk through digital models and use motion to tell a story.

A Question of Technology

Early computer hardware was unable to depict complex shapes convincingly or to store them. Oscilloscopes were the first screens which were connected to computers. Based on vector displays, which were originally invented by Ferdinand Braun in 1897, and on experiments performed in the mid-nineteenth century,[3] these circular screens were used by the US military as radar screens at the end of the 1950s. Ivan Sutherland's famous Sketchpad program, the first CAD software, also ran on a TX-2 computer with a cathode-ray tube display (CRT).[4] The problem with these screens was that they could not display any static images and therefore the lines on the screen had to be continuously refreshed to create the impression of permanence. However, this could not hide the blinking of the screen, which worked against the notion of a stable image. It was only at the end of the 1960s, when Tektronix brought out a direct-view storage tube, that static drawings could be stored directly in the screen and that stationary images could be created.[5] Priced at less than US$10,000, these terminals were the first devices to prove attractive to architectural offices.[6] Like the earlier displays, these screens were limited to illuminated green vector drawings and could only display one static image, after which the whole screen had to be redrawn. With the invention in the early 1970s of frame buffers, local memory units integrated into the screen, it became possible to store more than one frame and hence show sequences of images.[7] A few years later these frame buffers were combined with raster-scan color screens that displayed raster points and 3-D color shading instead of vectors, which made it possible for them to show realistic three-dimensional images.[8]

It was not until the 1980s, however, that the fundamental problem of digital computers was solved, as moving digital images were constrained by another data storage problem in addition to their visibility on the display: the only way a moving image could be displayed was by filming individual images from the display with a film camera capable of photographing individual frames. Various devices were invented to automatically trigger an analog camera whenever a new digital image had been calculated by the computer and made visible on the display.[9] A few minutes' film of this type often took hours and many night shifts to create on mainframe computers with the required computing power. The result was an analog film comprising digitally programmed images. The process was not only time-consuming but laborious and costly.

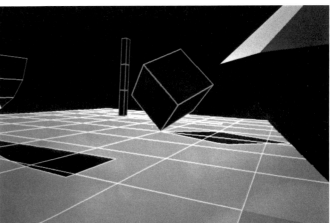

II   Solid model with a wireframe appearance

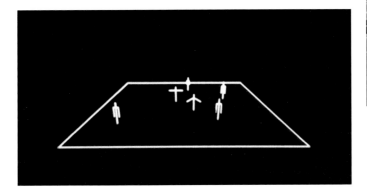

I   *Computer-Generated Ballet* by Michael Noll, 1965

TRON (1982) was the first and the only longer feature film to contain images made by this method; including about twenty minutes of spectacular computer-generated footage.[10]

The data storage problem remained until the invention of media with enough capacity to digitally store and play the large amounts of information generated for moving images. Until well into the 1970s, digital data for animations were fed into the computer using punch cards, which in their abstract, binary logic were an early form of storage for instructions to be executed on the computer. This technology stemmed from the nineteenth century and had originally been used for looms and other analog automated machinery, such as Charles Babbage's Analytical Engine.[11] This system was also used for digital computers, and the cards were often referred to as Hollerith cards, after their inventor, Herman Hollerith. Magnetic tape and drums took over the task of storing data in the 1960s, and floppy disks and hard drives transferred this technology onto portable and less expensive storage media. It was not until the 1980s, however, when optical storage media such as CDs and DVDs came onto the market, that larger and interactive data sets such as films and computer programs could be digitally played back.

From the Line to the Object

Ivan Sutherland's vector drawing program Sketchpad, the first CAD software, was developed in 1963 at the Massachusetts Institute of Technology (MIT) to facilitate technical drawing. The novelty of this program was that it graphically enabled the user to draw lines and shapes directly on a CRT, allowing immediate visual verification of the design. The program also contained a limited number of programmed modifications to be made on the drawn object, including scaling or rotating. In addition it was able to store shapes that had already been drawn and bring them out of storage

when needed, which greatly simplified repetitive processes. While the first program was two-dimensional, a 3-D version appeared a year later. For the first time, this enabled users to create digital objects without having to learn programming languages, which until then had dominated early computer art. In both versions the drawn objects were displayed only by their edges, as wireframes. They could not be filled, and the shapes remained transparent. Yet, the program made it possible for the first time to receive a preview of a designed object on a screen in real time.

Just one year after Sketchpad, Michael Noll created the first film with computer-animated, two-dimensional wireframe figures, *Computer-Generated Ballet*, at the Bell Lab in New Jersey, on the Graphic 1 computer ▶ Fig. I. Noll used the program BFLEX, developed in-house, to draw a "stage" and several stick figures that executed a simple dance choreography.[12] With the invention of solid modeling, which made its first appearance on the market as part of the SynthaVision 1967 software package, it was soon possible to create three-dimensional objects whose hidden edges could be blanked out according to the perspective of the observer. The visibility problem of the early wireframes was solved by a hidden-surface determination algorithm ▶ Fig. II.[13] A little later, materials could be represented on the outer skin of these shapes.

1   Nadia Magnenat Thalmann and Daniel Thalmann, *Computer Animation: Theory and Practice* (London: Springer, 1990), vii.
2   Tom Sito, *Moving Innovation: A History of Computer Animation* (Cambridge, MA: MIT Press, 2013), 232.
3   Jon Peddie, *The History of Visual Magic in Computers* (London: Springer, 2013), 294.
4   See the section about Sketchpad in this book, pp. 34–37.
5   Peddie, *The History of Visual Magic in Computers*, 321–22.
6   Ibid., 323.
7   Ibid., 325.
8   Ibid., 333.
9   Susan Doubilet, "The Big Picture," *Progressive Architecture*, May 1984, 144.
10 Sito, *Moving Innovation*, 163–64.
11 George Fierheller, *Do Not Fold, Spindle or Mutilate: The "Hole" Story of Punched Cards* (Markham, ON: Stewart Publishing, 2014), 14.
12 Michael Noll, "Computers and the Visual Arts," *Design Quarterly* 66/67 (1966): 65–71.
13 Ray Hill, "Synthavision: How a Computer Produces Movies," *Popular Science*, November 1973, 108–9.

At the University of Utah, where Sutherland taught as a professor after he left MIT and which was one of the centers for research into computer graphics in the 1960s and 1970s, Jim Blinn and Martin Newell made a groundbreaking step forward in 1976: texture mapping.[14] This technique allowed digital photos to be projected onto a three-dimensional form, which gave the object the appearance of materiality and therefore greater realism. The addition of textures and materials—today described as rendering—was, however, not the only realistic aspect. Being able to represent the effects of light, shadow, and reflections on the surfaces of objects was an important step in the search for photo-realistic images ▶ Fig. III. It was this realism that would prove to have an enormous influence on the development of new animation techniques in the film industry.[15]

Morphing: Deforming Objects

Ever since animated cartoons were invented in the early twentieth century and later made famous by Walt Disney, traditional handmade animations have been based on the creation of slightly altered images that simulate the impression of movement when played at high speed. The individual images were created in rapid succession by trained animators, who drew the intermediate steps between key frames from their imagination, converting the imagined 3-D objects into 2-D images.[16] With the advent of the computer, this work was greatly simplified by a technique that adopted the name used in analog animated films: interpolation, or inbetweening. Inbetweening or, as the name suggests, "putting something in between" perfectly describes the steps in the process: the computer calculates all the individual intermediate steps between key frames. This technique was initially based only on two-dimensional vector drawings, since the computer, unlike the human brain, had great difficulty in converting complex moving objects from 3-D to 2-D. The first freely available two-dimensional software aimed at architects and artists was the Graphics Symbiosis System (GRASS) by Thomas DeFanti (1974), which could perform simple movements, color changes, and rotations.[17] A 3-D version was released under the name ZGRASS in 1978. Another way to produce moving images was to script a motion sequence, but this required knowledge of programming languages, which only a few architects possessed. One of the most well-known programs was ASAS, which was used to animate many of the sequences in *TRON*.[18] In the 1980s the term *morphing* came into use. It had the same meaning as the older names, but it implied more complex transformations that could be performed on the basis of polygon meshes. The earliest demonstration of such a process took place at the SIGGRAPH conference in 1982.[19] The film *Terminator II* (1991) introduced this technique to a worldwide audience using the software Alias. In several scenes the Terminator T-1000, a humanoid robot, seamlessly transforms from a human figure into liquid metal and back ▶ Fig. IV.

While early computer animations such as Michael Noll's dancing stick figures were based on simple two-dimensional, and later three-dimensional, shapes, the discovery of new geometric calculation methods made it possible to display complex, doubly curved and non-Euclidean shapes such as NURBS curves onscreen. This development in the field of topology, a branch of mathematics dealing with the behavior of surfaces under deformation, took place on both sides of the Atlantic in the automobile industry. It was taken forward by General Motors with the invention of B-splines, and further developed by the aerospace industry with the invention of NURBS curves.[20] In the film industry these methods and the software applications based on them have been used, for example, to create smoother, more controllable surfaces for complex 3-D objects or for the skin of the faces of

14 Wayne E. Carlson, *Computer Graphics and Computer Animation: A Retrospective Overview* (Columbus, OH: n.d.), 610–11, ohiostate.pressbooks.pub/ graphicshistory/, accessed February 28, 2020.

15 John Hollar, *Oral History of Edwin Catmull: 2013 Computer History Museum Fellow* (Emeryville, CA: 2013), 8, CHM reference number X6771.2013.

16 Sito, *Moving Innovation*, 218.

17 Carlson, *Computer Graphics and Computer Animation*, 105.

18 Ibid., 236.

19 John McCann and Alessandro Rizzi, *The Art and Science of HDR Imaging* (Chichester, UK: 2012).

20 Alastair Townsend, "On the Spline," *International Journal of Interior Architecture + Spatial Design* 3 (2014): 48–59.

III Reflections and distortions on three-dimensional objects
    by J. Turner Whitted, 1979

IV Morphing scene from *Terminator II*, 1991

humans or animals. *Toy Story* was the first feature film to use this technique to great effect. The round face of the main character Woody, the sheriff among the toys, could thus be modeled almost lifelike and show even the smallest muscle movements. Only with the film *Geri's Game* (1997) and new techniques for subdivision surfaces—that is, polygonal surfaces that could be divided into infinitely small subsections to give the appearance of a continuous surface—did it become possible to create completely smooth surfaces without edges.[21]

The 1980s marked the beginning of architecture's adoption of computer visualizations, morphing, and animations, which were based on the technical developments of previous decades and for the first time allowed the creation of simulations previously found impossible. What was new was that architects no longer used the traditional representations—plan, elevation, and section—but created 3-D models that were viewable from any angle. Outside the film industry, art and architecture schools were among the first to install computers and commercial software and to offer students the opportunity to experiment with the new animation programs. The most successful programs at the beginning of the 1990s were the Canadian software Softimage (1988), Alias (1985), and later Maya (1998), which enabled the deformation of three-dimensional objects based on given parameters and concepts, such as fluid dynamics between key frames. On this basis a completely new architectural language emerged in the 1990s, which increasingly made use of non-Euclidean shapes created by morphing. The blob is certainly the best known of these digitally conceived forms ▶ Fig. V.[22] They all had one thing in common: their creation in the computer. Individual shapes were created as 3-D models and then stretched, compressed, turned, or otherwise deformed over a finite period of time. Significantly, Greg Lynn, one of the pioneers of this movement, called his first published work *Animate Form* (1000). This new design method, however, was not without its own problems. One of the main questions facing architects was when to stop the morphing process for a design, also known as the stopping problem.[23] Because, despite the software, it was always architects who ultimately had to select and finalize a design—a key frame—from the multitude of options created over a certain period of time.

Animation: Moving Objects

Digitally created objects were freed from their static existence in the 1980s and began to move. Motion path animation made it possible for the first time to have simple objects such as cubes, columns, or even cars perform a precisely defined motion based on a given path, as in a script ▶ Fig. VI. This innovation offered the opportunity to produce short animations using digital models. Crucial to obtaining the most realistic representation possible was that the moving objects obeyed physical laws, the effects of which were simulated on three-dimensional objects in a simplified form, as in the animation *Rigid Body Dynamics Simulations* by James Hahn (1987), in which, although the movement of falling objects is simulated, no deformations caused by it can be recognized.[24] Early computer animations in architecture, such as Skidmore, Owings & Merrill's *9 Cities* or *Cornell in Perspective* by Donald Greenberg, had experienced the previously mentioned problem of inadequate digital storage media, so they were filmed directly from the screen as single images. The appearance of movement was created only on the 16mm film.

This changed in the 1990s with the advent of programs that could both animate the shapes themselves and take pictures in and around objects along predetermined routes with a virtual camera. The entries for the Eyebeam Center in New York (2001), one of the first architectural competitions in which an animation was explicitly required as part of the design, were an early highlight of this new form of narrative.[25] Many of these early animations used simple flights around a model or through its interior. They often opted for movements that would be impossible in reality, such as penetrating the outer skin of the building or flying through walls and ceilings. Others, such as Greg Lynn, used animation to illustrate the process of creating a morphed form, making the design concept of the building understandable. What they all have in common is that the architects themselves were able, as directors, to decide what was to be shown by choosing the digital camera positions.

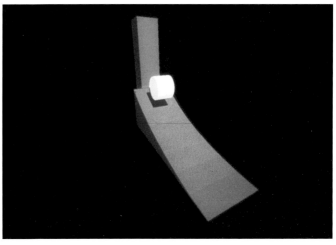

VI Moving simple shapes in space with rigid body dynamics

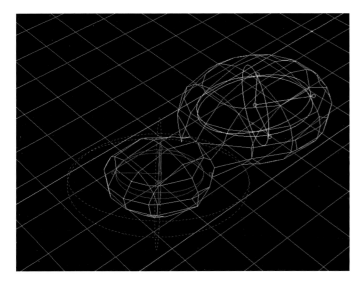

V Bubble master geometry by Bernhard Franken, 1991–99

The Fourth Dimension: New Worlds

The ability to create virtual models that can realistically render and faithfully reproduce an object provides architects with a tool not only to get a digital preview of their work onscreen, but also to create a whole new genre of architectural visualization. For the first time it is possible to enter a building digitally, move around in it with ease, and observe a high degree of detail before it has been completed. Due to their complexity, living beings were for a long time the most difficult entities to model and animate. The animation of three-dimensional representations of people was and remains the supreme discipline within animation, due to the high number of degrees of freedom and independent movements of individual joints and muscles. William Fetter was the first to draw a 3-D computer model of a seated human body, the Boeing Man ▶ Fig. VII.[26] Further groundbreaking work on the way to animating a human body followed. In 1972, Edwin Catmull and Fred Parke created a computer-animated and -textured hand that, together with a rotating digital face, was used in the science fiction film *Futureworld* (1976); it was even possible to move individual fingers.[27] David Zeltzer and Donald Stredney created an animation in the mid-1980s in which a human skeleton was able to perform a few movements such as running and jumping in a fluid manner.[28] Moreover, at the New York Institute of Technology, Garland Stern developed a similar program called BBOP, which allowed interactive control of joints and interpolation of movements between key frames.[29] Woody and Buzz Lightyear, the main characters in the film *Toy Story*, were among the first digital beings whose appearance and movement came close to reality. Woody was so complex that he had hundreds of individual motion controls, including nearly three hundred for his face. For a long time, despite detailed digital

models, it had remained impossible to capture human perspectives in moving computer models. In 1957 the architect Gordon Cullen coined the term *serial vision*, which described a sequence of seven images that represented what a person sees when moving through a space.[30] Only after the technology had developed enough to allow the film character Woody to move around in digital spaces were designers able, by means of a digital camera placement or an avatar, to take a new viewpoint from the pedestrian's perspective in other 3-D models. They could also explore spaces that would be impossible to enter in the built reality due to their geometry or impossible structure. These virtual realities convey the possibilities of a spatial experience accessible only in the digital space of the screen or VR glasses. An early example of this is the design for an online branch of the Guggenheim Museum (1999–2001) by Asymptote, in which the digital building constantly changes shape and contains spaces through which the visitor can move only via an interface ▶ Fig. VIII.[31]

For many other architects who are interested in alternative spaces, the foundations for this new outlook lie in developments that took place outside architecture: in Albert Einstein's quantum theory and in chaos research. In loose interpretation of these concepts, space

21 Tony DeRose et al., "Subdivision Surfaces in Character Animation," *SIGGRAPH '98: Proceedings of the 25th Annual Conference on Computer Graphics and Interactive Techniques*, July 1998, 85–94.

22 Greg Lynn, "Blobs, or Why Tectonics Is Square and Topology Is Groovy," *ANY* 14 (1996): 58–61.

23 Richard Garber, "Building Information Modeling," in *The Digital Turn in Architecture 1992–2012*, ed. Mario Carpo (Chichester, UK: Wiley, 2013), 232.

24 James Hahn, "Realistic Animation of Rigid Bodies," *Computer Graphics* 22, no. 4 (August 1988): 299–308.

25 See the section about the Eyebeam Center in this book, pp. 142–46.

26 Peddie, *History of Visual Magic*, 101.

27 Sito, *Moving Innovation*, 64, 154.

28 Charles Csuri and David Zeltzer, "Goal-Directed Movement Simulation," *Proceedings of the 7th Canadian Man-Computer Communications Conference*, Waterloo (Ontario), 1981, 271–80.

29 Carlson, 237.

30 Madis Pihlak, "Revisiting Animation," *Landscape Architecture Magazine* 92, no. 3 (March 2002): 48.

31 Hani Rashid and Lise Anne Couture, *Asymptote: Flux* (New York: Phaidon, 2002).

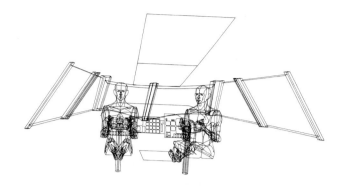

VII Boeing Man by William Fetter, 1966–69

is no longer seen as static and fixed, as it had been since Descartes and the Cartesian coordinate system, but as polymorphic, changeable, and flexible.[32] Space, according to this view, is relativistic, and time becomes an important dimension in the experience of architecture. Movement, time, and architecture influence and depend on each other in this virtual architecture. Since the 1990s this digital, moving architecture has allowed people, with the help of new technologies, to create stories, spaces, and experiences that have only become fully accessible through the computer and that are strongly reminiscent of the virtual space Michael Benedikt described in his 1991 book *Cyberspace: First Steps*: "Cyberspace: The tablet become a page become a screen become a world, a virtual world. Everywhere and nowhere, a place where nothing is forgotten and yet everything changes."[33]

32 Gregory More, "Animated Techniques: Time and the Technological Acquiescence of Animation," *Architectural Design* 71 (April 2001): 20–27.
33 Michael Benedikt, ed., *Cyberspace: First Steps* (Cambridge, MA: MIT Press, 1991), 1.

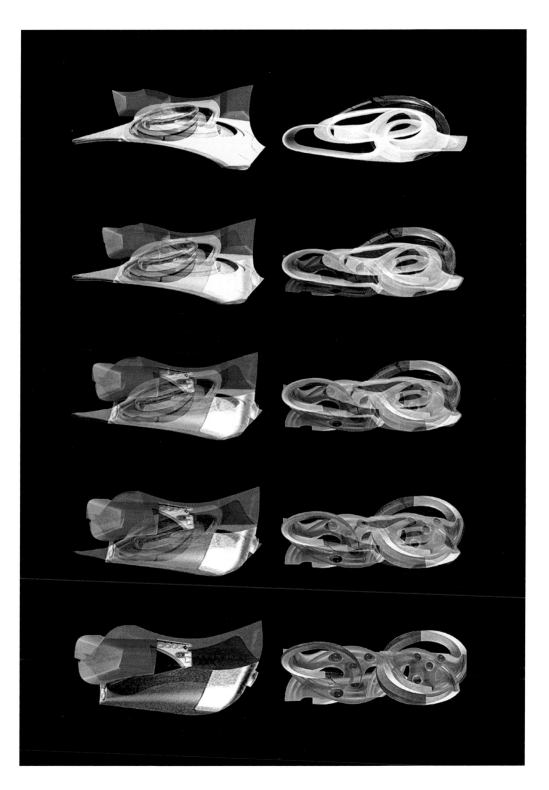

VIII Moving architecture of the Guggenheim Virtual Museum, 2001

Cornell in Perspective

Donald P. Greenberg, Students at Cornell University College of Architecture, Art, and Planning

1969—1972

HARDWARE
color TV screen

PURPOSE OF SOFTWARE
Purpose of software: 3-D modeling, rendering

Cornell in Perspective was one of the first walk-throughs of a digital architectural model. It was created at Cornell University College of Architecture, Art, and Planning by Donald P. Greenberg and his students. The video is eighteen and a half minutes long and shows the evolution of the Arts Quadrangle at Cornell from 1865 to 1875, with all buildings fully rendered and textured. Greenberg had started working with computers in the 1960s and began teaching computer-aided design at Cornell in 1965. He received his PhD in Engineering in 1968 and is now director of the Program of Computer Graphics at Cornell University. For *Cornell in Perspective* Greenberg wrote his own programs and used the computer facilities at the nearby General Electric Visual Simulation Laboratory at Syracuse University at night to render the images. All programmed information had to be input via IBM punch cards, and it took forty-five seconds to render a single frame. The 3-D model was based on hidden surface algorithms with which opaque planes were built up from the background to the foreground, with each successive layer obscuring hidden lines depending on the location of the viewer. There were sixty-four color choices available for each frame. The rendered images were displayed on a color TV screen—a technique invented by the Visual Simulation Laboratory for astronauts training for docking maneuvers in space. The walk-through of the quadrangle was created by determining a starting and ending point as well as the number of frames per second after which the computer could generate the whole sequence. The final 16mm film was shot frame by frame directly from the TV screen.

Greenberg's work can be seen in the context of new developments in the treatment of computer-generated images, including halftone images, smooth shading, and illumination techniques. The project was meant as a preview and testing ground for the use of colored images as an architectural tool for visualizing designs from various viewpoints. Movement was meant to increase realism in portraying the experience of proposed additions to the built environment. Greenberg demonstrated this effect by moving I.M. Pei's proposed Herbert F. Johnson Museum of Art around the quadrangle to show the potential of the new technique. — *Teresa Fankhänel*

Greenberg, Donald. "Computer Graphics in Architecture." *Scientific American* 230, no. 5 (May 1974): 98–107. ● Greenberg, Donald. "Computers and Architecture." *Scientific American* 264, no. 2 (February 1991): 104–9.

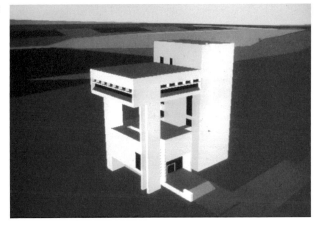

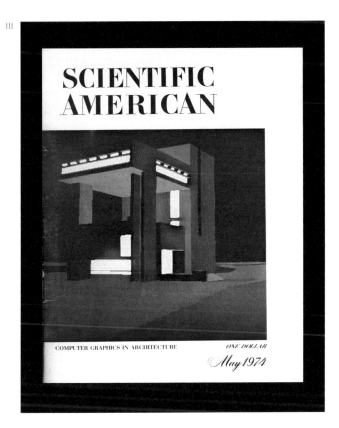

I   Arts Quadrangle at Cornell University
II–III Digital model of Herbert F. Johnson Museum of Art by I.M. Pei
IV   Donald Greenberg with Evans and Sutherland's Picture System I

Skeleton Animation System

David Zeltzer, Donald Stredney,
Judy Sachter (landscape model)

1983 — 1984

SOFTWARE
Skeleton Animation System, written in C
in Unix environment

HARDWARE
VAX 11/780 computer

PURPOSE OF SOFTWARE
animation

The Skeleton Animation System is an early digital animation of a human figure walking through a landscape and architectural setting. The animation uses "George," a three-dimensional skeleton that was developed by Donald Stredney and David Zeltzer as part of the Computer Graphics Research Group at Ohio State University, which had been founded by computer artist Charles Csuri in 1971. In the 1980s animations were based on the traditional 2-D animation technique of "in-betweening"—of interpolating changing shapes between key frames in the human animator's mind and then drawing them by hand. Computers, on the other hand, were unable to correctly calculate the appearance of moving or rotating three-dimensional shapes into two-dimensional representations between key frames. Therefore, movements in computer animations remained awkward and time-consuming.

To find a new solution, Zeltzer created a 3-D software called Skeleton Animation System that focused on autonomous legged motion animation of complex figures moving in nonlinear and variable ways. Studying animals to learn more about motion control, Zeltzer broke down these complex activities into smaller steps and used clinically recorded joint motions of walking humans to create a set of motor tasks for George. The skeleton's 3-D model was based on the measurements of a real human skeleton that Zeltzer and Stredney had obtained from a mortician, who had named the specimen George. With the help of Zeltzer's software the figure could follow a predetermined movement script. In several animations George can be seen walking and jumping through even and uneven terrain, landscapes, and fully textured and rendered architectural settings. His movements were described procedurally, which meant that individual joints could move in relation to all other parts of the skeleton, resulting in more realistic motion.

Zeltzer completed his PhD on the "Representation and Control of Three Dimensional Computer Animated Figures" in 1984 and later continued research into animated 3-D models at Computer Graphics and Animation Group at MIT.—*Teresa Fankhänel*

Csuri, Charles, and David Zeltzer. "Goal-Directed Movement Simulation." In *Proceedings of the 7th Canadian Man–Computer Communications Conference*, 271–80. Waterloo, Ontario, 1981. ● Hammond, Allen. "A Palette for Computers." *Mosaic*, November/December 1982, 35–40. ● Jones, Angie, and Jamie Oliff. *Thinking Animation: Bridging the Gap between 2D and CG*. Independence, KY: Cengage Learning PTR, 2006, 123. ● Carlson, Wayne. *History of Computer Graphics and Animation* (Ohio State University). Accessed January 27, 2020. ohiostate.pressbooks.pub/graphicshistory/chapter/4-4-the-ohio-state-university/.

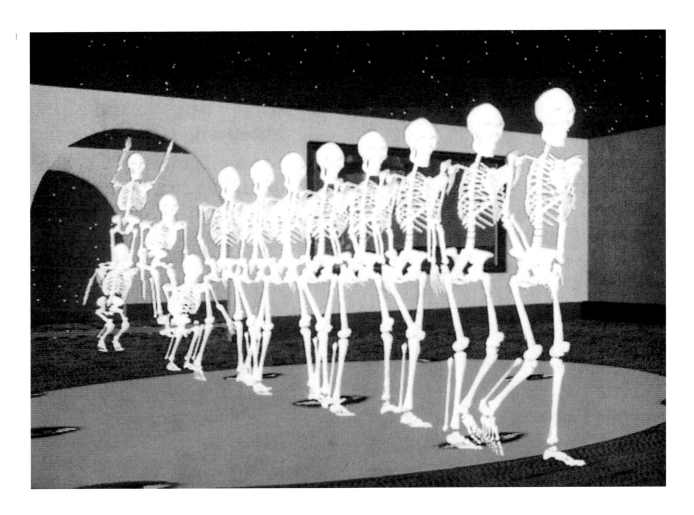

I   Stills of George jumping and walking
II George rotating

9 Cities

Skidmore, Owings & Merrill,
Robert Abel / William Kovacs Inc.

1984

SOFTWARE
DRAFT

HARDWARE
DEC PDP 11/70 minicomputer,
Tektronix 4014 terminal

PURPOSE OF SOFTWARE
3-D modeling, fly-through animation

9 Cities was meant as a marketing tool showcasing several of Skidmore, Owings & Merrill's iconic buildings in a wireframe fly-through of the locations of its nine branches in the early 1980s. SOM was a pioneering firm that began using computers in 1963 for engineering analysis. Since no commercial software was available at the time, the office developed its own solutions to tackle time-consuming tasks such as estimating costs and structural calculations. To assess square footage and costs for O'Hare Plaza in Chicago, Neil Harper and David Sides first developed a program called Building Optimization Program (BOP) in 1967, which ran on IBM 1130 terminals. As the client only cared about maximum return on investment, the software was based on calculating costs for four aspects—structure, exterior wall, mechanical system, and elevators—to find the most economic version. The text-based program was used for all subsequent buildings until 1990.

By 1980 the Computer Group within the firm had grown to include more than a hundred computer terminals in various branches. Research into software was headquartered in Chicago. A vast range of programs were written in-house to address managerial as well as design and engineering problems. They included precursors to today's BIM software such as BOP, Storage and Retrieval of Architectural Programming Information (SARAPI), and Architecture and Engineering Services (AES). Among the programs written in the 1970s and 1980s were several drawing programs, including an early 3-D modeling software called DRAW3D by Nicholas Weingarten, a former student of Donald Greenberg's at Cornell, and DRAFT by Mirsante and Huebner. For decades SOM cultivated a close research partnership with IBM, which eventually bought out AES in 1986.

While all the buildings in *9 Cities* had been designed using some of SOM's in-house software tools, the video shows them as simple mass models in their urban surroundings. All lines of the wireframes, even those that would normally be hidden, are clearly visible. In its aesthetics the animation was reminiscent of the simulation of a control display in an airplane approaching New York in the film *Escape from New York* (1981). Despite its futuristic look, *9 Cities* was filmed as a series of stills from a Tektronix display with a 16mm camera and dubbed with the Superman theme song.—*Teresa Fankhänel*

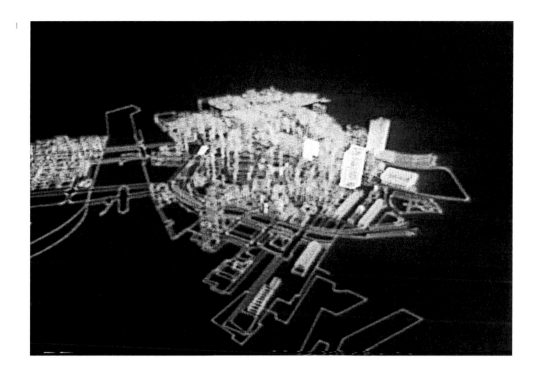

I   Still from *9 Cities*, Boston
II Still from *9 Cities*, Houston

Doubilet, Susan. "The Big Picture." *Progressive Architecture*, May 1984, 140–45.
● Fallon, Kristine. "Early Computer Graphics Developments in the Architecture, Engineering, and Construction Industry." *IEEE* 20, no. 2 (1998): 20–29. ● Adams, Nicholas. "Creating the Future (1964–86)." In *SOM Journal 8*, edited by Peter MacKeith. Berlin: Hatje Cantz, 2013. ● Liu, Ann. "Data Dreams: The Computer Group and Architecture by Spreadsheet, 1967–1984." In *Drawing Futures*, edited by Laura Allen and Luke Pearson, 224–33. London: Bartlett School of Architecture, 2016.

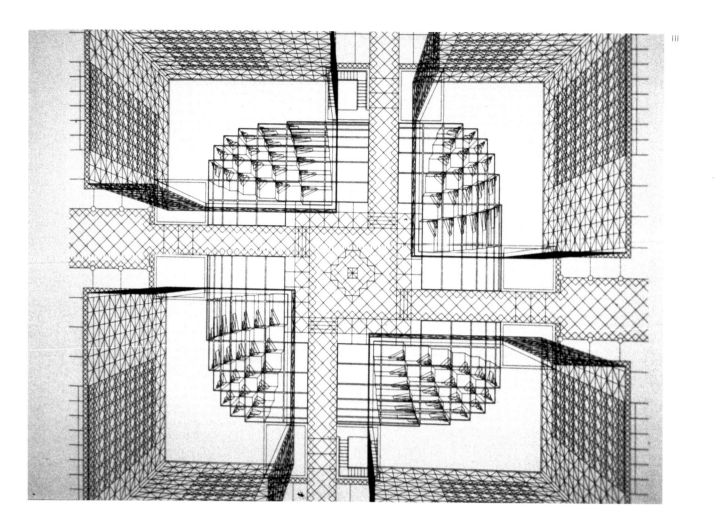

IV

DRAW3D	SYSTEM
SKETCH3D	DIGITIZER INPUT
DUAL3D	DUAL DIGITIZING PAIRS OF DRAWINGS OR PHOTOGRAPHS
TEXT3D	LABELING, DIMENSIONING AND TITLING
GROUP3D	GROUPING, EXTRUDING, ROTATING AND REPEATING OF ELEMENTS
GLOBAL3D	GLOBAL SCALING, ROTATING, TRANSLATING AND DELETING OF ELEMENTS
AREA3D	CALCULATIONS OF AREA, PERIMETER AND ANGLE
POLY3D	SCALING, ROTATING, TRANSLATING, DELETING AND REVERSING OF POLYGON ELEMENTS
MATH3D	LINE/LINE, LINE/PLANE, AND CIRC/CIRC INTERSECTIONS & OTHER MATH FUNCTIONS
CURVE3D	CIRCLES, CIRCULAR ARCS, SPIRALS, LOFTS, B-SPLINES, PATCHES & LOFTED SURFACES
PLOT3D	PLOT AND HIDDEN LINE OUTPUT FILES

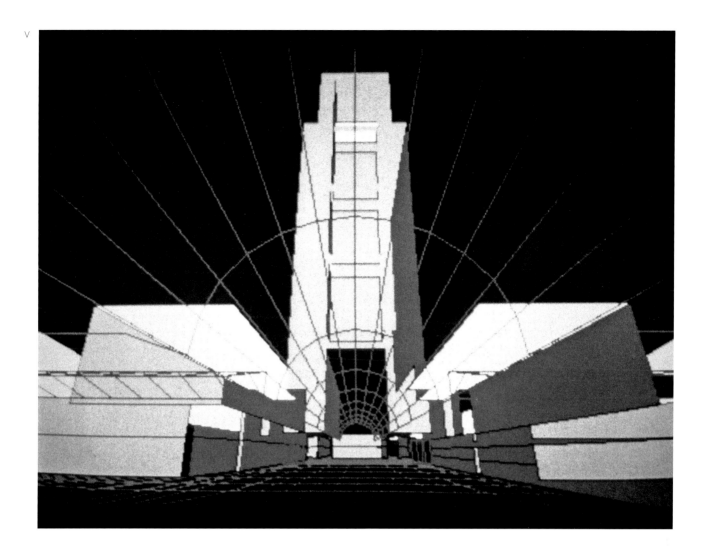

III Wireframe of proposed Kuwait Insurance Company building, 1984
IV Subprograms for DRAW3D, a predecessor of DRAFT
V Rendered image of proposed inner-city development with human vantage
    point, 1984

Locomotion Studies /
Evolved Virtual Creatures

Karl Sims

1987 / 1994

SOFTWARE
custom inverse kinematics and locomotion
software programmed in PL/1 *Locomotion
Studies*; evolutionary algorithms in C Programming
Language (*Evolved Virtual Creatures*)

HARDWARE
PDP11 computer (*Locomotion Studies*); Connection
Machine CM-5 (*Evolved Virtual Creatures*)

PURPOSE OF SOFTWARE
interactive evolution of animated forms

As landmarks in animation design and evolutionary algorithms, *Locomotion Studies* (1987) and *Evolved Virtual Creatures* (1994) show three-dimensional "evolved" creatures that were developed through genetic algorithms with limited human intervention. Karl Sims received his bachelor's degree in Life Sciences from MIT. In 1984 he left the university to work as an artist-in-residence at Thinking Machines Corporation (TMC). The supercomputer manufacturer and artificial intelligence company had been founded just a year earlier by MIT colleagues Sheryl Handler and Daniel Hillis, who developed the Connection Machine (CM). After his experiences at TMC, Sims returned to MIT's Media Lab and continued his research on graphics and animation, earning a master's degree in Visual Studies in 1987. Since then he works as a digital media artist and visual effects software developer.

His animations illustrate novel systems in the visualization of movement that show animallike creatures moving through a simulated three-dimensional space. In *Evolved Virtual Creatures*, Sims's critters are based on artificial evolution, a system that selects, varies, and re-creates them based on their ability to master different tasks. In analogy to Darwin's theory of biological evolution, a set of algorithms functions like a genotype, expressing a certain phenotype—in Sims's case cuboid-shaped creatures with various limbs and moving abilities, tubular inchworms or stick figures with up to six legs. Placed in a hilly landscape or in water, they need to move, working against the forces of gravity or resistance. They jump, roll, swim, shuffle, hobble, and crawl, sometimes hunting a red dot, testing their light sensibility. Some phenotypes prove successful, others do not. And as in nature, the survivors get to reproduce and their algorithmic genotypes get mixed at random to maintain the population, and the experiment starts again.

Locomotion Studies features a soundtrack that was likely produced on an early 1980s drum machine. *Evolved Virtual Creatures* has a descriptive, empathic, deep male voice-over—a cheeky nod to TV wildlife documentaries. Musical or verbal, both soundtracks underline the two animations as distinct places in the history of algorithmic design and digital storytelling.
—Sina Brückner-Amin

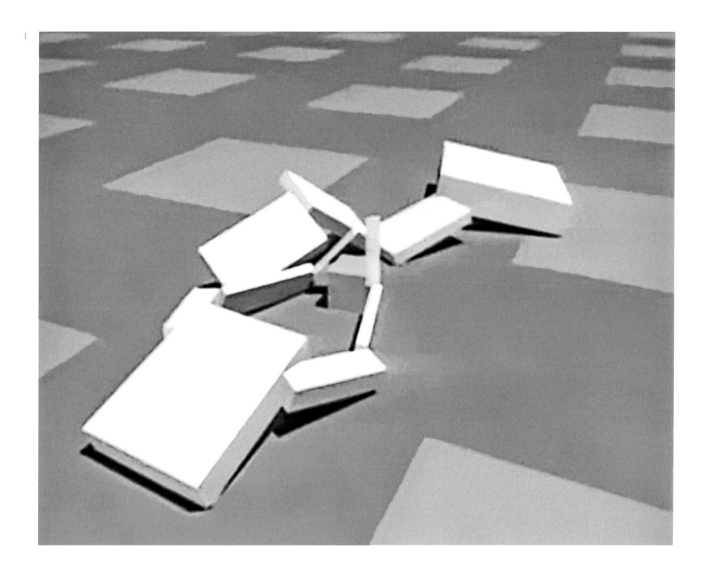

| Two Evolved Virtual Creatures competing for a green block

Sims, Karl. "Interactive Evolution of Equations for Procedural Models." *Visual Computer*, 1993, 466–76. ● Sims, Karl. "Evolving Virtual Creatures." *Siggraph '94 Conference Proceedings: Computer Graphics*. New York: ACM Siggraph, 1994, 15–22. ● Casti, John, and Anders Karlqvist, eds. *Art and Complexity*. Amsterdam: JAI Press, 2003, 23–24. ● Wünsche, Isabel, and Wiebke Gronemeyer, eds. *Practices of Abstract Art: Between Anarchism and Appropriation*. Newcastle upon Tyne, UK: Cambridge Scholars Publishing, 2016, 152–53.

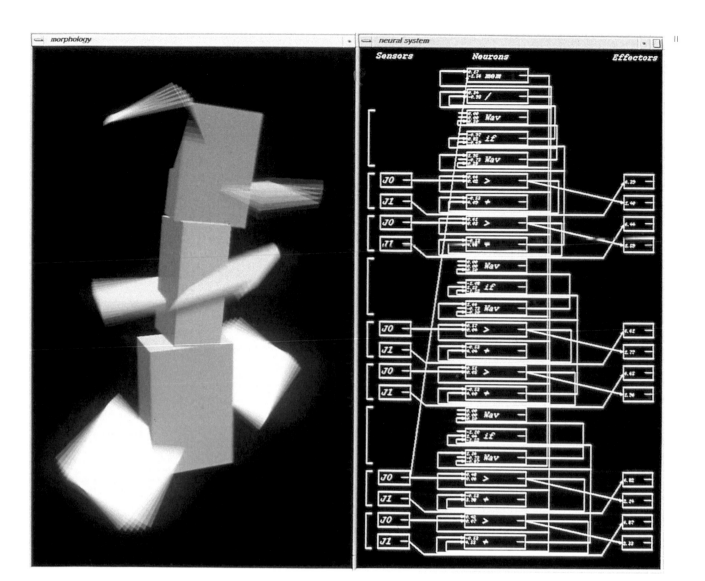

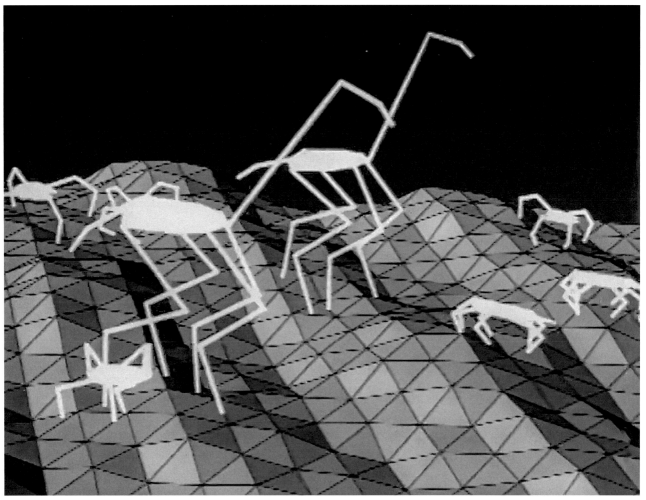

II   Morphology on the left and neural system of the phenotype on the right
III   Stick figures walking and jumping in *Locomotion Studies*

Eyebeam Atelier

Architecture Research Office, Asymptote Architecture, David Chipperfield Architects, Diller + Scofidio, Foreign Office Architects, Gluckman Mayner Architects, Greg Lynn FORM, Leeser Architecture, MVRDV, Neil M. Denari Architects, Preston Scott Cohen, Reiser + Umemoto, Rogers Marvel Architects, Steven Holl Architects, UNStudio

2000—2001

SOFTWARE
Quicktime, form·Z, Discreet, Photoshop, After Effects, Premiere, Radiosity (Leeser Architecture)

PURPOSE OF SOFTWARE
rendering, animation

The competition for the new Eyebeam Atelier was one of the first large-scale projects that asked for animations in the design brief. Eyebeam was a nonprofit museum of art and technology on West 21st Street in New York City that had been founded by filmmaker John S. Johnson in 1996. Thirty international offices were invited to a three-stage competition in 2000–2001. The goal was to explore a novel museum typology that catered to the presentation of new media, the connection between virtual and real spaces, and the ephemeral nature of born-digital content. The designs were meant to challenge the inherently static nature of gallery spaces that were now facing temporal, ever-changing digital artworks. The museum was supposed to include artist studios, classrooms, offices, exhibition and performance spaces, and a museum shop. Many of the entries built on the idea of folded and layered ribbons to visualize the program. For the second and third stages of the competition, short animations had to be handed in. They were meant to showcase movement through the spaces and the development of the formal and organizational structure of the building. Diller + Scofidio were announced as winners in early 2002. In the aftermath of 9/11, however, the museum was canceled.

Many of the entries used fly-throughs and simple movements around the building. Leeser Architecture's work is exemplary for the pioneering use of moving images. For their final animation they montaged several layers into a video of Lower Manhattan with the Twin Towers of the World Trade Center in the background. The model of the building had been constructed in form·Z. It was rendered and animated in Discreet, a predecessor of 3ds Max. Rendering remained a tedious undertaking; it took ten hours to create one HD image. Leeser's animations were inspired by movies as well as music videos. Their final video used "Keepin' It Steel" by Amon Tobin as a soundtrack.—*Teresa Fankhänel*

Muschamp, Herbert. "Art/Architecture: An Elegant Marriage of Inside and Outside." *New York Times*, October 21, 2001, 34. Kristal, Marc. "Measuring the Competition." *Metropolis*, November 2002. ● Meissner, Irene. "Projekt Eyebeam Museum of Art and Technology, New York." In *Exemplarisch. Konstruktion und Raum in der Architektur des 20. Jahrhunderts*, ed. Winfried Nerdinger, 164–65. Munich: Prestel, 2002. ● Turner, Grady, and Johnson, John. *Bomb Magazine*, February 19, 2004. Accessed November 20, 2019. bombmagazine.org/articles/john-johnson/. ● Canadian Centre for Architecture, ed. *Preston Scott Cohen, Eyebeam Atelier Museum*. Montreal: Canadian Centre for Architecture, 2017.

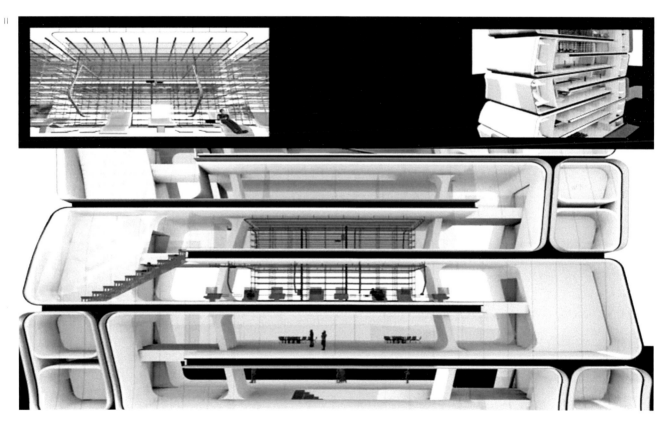

I Opening sequence by Leeser Architecture
II Still from animation by Leeser Architecture

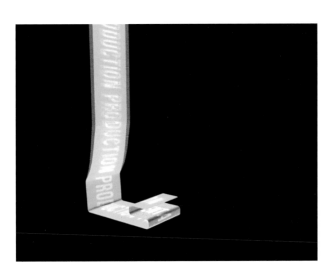 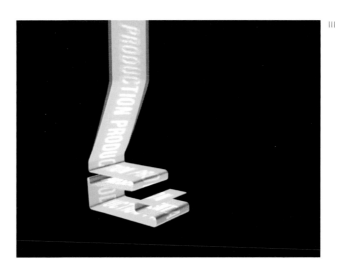

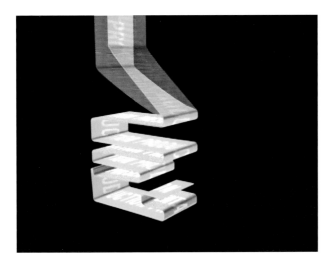 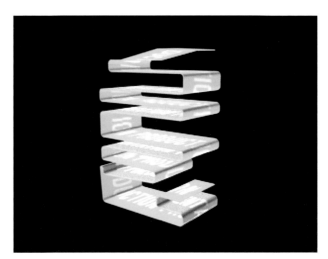

III Stills from Diller + Scofidio's first animation
IV Flight through the animated facade by Reiser + Umemoto

Arctic

Lucia Frascerra

2014

SOFTWARE
3ds Max, V-Ray, Photoshop

HARDWARE
laptop

PURPOSE OF SOFTWARE
rendering

Italian architect Lucia Frascerra sees visualization as a way of expressing emotions through the creation of photo-realistic works of art. *Arctic* was first introduced on the online platform CG Architect and was named Pro of the Week in 2015. The work also received a CG Architect 3D Award. Frascerra achieved her professional breakthrough with this visualization, not least from its widespread distribution on the Internet.

Her approach to creating this architectural visualization was similar to that of other architects. The first step was online research, in which she sought suitable references for the image composition, lighting situation, and mood. Once the crucial image references were found, Frascerra made sketches in graphite or pencil, which was helpful, among other things, in aligning the perspective. The sketches are first studies and can be compared in their approach to those used in painting. This intermediate step was the only analog, manual step before the digital phase.

In the subsequent raw rendering phase, the volume was modeled using a 3-D computer graphics program. The scenery was built up in three dimensions, and the problems of light sources, the effect of light, perspective, and composition were investigated. The generated images were further processed, including with the image-processing program Photoshop, and first moods were produced. Scenes for foreground and background were worked out to tell as interesting a story as possible. In this case an image file for the sky motif was placed behind the building as background scenery, and object surfaces in the 3-D model were covered with different materials. As in reality, each material can have different physical properties, so that transparency, relief, reflectance, gloss, or refraction of the surfaces had to be individually adjusted. The image-processing program Photoshop was used again in the last phase: postproduction. In this example the raw image material of the water surface was interwoven with the ice floe motifs. To make the picture more vivid, accessories such as people, a flock of birds, mountains, or the lettering on the building was added. Frascerra tried to produce as dramatic a scene as possible, using filters to create brightness gradients to evoke the right mood. Another stylistic device repeated in the architect's work is her use of vignetting. In photography, this refers to darkening at the edges of a photo. A vignette directs the viewer's eye

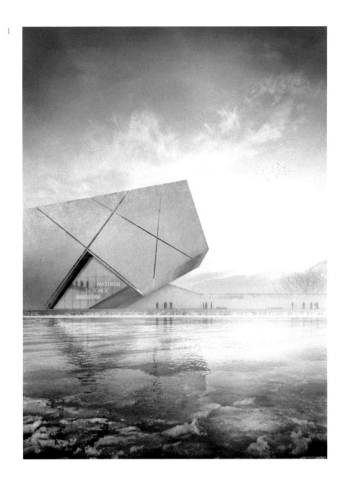

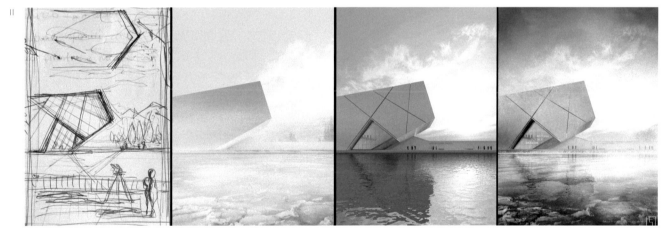

I   *Arctic*
II Workflow for *Arctic*

toward the center of the picture and weakens the less significant elements in the work. The final picture always possesses a representational character, since the design process has already been concluded by the time the visualization is complete.—*Lluis Dura*

"Lucia Frascerra." AREA (online community). Autodesk.com, August 24, 2017. area.autodesk.com/gallery/featured-story/lucia-frascerra.

Villa R

Dyvik Kahlen

2015—2020

SOFTWARE
Rhinoceros

HARDWARE
iMac, 3.2 GHz Intel Core i5

PURPOSE OF SOFTWARE
design, representation, communication

The London-based architecture firm Dyvik Kahlen, founded in 2010 by Christopher Dyvik and Max Kahlen, develops series of perspectives for its architectural projects that depict the path through the building and thus help to develop and communicate complex design ideas. Villa R is part of the new building ensemble in Arnhem, the Netherlands. It is built on a rectangular grid of 3 × 3 rooms, with the central space functioning as an inner courtyard. The middle rooms on each side assume a special significance, while the corner rooms serve as private rooms. The building takes up the topography of the landscape, so that each room is on a different level and connected to the adjacent room by steps. The perspectives—screenshots from the virtual reality tour—depict this circular movement and allow the design to be experienced as "film stills." Dyvik Kahlen uses these images both for the design process and for communication with the client. The renderings, based on quick hand-drawn sketches, are therefore created at an early stage in the design and serve, among other things, to check the proportions of the rooms and the positions of the window openings. The perspectives are rendered in Rhinoceros and are neither reworked nor supplemented with colors or materials, which makes them interesting as a quick and viable mode of representation. The reduction of the color palette to shades of gray recognizes all elements of the building—not only the walls, floor, ceiling, and doors, but also furniture, plants, objects, and landscape—as part of the architecture and combines them into an image that avoids abstraction and thus directly and intuitively illustrates the design idea.—*Anna-Maria Mayerhofer*

I   Villa R, external view

II–IV Villa R, internal view

Prince Claus Bridge

Mir Studio (visualization),
Powerhouse Company (design),
Miebach (structural engineering)

2015

SOFTWARE
Photoshop

PURPOSE OF SOFTWARE
rendering

The panorama of the Dutch port city of Dordrecht with an unrealized bridge seems to shimmer between past and future. The composition and aesthetics of the visualization with the spectacular, overcast sky and dramatic lighting effects are strongly reminiscent of oil paintings by seventeenth-century Dutch masters and at the same time focus on an architectural monument that does not yet exist. This tension between new and old is also reflected in the design for the future Prince Claus Bridge, which the Dutch architects Powerhouse Company developed together with the German engineering consultancy Miebach for an international competition. The location of the bridge is steeped in history, yet the structure itself is iconic in its simplicity: a 130-meter-long pedestrian and cycle bridge made of wood and steel, which will connect the Stadswerven district directly with the historic center of Dordrecht while creating a new gateway to the city. The port city near Rotterdam was visited by many Dutch painters. Because of its picturesque townscape by the water, it is famous as the subject of numerous works of art, such as the masterpiece *View of Dordrecht* (1644–53), which the Dutch painter Jan van Goyen painted in many variations, or Aelbert Jacobsz Cuyp's painting *The Maas at Dordrecht* (ca. 1650). As a reminiscence Mir Studio uses stylistic elements and the aesthetic language of the Old Masters for the rendering, which was based on a design by Powerhouse Company. Unlike conventional renderings, the entire view was digitally "painted" in Photoshop and is not based on a previously created 3-D model. The bridge serves as a central, continuous connecting element—concrete between two places and abstract between times. The rendering combines individual snapshots of the city of Dordrecht at different moments in a single image, spanning an arc between different eras.—*Myriam Fischer*

I Visualization of the Prince Claus Bridge in Dordrecht
II Aelbert Cuyp, *The Maas at Dordrecht*, ca. 1650, oil on canvas, National
   Gallery of Art, Washington, DC
III Jan van Goyen, *View of Dordrecht*, 1644–53, oil on canvas, Musées
   royaux des Beaux-Arts, Brussels

The Elephant and the Corsair

Dennis Allain

2017

SOFTWARE
Cinema 4D, Photoshop

HARDWARE
Windows 10 64-bit version, Boxx Apexx 2,
Intel Core i7 microprocessor

PURPOSE OF SOFTWARE
drawing, rendering

The digital works of Dennis Allain include some of the pioneering projects in the digital representation of architecture. He completed his studies in architecture and engineering at the Wentworth Institute of Technology in Boston, Massachusetts, in 1990, and worked for several architectural and design offices, including ten years at Elkus Manfredi Architects. In 2004 he founded his own practice and has since created visualizations and illustrations for numerous companies, including Disney, Lego, and Universal Studios Hollywood, as well as his own projects, many of which have been published.

The Elephant and the Corsair is a piece of independent work by Allain, which he created with Photoshop and Cinema 4D. He was using the image-editing program Photoshop as early as the mid-1990s for digital editing of scanned manual drawings. Ever since it has been possible to create works directly in Photoshop, he has used the program for the complete creation of his digital image worlds. In 2000, motivated by the need to save time, Allain began to develop three-dimensional forms with Cinema 4D. The combination of the two programs enabled him to create the graphic design almost simultaneously with the narrative visual world. Occasionally, he prepares manual sketches to support the development process and simplify compositional decisions. For Allain, each rendering begins with a narrative intent that can be based on a location, historical time, or object.

In the case of *The Elephant and the Corsair*, it is the scene of an ancient temple structure in a desert landscape, from which a technoid structure of columns, bars, and polygonal shapes grows. The arrangement of the depicted objects reveals hardly anything about their temporality; like a palimpsest, the structures lie on top of one another. The ancient architecture is surrounded by a dilapidated border of barbed wire and watchtowers on which stag figures are enthroned; a well-lit shipwreck bears witness to a recent devastation. The futuristic framework seems to be in the making but perhaps also in its dissolution. The enigmatic representation is enlivened only by the caravan of camels, decorated elephants, and pitched tents—signs of human life in an almost post-human environment. A white blue light source from inside the temple ruins characterizes the entire sheet and immerses the postapocalyptic scene in a mysterious atmosphere. The light seems to be the origin of the skyward-reaching edifice, the tangled structure

I   Final rendering
II   Preliminary hand sketches
III 3-D structure integrated in Photoshop
IV   Digital preliminary version with composition sketches in Photoshop
V   Digital preliminary version with detailed design of the sky in Photoshop

of which towers above the landscape. It is the expression of the digital, the machine, that communicates an architectural design of the future and, in doing so, makes reference to its own medium of creation.

The preliminary versions of the work reveal the compositional process as well as the conceptual proximity to capriccio, art history's earlier architectural fantasy. Not least because of the elaborate design of the sky, which is digitally reminiscent of the highly analogous phenomenon of patina, in Allain's work the boundary between past and future, between manual work and computer rendering, becomes blurred, and it remains a mystery which of the two existed first.
—*Franziska Stein*

Schillaci, Fabio, ed. *Architectural Renderings: Construction and Design Manual. History and Theory, Studios and Practices.* Hoboken, NJ: Wiley, 2009. ● Fankhänel, Teresa. "Examining a Creative Process." Unpublished interview with Dennis Allain, October 20, 2019

Hilma af Klint Museum,
A Temple for the Pictures

Jana Čulek

2017

SOFTWARE
Rhinoceros, AutoCAD, Illustrator, Photoshop

HARDWARE
Windows 10, AMD FX(tm)-8120 8-core processor,
NVIDIA GeForce GTX 770 graphics card, ASUSTeK
M5A97

PURPOSE OF SOFTWARE
drawing, rendering, design

Croatian architect Jana Čulek creates fantasy scenes and idealized versions of the designed physical reality with her perspective images. Her renderings make no claim to volumetric accuracy but communicate impressions of the spatial environment and are therefore, first and foremost, telling a story. Her entry "A Temple for the Pictures" for the architectural design competition, seeking a museum for the works of Hilma af Klint, consisted of four digital illustrations (*Childhood*, *Youth*, *Maturity*, and *Old Age*), which represented the four stages of life in abstract paintings by the artist. The images not only function as methods of presentation but also as a design instrument. Čulek considers the perspective image as a tool that, unlike traditional renderings, "allows for spatial manipulations, additions, and exaggerations."[1] Her perspectives show a subjective view of the observer's environment. They are free from the objective, precise reality of design, which generally involves sections and plans, and therefore are capable of directly communicating the project's key ideas.

To create the images, Jana Čulek used a range of software, which was also employed to develop and present the archi-

tectural forms. Beginning with the written text and sketches, she first created the perspective based on a volume model with Rhinoceros, which did not depict the designed buildings accurately. She changed the dimensions of objects and their distances away to produce a much more exciting perspective. She refined the scenes in AutoCAD, enhancing smaller objects, environments, and shadows. In the exported line drawings, she built sets of colors with Illustrator on palettes based on those in Klint's paintings and added figures as well as vegetation used by the artist. Finally, she finished the image with Photoshop, enhancing it with textures and color gradients to lend a certain depth to the flat surfaces. With her work, she won the Editor's Choice Award 2017.—*Anna-Maria Mayerhofer*

1 Jana Čulek, "Entry for Combo Competitions—A Temple for Hilma" (unpublished manuscript, March 2017), n.p. ● Allen, Laura, and Luke Caspar Pearson, eds. *Drawing Futures: Speculations in Contemporary Drawing for Art and Architecture*. Cambridge, Canada: Riverside Architectural Press, 2016. ● Wilson, Rob, et al., eds. *The Site: A Field Guide to Making the Future of Architecture*. Vol. 3 of *Archifutures*, edited by &beyond collective. Barcelona: dpr-barcelona, 2016. ● Frausto, Salomon, ed. *Lexicon No. 2 Agency—Advocacy—Authorship*. Self-published, The Berlage, 2016.

Hilma af Klint Museum

I–IV Four renderings: *Childhood*, *Youth*, *Maturity*, *Old Age*
V   Color palette for Čulek's *Maturity*: Group IV, The Ten Largest, No. 7,
        Adulthood, Hilma af Klint, 1907

Sørli Visitor Center

Brick Visual Solutions (visualization), Saaha AS (design), Asplan Viak AS (landscape architecture)

2018

SOFTWARE
3ds Max, V-Ray, Forest Pack, Photoshop

PURPOSE OF SOFTWARE
rendering

The renderings produced by Brick Visual Solutions show the impossible: inhabited architecture even before the foundation stone of the building is laid. Quiet and idyllically situated in the middle of a forest in Østmarka near Oslo, the historic farm will be given new life as a visitor center for children and young people. Bright sunbeams penetrating thick clouds wrap the scenery in a breathtaking play of light. Small groups, different characters, and individual nuances bring the composition to life. Brick Visual shows architectural representations in a different way: the focus is on the communication of architecture. Embedded in this natural and lifelike context, the building almost seems to fade into the background. Unusual for visualizations, the focus here is not on the presentation of a building, but rather on conveying emotions, in particular a strong sense of community which was important to the architects and the client. This visual way of storytelling, which translates ideas into images, makes the experience of future life on the farm tangible. The architects added two new buildings to the landmarked small farmyard. However, the infrastructure of the property has been retained so that the existing house and the area in front of it can be used as an arrival and meeting point for visitors, while the existing and renovated barns can be used for keeping animals. Architectural models from the architects Saaha AS, which created the design for the future Sørli Visitor Center, served as a basis for the image visualization. Brick Visual Solutions uses age-old artistic principles—composition, perspective, mood, contrast, and color—which are visualized using highly modern techniques. Lifelike characters and interactive scenery illustrate the future life and community at this special place.—*Myriam Fischer*

I   A look into the future of the Sørli Visitor Center
II   Visual storytelling through the precise, detailed representation of small scenes

Chapter 4
The Computer as an Interactive Platform

Essays

Playing Architect.
Designing with Computer Games

Felix Torkar

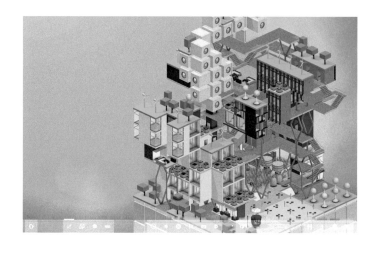

I   A mega-structure simulator with autonomous economic and ecological cycles, *Block'hood*, 2017

Whether as an urban planner in *SimCity*, time-traveling architectural historian in *Assassin's Creed*, or block-world builder in *Minecraft*, computer games allow players access to new forms of architectural appropriation and representation ▶ Fig. I. Even if the developers in most cases only want to produce a creative form of entertainment, computer games change the access to architecture. They give every player a virtual agency to act to which otherwise only a tightly defined group of professionals are entitled. Virtual design processes are free of physical and commercial constraints. But at the same time the games' worlds always reflect the view of their creators in their rules, which control the possible creations.

Playing Architect

The idea of translating architectural design into games goes back a long time. The first pedagogical modular system with distinctly architectural aims was developed in the 1870s by the brothers Gustav and Otto Lilienthal, who are more famous today for their flying experiments, and marketed from 1880 by the company Friedrich Adolf Richter as Anker Steinbaukasten (Anchor Stone Blocks) ▶ Fig. II.[1] The sets consist of stone blocks of various shapes and colors. Accompanying booklets show perspectival views and floor plans of architectural models to be constructed, which do not represent existing buildings but archetypal building forms. Rather than interlocking, the building blocks rest on one another and thus reproduce the principles of architectural tectonics. At the same time, the templates demonstrate the principles of classical architectural style. Having only a few recognizable elements, such as circular or pointed arches, the stones permit designs that do not have to be tied to architectural styles. However, on closer consideration, the assumed design freedom is channeled in specific directions. For the most part cuboid, the blocks connote conventional, right-angled masonry courses and traditional perforated facades. Creating cantilevers is hardly possible because the blocks are not joined by a force-transmitting connection such as happens with, for example, Lego. What initially appears as a largely neutral collection of basic shapes embodies the traditional architectural values prevailing at the close of the nineteenth century. Aesthetic neutrality is impossible. Between free play and guided learning lies a dichotomy.

The concept of experiencing architecture through guided play is also a core idea in the context of computer games. Contrary to the intention of Anker Steinbaukasten, most games that will be mentioned here have no thoughts of didactics behind them. An analysis of such games assumes that their developers conceived them as entertainment media. That they can also be used as teaching materials was therefore not considered at the outset. At the same time, they give players a new architectural agency. They invite them to experiment with architecture without physical or commercial constraints. Here, only the developers decide the general conditions and rules; the players can follow, bend, or sometimes even break them.

Perhaps the most extensively analyzed game is *SimCity* ▶ Fig. III. Its inventor, Will Wright, studied architecture for a few semesters before he gave up the course to concentrate on developing computer games. The original idea came to him while he was working on the concept for a helicopter battle game; building cities using the level editor he had designed was more entertaining to him than the game itself. The first version of the city simulator appeared in 1989, after Wright had encountered considerable difficulties in finding a publisher for this new type of conflict-free game. After his first market successes, the next game in the series, *SimCity 2000*, appeared in 1993, and it remains the most well-known and influential version, despite numerous sequels.

The basic concept can be described as an urban planning simulation. The player is formally known as the mayor and has absolute power. The general objective is to create a flourishing city. Road and rail grids intersecting at 90 degrees are designed from an isometric perspective. Development zones are strictly defined and divided into areas for residential, business, and industrial use and supplied with electricity and water through a network of power lines and pipes. Public parks, schools, and police and fire stations must be distributed to avoid problem neighborhoods. The city's budget must be balanced by taxes. The more attractive the city becomes,

III The best-known city building simulator is based on real principles of urban planning: *SimCity 2000*, 1993.

II The first didactic architecture building blocks, Anker Steinbaukasten, 1880 onwards

the more inhabitants and companies settle in the predefined zones and bring life to their districts. Public utilities can be visualized with graphical and analytical overlays. What at first sounds like a fairly dry economic simulation inspired millions of players thanks to its charming Where's Waldo aesthetics and a game flow that never comes to an end and continually motivates users to extend and improve their creations.

As the architectural theorist Daniel G. Lobo concluded from his analysis, some of the basic influences can be traced back to Wright's time studying architecture.[2] In 1969, MIT professor Jay Forrester published his idea of *system dynamics*, a computer model for the variables in urban planning.[3] *SimCity*'s view modes for crime rates and land values stem directly from this approach. Some people would say that *SimCity* is like the geographic information systems programs that have been in use since the 1990s for urban planning. Both could be seen as the inheritors of Forrester's system dynamics. The urban planner Christopher Alexander advocated a dispersed form of zoning in which the various areas can be interlocked with one another in small pieces—a model that *SimCity*'s basic rules at least resemble.[4] The fundamental design proposition of the game—establish a new city with a rectangular road grid in virgin countryside—has its roots in colonial, in particular US-American, city planning such as can be found above all in the Midwest (e.g., Salt Lake City) and on the west coast. However, with all these

directions of thought, it is important to emphasize that Will Wright did not necessarily seek to promote these simplified rules as the best system for urban planning. It is more likely that these were principles in which he had confidence and that were comparatively easy to implement and explain in a game intended to provide an entertaining gaming experience.

Since the early 1990s, *SimCity* and its subsequent versions have been used in schools and universities as learning materials to communicate the basics of urban planning and municipal politics—a use never intended by Wright. David Lublin, a professor at the American University in Washington, DC, had his students use *SimCity*, for example to build virtual cities, and then analyze the theories behind it.[5] Because of the game's widespread popularity, it is often said that *SimCity* has a broader influence on the subject than any book.[6]

The *MagnaSanti* (2007–9) project by Vincent Ocasla, an architecture student at the time, shows that the game can also lead to quite different creations ▶ Fig. IV. Ocasla experimented for two years with *SimCity 3000* (1999), trying to achieve the greatest possible number and density of inhabitants. The result was a dystopian city with a population of six million that was mercilessly optimized for population density. The project was made popular as a YouTube video set to a menacing, dramatic soundtrack.[7] The dystopian atmosphere lends *MagnaSanti* a concept-art character and immediately calls to mind the high-density living spaces

1 Bernd Lukasch, "Lilienthal und der Baukasten," 2018, accessed November 27, 2019, www.lilienthal-museum.de/olma/baustein.htm.
2 Daniel G. Lobo, "Playing with Urban Life: How SimCity Influences Planning Culture," in Friedrich von Borries et al. (eds.), *Space Time Play: Computer Games, Architecture and Urbanism* (Basel: The Next Level, 2007), 206–13.
3 Jay Forrester, *Urban Dynamics* (Cambridge, MA: Pegasus Communications, 1969).
4 Lobo 2007 (as note 2), 208.
5 Ibid.
6 Gerrit Vermeer, "Games: Designing Cities and Civilizations," in *The Architecture Co-Laboratory: Game Set and Match II. On Computer Games, Advanced Geometries, and Digital Technologies*, ed. Kas Oosterhuis and Lukas Feireiss (Rotterdam: Episode, 2006), 90–97.
7 SimCity 3000, accessed November 24, 2019, www.youtube.com/watch?v=NTJQTc-TqpU.

V   Virtual architecture simulator and dollhouse,
The Sims 4

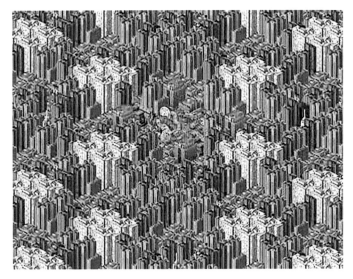

IV   Maximizing rewards by bending the rules: *MagnaSanti*,
2007–9

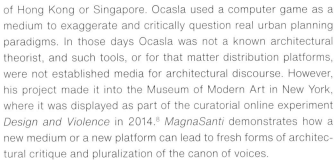

of Hong Kong or Singapore. Ocasla used a computer game as a medium to exaggerate and critically question real urban planning paradigms. In those days Ocasla was not a known architectural theorist, and such tools, or for that matter distribution platforms, were not established media for architectural discourse. However, his project made it into the Museum of Modern Art in New York, where it was displayed as part of the curatorial online experiment *Design and Violence* in 2014.[8] *MagnaSanti* demonstrates how a new medium or a new platform can lead to fresh forms of architectural critique and pluralization of the canon of voices.

Building on the basic idea of *SimCity*, increasingly complex city simulators have appeared over the years. The simulators not only further develop existing points of criticism, such as the highly rectangular grid and the original core concept, but also experiment with the known formula and recontextualize it. As the most successful *SimCity* inheritor, *Cities: Skylines* (2015) expands the basic idea with many other systems, such as solid waste and waste water management or detailed traffic models, and allows less strict curves instead of rectangular street grids. An add-on system allows players to create and share building and planting models. The diversity of possibilities leads to a community, one which—not unlike model-railway enthusiast clubs—embarks on huge urban planning projects or, for example, works together to produce a highly accurate virtual copy of Berlin.

In *Tropico* (2001), on the other hand, the *SimCity* principle is transposed onto an unidentified island and, without more ado, the player becomes its dictator. This banana republic simulator game is based on a detailed model of various forms of government and population dynamics, with riots and attempted coups. On closer inspection, the satirical viewpoint concisely demystifies the political and economic constraints of island economies and small states. Real patterns of behavior and the consequences flowing from them become an experimental field in game form, enabling the player to look into the planning challenges.

Will Wright remained the most influential figure in this game genre during the 1990s and 2000s. In *The Sims* (2000), the focus of his games shifted onto suburban homes ▶ Fig. V. This game was conceived as a type of digital dollhouse. In addition to playing with people's life paths, users soon came to see the building mode as a main attraction of the game. Users can create interior fittings and furniture or even the whole house in great detail. The large catalog of various building styles, interior furnishings, and furniture, whether postmodern, neo-modern, Mediterranean, Victorian, or neoclassicist, looks very much like real-life catalogs for suburban homes. Wright actually meant his game as a satire on the predominantly white, consumerist lifestyle in the city suburbs of the USA, although, according to the original concept, the game was to have been a type of architecture simulator in which the virtual residents could test out the plausibility of the house design.[9]

The most important theoretical influence was the 1977 bestseller *A Pattern Language: Towns, Buildings, Construction* by Christopher Alexander, Sara Ishikawa, and Murray Silverstein.[10] Using their pattern of language, the authors sought to enable a participative architecture, with residents being able to design or take part in the design. This investigation of architectural problems in a game environment turns *The Sims* into a testing zone in which players can experience domestic architecture as a changeable space. With 175 million copies sold to date (to say nothing of countless pirate copies), the game opens new opportunities for architectural experimentation. Players tackle the question of what makes a good home. Like *SimCity* before it, *The Sims* operates in a special local reference system—in this case that of the traditional US-American suburbs. However, the time-honored distribution of roles between architect and client is called into question.

It is perhaps no accident that this shift is currently inspiring the architecture of self-build projects as well. The *WikiHouse* initiative (2011) promotes the construction of residential buildings through freely available construction plans with a Creative Commons license.[11] Its objective is to popularize resource-conserving, simple-to-erect houses with components made from materials such as plywood that can be built by the future occupants themselves by following the instructions provided. Alejandro Aravena's Elemental houses in Iquique, Chile (2004), are based on the idea of upgrading the Quinta Monroy slum through social housing. To give the inhabitants, who had an extremely small budget for their plans, the possibility of long-term further development, Aravena designed simple "half" houses equipped with only the most essential elements, which the inhabitants could gradually extend to create a larger house by self-building.[12] What happens virtually in *The Sims* is found in these real construction projects. An increasing number of residents are architecturally thinking for themselves in this environment.

While built architecture was a key aspect in Will Wright's simulations from the beginning, it played hardly any role in the concept of *Minecraft* (2009). However, over the last ten years, *Minecraft* has advanced to become perhaps the most influential architectural tool based on a computer game. Its Swedish inventor, Markus Persson, has no personal connection to the architecture world; his background is in programming. *Minecraft* began as an adventure game in which players explore, collect raw materials and objects, and erect simple dwellings to protect themselves from looming dangers. The distinctive block aesthetic, generated in the game environment from one-by-one-by-one-meter cubes of various materials, reminiscent of Lego blocks.

At an early stage, the developers recognized the potential of a creative mode in which players are invited to assemble the blocks in a virtual world free of the element of danger. However, the game soon became an open-source modular system in which players collaborate to create huge building projects, way beyond the author's original idea. On anything from high-rises to whole cities or mini-planets, players work together to create game worlds, which, with self-designed and freely distributed textures, components, and instructions, represent their own micro-cosmos. As seen before with *The Sims*, this creates connections to the DIY architectures of Aravena or *WikiHouse*. The structures enable laypeople to design architecture themselves while supporting one another through networks. In addition, *Minecraft* allows users to become familiar with digital design tools in the course of the game. As Cody Sumter from MIT Media Lab said in 2012: "[Persson] hasn't just built a game. He's tricked 40 million people into learning to use a CAD program."[13] Development tools such as level editors and rendering environments such as *Maya* work in a similar way as architecture software such as *Revit*.[14]

In *Second Life* (2003), the boundaries between game and online community are blurred and virtual architecture gains market value for the first time. Players walk as self-designed avatars through virtual worlds created by fellow players. These worlds contain businesses, housing and complete cities. In a virtual economy linked to real monetary values, players can deal in objects such as clothing or whole houses they have created themselves. Thus it is possible to buy a virtual home of your own from *Second-Life* architects. The range on offer reflects current architectural trends and preferences to an astonishing degree. Anyone can now find and purchase their dream villa in Richard Meier style or an idyllic castle. In this environment, architecture becomes a virtual economic commodity and reflects real economic processes.

Following a period of rapidly growing technical capabilities in the 1990s and 2000s, a period in which developing computer games became increasingly complex and expensive, recent decades have seen new, more accessible development environments that

8   Paola Antonelli and Jamer Hunt, *Design and Violence* (New York: Museum of Modern Art, 2015), 74–77.
9   Jon Astbury, "Playing the Architect: Why Video Games and Architecture Need Each Other," in *Architectural Review*, 2014, accessed November 29, 2019, www.architectural-review.com/essays/playing-the-architect-why-video-games-and-architecture-need-each-other/8664135.article.
10 Christopher Alexander et al., *A Pattern Language: Towns, Buildings, Construction* (New York: Oxford University Press, 1977).
11 WikiHouse, accessed November 29, 2019, www.wikihouse.cc.
12 Alejandro Aravena and Andrés Iacobelli, *Elemental: Incremental Housing and Participatory Design Manual* (Ostfildern, Germany: Hatje Cantz, 2012), 85.
13 Tom Cheshire, "Want to Learn Computer-Aided Design (CAD)? Play Minecraft," *Wired*, November 2012, accessed November 27, 2019, www.wired.co.uk/article/minecrafted.
14 Astbury, "Playing the Architect."

have given rise to a renaissance of smaller games. These "indie games" widen the audience by including new game cultures and projects that do not always have to be judged from the point of view of maximizing profits. (Even *Minecraft* began as a hobby project like this before it was bought by Microsoft in 2014 for US$2.5 billion.) Some of these games show a new, critical consideration in their reflection of architectural realities. One example is the game *Block'hood* (2017), designed by the architect and games developer Jose Sanchez. In a mixture of *SimCity* and *SimTower* (Will Wright, 1994), players build a vertical mixed-use mega-structure, a type of autonomous city in the form of a single building. What is new here is an emphasis on aspects such as sustainability, environmental pollution, resource consumption, waste reduction, and socioeconomic factors as central gameplay components. Like all games, even *Block'hood* proves to have a defined scope of action. With an aesthetic resembling Kengo Kuma's timber latticework and metabolistic ideas, replaceable and expandable construction modules provide the framework for a type of design that, as Sanchez puts it, draws on the DIY mentality of the *Whole Earth Catalog*.[15] In contrast to the earlier-mentioned games, the developer adopts a didactic role. Building on the previously, almost accidentally discovered architectural potential of computer games, Sanchez consciously chose this system as the starting point for the game experience. The game intentionally creates a stage for players to practice sustainable, participative planning.

What all of these games have in common is that players are empowered to design and build their own worlds. In this way, the games activate powers of imagination and give laypeople access to a multitude of new fields of experience, and this in turn encourages a wide range of architectural approaches.

Architects Playing

In a similar way, games also influence architects and architecture students. At this point, it is worth taking a quick look back over modular systems of the past. Construction games have always reflected the contemporary architectural paradigms of their age;

and, in reverse, they have influenced generations of architects. Frank Lloyd Wright describes his experience with Fröbel building blocks in his childhood and how important this was for his later architectural language.[16] This begs the question: how will the change from physical to digital block games influence future generations of architects? Computer games do not in any way completely supersede physical toys. In most children's rooms Lego blocks are still to be found alongside game consoles, and they are an important early point of contact and influence. However, digital imagery and gaming worlds create a new frame of reference for architects who grow up with computers.

Both computer games and architectural design software serve the purpose of creating spaces for their users. The design and functions of level editors and of CAD software resemble each other in the way they go about creating three-dimensional environments. 3-D software is used in games to generate and texturize three-dimensional objects, a form of virtual design now considered an essential part of architectural design. A crucial change is the shift in the design perspective. The first-person perspective, in particular, allows a new, radical design experience. In contrast to traditional design practices using a combination of paper and models, the first person perspective leads to an embodied approach that allows more direct experience in the early design stages. Increasingly popular VR technologies further intensify these new forms of representation. It remains to be seen how far the resulting designs actually diverge from traditionally designed projects. For example, the result may be a more intensive exploration of aspects of spatial perception and atmosphere.

Elwin Koster was experimenting with VR technologies in teaching as early as the start of the new millennium.[17] Through virtual reconstructions of historical town structures, he and his students investigated how they had developed over time. *Disentanglement and Gates* (2012) was a game developed at the Savannah College of Art that concerns itself with the transition from architectural study to architectural practice.[18] It recognizes the problems inherent in the change of focus from creative to technical design that are experienced by architectural professionals at the start of their career. Using models of decision-making processes, actors,

VI   St. Mark's Basilica in Venice, built in the late fifteenth
      century—re-created virtually, *Assassin's Creed II*, 2009

fields of work, and socioeconomic factors, the game creates scenarios with the aim of ensuring that students are better prepared for practical work in architectural offices. The project of developing the game shows how architecture departments at universities and colleges can not only use existing computer games to impart knowledge but also develop their own.

In recent years, games in the *Assassin's Creed* series have taken the potential of historical re-creation an impressive step further ▶ Fig. VI. In these action adventures, gamers control an avatar that can move freely through populated reconstructions of historical towns. Parkour elements make climbing and clambering over the architecture a key part of the game. With the help of architectural historians, the designers created an authentic atmosphere with accurately re-created famous historical buildings like St. Mark's Basilica in Venice. However, historical urban layouts are shrunk for the sake of the game's flow and the proportions of the featured structures are subtly altered. For example, Florence Cathedral is slightly reduced in size and the nearby baptistery omitted; the Rialto Bridge is moved closer to St. Mark's Square. Playability is far more important in these games than 100 percent accurate reproductions. However, the atmosphere and the novelty of moving freely in these graphically impressive bustling replicas of historical epochs are crucial. Moreover, the aspect of acrobatically traversing buildings gives users a new way of experiencing the architecture, and one that cannot be matched in reality. What began in this case as not much more than a form of entertainment has gradually become useful in teaching.[19]

The potential was recognized recently by the development team. As a result, the two latest titles have conflict-free playing modes with virtual tours of the Acropolis in Athens and the Giza Pyramids at the time they were built. Since then, the growing sales of the series have made it one of the entertainment industry's biggest blockbusters, with a development budget in no way inferior to those of major Hollywood productions. Even though virtual re-creations are used increasingly by museums and educational establishments, these institutions do not have the financial resources of an eight- or nine-figure budget to create anything on this scale. Popular computer games are not subject to the economic constraints placed on cultural or educational institutions and can push the technological boundaries. In this way, today's generation of archaeologists and architectural historians is growing up with new, direct experiences that change and extend their approach to their research objects. On a different note, buildings acclaimed for their interactivity and transformability have been around since the 1990s. Earlier

15   Jose Sanchez, ed., *The Blindspot Initiative: Design Resistance and Alternative Modes of Practice* (New York: eVolo, 2019), 130.
16   Robert McCarter, *Frank Lloyd Wright* (London: Phaidon, 2006), 18 ff.
17   Elwin Koster, "How VR Can Help Studying Urban History," in *Game Set and Match II: On Computer Games, Advanced Geometries, and Digital Technologies*, ed. Kas Oosterhuis and Lukas Feireiss (Rotterdam: Episode, 2006), 582–87.
18   Astbury, "Playing the Architect."
19   Justin Porter, "Assassin's Creed Has a New Mission: Working in the Classroom," *New York Times*, May 16, 2018, accessed November 27, 2019, www.nytimes.com/2018/05/16/arts/assassins-creed-origins-education.html.

examples from Lars Spuybroek or Marcos Novak consider the user as an interactive component of the architecture. In his *Freshwater Pavilion* (1997), Spuybroek allows visitors to dynamically change the lighting and sound environment. Novak's algorithmic compositions create "transarchitectures," which are generated procedurally the way they are in many games, and have embedded sensors and mechanical elements.

More recent participative architecture projects relate quite specifically to computer games or build directly on them. London studio You+Pea uses video game development software to create interactive architectural experiences. They created a game for the *Disappear Here: On Perspective and Other Kinds of Space* exhibition at the Royal Institute of British Architects in London in which four players, each with a different viewpoint—perspective, elevation, plan, and a collection of images—are in control. The objective is to work together and puzzle out a Renaissance view reminiscent of Hans Vredeman de Vries's compositions. In *Everyone Is Architecture* (2019), people themselves are architectural blocks, following on from Hans Hollein's "*Alles ist Architektur*." Players can contribute to the provided public locations using an augmented-reality app to become a column, a staircase, or a window and create a virtual architectural assemblage through their positions relative to one another. In this way You+Pea melds video game aesthetics with contemporary architectural theory in its projects.

ETH Zurich developed a flexible design tool in the form of *Kaisersrot* (2001–10). The software allows users to organize space in anything from residential buildings to complete urban quarters. The software algorithmically generates configurations based on various preferences, such as available space, noise levels, or nearness to buildings like churches. Not unintentionally, the user interface is similar to *SimCity*, offering a low entry barrier for participants. Over a period of nine years the tool has been successfully used in the design of several real projects. One such project involved the resettlement of the flood victims of Kehlbach in Upper Austria. The software helped to contractually divide land between agricultural use and the new housing while balancing the interests of the existing population and the incomers by creating spatial configurations that, as far as possible, satisfied the wishes of

everyone.[20] Although *Kaisersrot* is certainly like a game, it does not always succeed in breaking through what is possibly the greatest barrier to participative models in architectural design: cooperative participation initiated by architects does not place all participants on an equal footing. The mixture of unequal backgrounds—on one side the experts, on the other laypeople—can be enough to stifle involvement.

As the architects at BlockWorks show, one possible solution to this is the use of computer games.[21] With a team of over sixty employees, BlockWorks designs interactive architectural environments using *Minecraft*. Reproductions of British castles were created for the country's heritage protection authorities. Visitors could virtually explore and alter the monuments. The Museum of London had a virtual copy of the center of the city made to reflect what it was like before and after the Great Fire of London in 1666. Communal building plans can be taken forward using this system as well. The most ambitious project to date was completed together with UN Habitat, the United Nations Human Settlements Program. In order to design public spaces in developing countries, BlockWorks modeled existing situations in the project *Block by Block*. This allows residents to visualize ideas and suggestions. Thus it is possible to discuss proposals not only on functional levels ("we need shady places to sit") but also directly in terms of the architecture itself ("this is what we imagine it should look like").

The important point here is that *Minecraft* is not architectural software. Indeed, some of the participants may have more knowledge of *Minecraft* than the architects with whom they are in discussion. *Block by Block* builds on a less unequally divided common body of experience of all stakeholders. In this way it is possible to at least partially level the uneven playing field in terms of the experience of the partners to the discussion. Architects and residents can collaborate more as equals on a neutral platform, which allows the discourse to be more diverse and pluralistic. Adolescents and young people in particular learn how to use this tool more quickly, which promotes their voices.

Computer games create narrative experience spaces. If players in *SimCity* build worlds and architects develop software like *Kaisersrot* influenced by it, the two groups move closer together. Both create spatial designs of built environments. In some ways it is only logical that *The Sims* was thought of originally as an architecture simulator; and today, after its change of direction to become a life simulator for players, it has once again been repurposed by players to function as a design game.

Computer games are capable of producing new views of architecture and ways of accessing it. Studios such as BlockWorks clearly demonstrate how players and architects work with the same types of systems. Games are used as architectural experimentation fields for utopias and as discussion platforms. In these games, failure is inherently desirable, allowing unrestricted consideration of what-if scenarios.[22] New ways of participating are possible when the playing field for architects and nonarchitects is leveled as with *Block by Block*, not least because this provides new opportunities for democratization and gives rise to new models of architectural representation.

Even though *SimCity* is already thirty years old, it appears, in the light of current developments, almost as if its architectural potential has not really been discovered, researched, and fully exploited until recently. Thus, after three decades, we are once again standing at the threshold of a new generation of interaction between architecture and computer games.

20 Kehlbachsiedlung, accessed November 27, 2019, www.kaisersrot.ch/kaisers rot-02/2003_Kehlbach.html.

21 BlockWorks, accessed November 27, 2019, www.blockworks.uk.

22 Luke Caspar Pearson, "Architectures of Ironic Computation: How Videogames Offer New Protocols for Architectural Experimentation," 2017, accessed November 29, 2019, discovery.ucl.ac.uk/id/eprint/1550096/1/Pearson_Archi tectures%20of%20Ironic%20Computation%20RPS%20Upload.pdf.

Computing Choice:
Self-Design, Configurators, and
the Enumerative Imagination

Theodora Vardouli

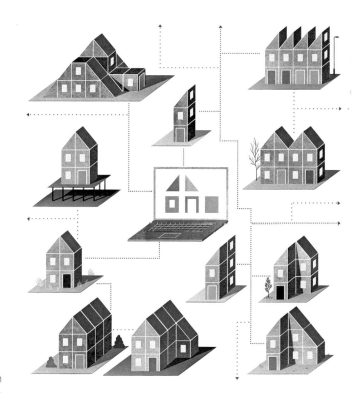

I Illustration of a kit of digital parts that are combined
in different ways to produce open-source houses

In his 1980 futurological compendium *The Third Wave*, Alvin Toffler forecast the return to a preindustrial condition in which the divide between the consumer and the producer would collapse, giving rise to the new persona of the *prosumer*.[1] Signals of the prosumer's rise, he argued, were distinct yet converging tendencies—from self-help movements and do-it-yourself trends, to computer-aided manufacturing technologies that turned products "outside-in" by involving consumers in their design and production.[2] Blending high technology with ideals of creative individualism that had variously been animating American culture since the 1960s, the "prosumer" encapsulated a vision of creative consumers with direct access to, and control of, their technological environment.[3] The image of empowered individuals shaping tools and products in collaborative communities—what Lewis Mumford had famously described as the condition of "democratic technics"[4]—has been, from the onset, central to emancipatory claims associated with the "participatory web." Also called web 2.0, the term describes the world wide web's shift from an information source to an interactive infrastructure dynamically populated by user-generated content.[5] Apart from being interactive and participatory itself, web 2.0 is also indirectly promoting prosumption through online product customization interfaces and, crucially, by igniting speculation on alternative "open" processes of design and production.[6]

In such endeavors to imagine the user as designer and producer, the participatory web has become both a tool and a metaphor for rethinking the potential of digital technologies in architectural design. In his 2011 *Log* article "Digital Style," for example, architectural historian Mario Carpo implored theorists and designers to tackle head-on what he identified as the most radical effect of the "digital": an "aggregatory" architecture made by "many hands"[7] through versions, patches, and reconfigurations. This architecture, he argued, would be the product of processes akin to those in place in open-source software development. In contemplating the implications of web 2.0 for architecture, Carpo laid out several interrelated possibilities, including architectures that always remain in "beta,"[8] the shift of architectural work toward the design of families of objects ("objectiles") instead of singular things with geometrically definite forms, and mass customization as an economic and technological paradigm entering architects' work.

Even though these scenarios have had limited effects on mainstream professional practice,[9] digitally enabled building systems such as Open Systems Lab's WikiHouse[10] and more than two hundred digital "configurator" tools in the housing industry[11] continue to promote a digitally enabled self-design and self-build. Configurators are digital interfaces that allow *configuration*, a specific case of design activity in which an artifact is assembled from a fixed set of component types interacting with each other according to specific rules.[12] The aim of the configuration is to arrange the components in such a way that it meets particular user-defined specifications or other global constraints.[13] These tools rely on kit-of-parts logics of discreteness, modularity, and combination to professedly make designing architecture as simple as choosing from a menu ▶ Fig. I.

The development of configurators is chiefly inscribed within pragmatic concerns of mass customization. However, a configurative process in which the designer provides an infrastructure that is made concrete through the assembly of parts or value assignments to certain variables is the standard way of thinking about the participatory or interactional potential of the digital in architecture today. The idea of "non-standard architecture"—as described by Frédéric Migayrou and Zeynep Mennan in their eponymous exhibition at the Centre Pompidou in 2003—relied on a more abstract definition of configuration. In projects such as Gramazio Kohler Architects' mTable or those pursued by Patrick Beaucé and

II   Tables designed by three users of Gramazio Kohler
      Architects' mTable mobile phone application

Bernard Cache at atelier Objectile, to name two salient examples, the parts to be configured by users are not building components but nested digital topologies. In the mTable, for instance, "people" were "empowered" to "affect the shape of a design object" ▶ Fig. II.[14] In this essay I argue that the idea of self-design and the recasting of design as a configuration historically constituted each other. They did so in the context of a "participatory turn" other than the one Carpo outlines [15] and which preceded the advent of web 2.0 by some thirty years. In this earlier turn, architects working with new mathematical techniques and in proximity to early versions of digital electronic computers approached design participation as an *informational* problem. Episodes from that history reveal a particular model of open-endedness embedded in current digital tools for self-design in architecture. Specifically, I suggest that the very idea of digitally powered participatory architecture can be inscribed within a historically specific *configurative* and *enumerative* understanding of design that stemmed from architects' engagement with particular cultures of abstraction in the postwar period. The shift from authoring the appearance of things to authoring their configuration is not an unrealized potential of digital technologies, but was in fact one of the key agendas that underpinned architects' initial engagements with computers and computation. I also argue that this configurative agenda was conceptually and technically tied to a historically specific shift from appearance to structure, from geometry to topology, as the locus of architectural authorship.

Participation, Information, and "Self-Decision"

In his 1929 work *The Quest for Certainty*, American pragmatist philosopher John Dewey attributed the pervasive philosophical separation between intellect and action to a generalized uncertainty aversion.[16] Uncertainty, he argued, is inherent to practical action, simply because "all activity involves change."[17] Regardless of how well informed one is, anticipation is therefore doomed to "precarious probability."[18] A few years later sociologist Robert Merton set out to systematize this phenomenon. "Unanticipated consequences," he argued, result from biases, errors, and knowledge limitations, but also from the impact of the action itself in changing the situation on which the prediction was made. In the 1960s this unsettling realization came to vex the architecture and planning professions. Put to use, the carefully calculated and socially visionary decisions of their predecessors presented unsettling and unanticipated effects: occupants of "functional houses" were not living by the "dwelling manuals,"[19] while the "functional city" was being perceived as "a world of massive urban misery."[20] Within a

1   Alvin Toffler, *The Third Wave* (New York: William Morrow and Company, 1980), 282.
2   Ibid., 290.
3   Fred Turner, *From Counterculture to Cyberculture: Stewart Brand, the Whole Earth Network, and the Rise of Digital Utopianism* (Chicago: University of Chicago Press, 2008); Fred Turner, *The Democratic Surround: Multimedia and American Liberalism from World War II to the Psychedelic Sixties* (Chicago: University of Chicago Press, 2013).
4   Lewis Mumford, "Authoritarian and Democratic Technics," *Technology and Culture* 5 (1964): 1–8.
5   Tim O'Reilly, "Web 2.0: Compact Definition?" 2005, accessed January 6, 2020, radar.oreilly.com/archives/2005/10/web-20-compact-definition.html; Grant Blank and Bianca Reisdorf, "The Participatory Web," *Information, Communication and Society*, no. 15 (2012): 537–54.
6   Carlo Ratti and Matthew Claudel, *Open-Source Architecture* (London: Thames & Hudson, 2015).
7   Mario Carpo, "Digital Style," *Log*, no. 23 (2011): 43–44.
8   Ibid., 44.
9   Mario Carpo, *The Second Digital Turn: Design beyond Intelligence* (Cambridge, MA: MIT Press, 2017), 144.
10   WikiHouse, accessed January 6, 2020, www.wikihouse.cc/About.
11   Paul Blazek et al., *Configurator Database Report 2016* (Vienna: CyLEDGE, 2016).
12   Daniel Sabin and Rainer Weigel, "Product Configuration Frameworks—A Survey," *IEEE Intelligent Systems*, no. 13 (1998): 43.
13   Ibid.
14   Gramazio and Kohler Architects, *mShape*, accessed January 6, 2020, www.mshape.com.
15   Carpo, *The Second Digital Turn*, 131.
16   John Dewey, *The Quest for Certainty: A Study of the Relation of Knowledge and Action* (New York: Capricorn, 1960), 10.
17   Ibid.
18   Ibid.
19   Le Corbusier, *Towards a New Architecture* (New York: Dover Publications, 1986), 122.
20   J. Nuttall, "How to Use Technology," in *Design Participation: Proceedings of the Design Research Society's Conference, Manchester, September 1971*, ed. Nigel Cross (London: Academy Editions, 1972), 19.

broad "crisis of professionalism"[21] certain architects and planners sought to include "users" in theories and methods in order to eliminate conflicts between anticipated and actual use and to mitigate the social and environmental "side effects" of design interventions ▶ Fig. III.[22]

From the onset of its popularity[23] the concept of participation was diagnosed as fuzzy and confused.[24] In an effort to clarify the idea in architectural design, architectural researcher Fredrik Wulz proposed a "passive–active" yardstick for ranking different participation forms according to the user's ability to make choices and changes on the design outcome.[25] On the "passive" side of the spectrum Wulz placed cases where designers employed questionnaires or dialogues to collect information about users' needs or desires. In the middle he listed forms of designer–user collaboration.[26] Finally, at the "active" end Wulz positioned "self-decision,"[27] which he vaguely described as a process where the architect ensured the "needs for security"[28] but gave up control over the final outcome of the design.

The "user passive" attitude to participation emerged in continuity with 1960s efforts to develop an anticipatory "design science"[29] through the aid of predictive decision-making techniques.[30] Proponents of this attitude assumed that replacing the statistical approximations used in modernist planning with *actual* user data would provide better knowledge of the present and therefore enable better predictions.[31] The argument for more and better information was quickly considered to be theoretically erroneous. In their influential article "Dilemmas in a General Theory of Planning" design theorist Horst Rittel and urban theorist Melvin Webber posited that errors in prediction had little to do with the quality of data.[32] Instead, they were a result of the unique and open-ended character of planning problems that were inherently "wicked"—irreducibly and inextricably linked with uncertainties and unanticipated outcomes. Aside from being flawed, "passive participation" was also argued to be ethically questionable, what Sherry Arnstein called an "empty ritual,"[33] performed to legitimize the decision-maker's choices rather than give choice to users.

"Co-decision" models of participation were developed to address these shortcomings, by positioning architects and planners as "facilitators" rather than controllers of the design. Processes following this model variously took the form of negotiation structures,[34] games and simulations,[35] or performance-based techniques.[36] Co-decision participation aspired to ameliorate problem setting and decision-making by combining different viewpoints and kinds of expertise in an argumentative process. One of the assumptions supporting this approach was that negotiation of perspectives would bring to light parameters inaccessible to a single individual. Participating in the making of a plan enhanced engagement and commitment to its execution,[37] thereby lowering the possibility of future discrepancies or conflicts. Most of the co-decision methods, however, did not escape controversy around the authority of the architect in "translating" the user's plans or decisions into actual designs.[38]

The more radical idea of "self-decision" claimed to remedy this issue by delegating design control to the user within "security" constraints.[39] "Self-decision" forms of participation that emerged in the 1960s placed the categories of "unpredictability," "uncertainty," and the "unknown" at their epicenter. Participatory design theories of this form professed to settle the inherent contradiction between user freedom and designer-imposed constraints by arguing that these constraints captured a necessary and invariant structural aspect of the built environment that every viable decision needed to comply with. The inceptors of these theories sought to accommodate uncertainty at the local level of use and ensure that "the unforeseen can be absorbed" at the global level of the built environment.[40]

Infrastructures and Combinatories

An influential approach to "self-decision" participation was the "support-infill" system pioneered by Dutch architect and design theorist John Habraken in 1961. The system claimed to promote liberty of choice and flexibility of change. Habraken imagined groups of prefabricated elements building up "innumerable dwelling types"[41] to match the user's preferences, supported by structures "growing, developing and changing"[42] to match the structure of the "living organism" that they contained.[43] The contradiction between

III Cover of the first Design Research Society International
Conference, themed *Design Participation*

21 Reyner Banham, "Alternative Networks for the Alternative Culture?" in *Design Participation: Proceedings of the Design Research Society's Conference, Manchester, September 1971*, ed. Nigel Cross (London: Academy Editions, 1972), 16.
22 Nigel Cross, "Here Comes Everyman," in *Design Participation: Proceedings of the Design Research Society's Conference, Manchester, September 1971*, ed. Nigel Cross (London: Academy Editions, 1972), 11.
23 One of the most influential articles arguing for participation in planning was Paul Davidoff, "Advocacy and Pluralism in Planning," *Journal of the American Institute of Planners*, no. 31 (1965): 331–38.
24 J. Johnson, "A Plain Man's Guide to Participation," *Design Studies*, no. 1 (1979): 27–30.
25 Fredrik Wulz, "The Concept of Participation," *Design Studies*, no. 7 (1986): 155, 162.
26 Ibid., 158.
27 Ibid., 159.
28 Ibid., 161.
29 Sydney Gregory, ed., *The Design Method* (London: Butterworth Press, 1966).
30 Geoffrey Broadbent, *Design in Architecture: Architecture and the Human Sciences* (London: David Fulton Publishers, 1988), xvii.
31 Michael Batty, "Limits to Prediction in Science and Design Science," *IPC Business Press*, no. 1 (1980): 153–59, 157.
32 Horst Rittel and Melvin M. Webber, "Dilemmas in a General Theory of Planning," *Policy Sciences*, no. 4 (1973): 155–69.
33 Sherry Arnstein, "A Ladder of Citizen Participation," *Journal of the American Planning Association*, no. 35 (1969): 216–24, 216.
34 Werner Kunz and Horst Rittel, "Issues as Elements of Information Systems," Working Paper No. 131, Institute of Urban and Regional Development, University of California at Berkeley, 1970.
35 Henry Sanoff, *Community Participation Methods in Design and Planning* (Hoboken, NJ: Wiley, 1999).
36 Lawrence Halprin, *The RSVP Cycle: Creative Processes in the Human Environment* (New York: Braziller, 1969); Lawrence Halprin and Jim Burns, *Taking Part: A Workshop Approach to Collective Creativity* (Cambridge, MA: MIT Press, 1975).
37 Peter Stringer, "A Rationale for Participation," in *Design Participation: Proceedings of the Design Research Society's Conference, Manchester, September 1971*, ed. Nigel Cross (London: Academy Editions, 1972), 26–29.
38 Charles Eastman, "Adaptive-Conditional Architecture," in *Design Participation: Proceedings of the Design Research Society's Conference, Manchester, September 1971*, ed. Nigel Cross (London: Academy Editions, 1972), 52; Nicholas Negroponte, *Soft Architecture Machines* (Cambridge, MA: MIT Press, 1975), 108.
39 Wulz, "The Concept of Participation," 161.
40 John Habraken, *Supports: An Alternative to Mass Housing* (England: Urban Press, 2011), 74.
41 Ibid.
42 Ibid., 94.
43 Ibid., 81, 86.
44 Ibid., 74.
45 *Yona Friedman Regarding the Machine That Invents Flats*, video recording, 1969, fresques.ina.fr/europe-des-cultures-en/fiche-media/Europe00061/yona-friedman-regarding-the-machine-that-invents-flats.html.
46 Yona Friedman, *Toward a Scientific Architecture* (Cambridge, MA: MIT Press, 1975), 10.

standardization of spatial modules or building components and erratic individual preferences was settled by the argument that combinations of these spatial or building units could produce "innumerable" choices.[44]

Hungarian-French utopian Yona Friedman voiced similar arguments about the limits of choice in his late 1950s proposals for a Spatial City (Ville spatiale)—a three-dimensional grid expanding over natural and urban landscapes and enabling a limitless mobility of architectural dwellings according to mutating social structures. In a series of articles throughout the 1960s—which led to his 1971 book *Pour une architecture scientifique*, a working manual of sorts for the Ville spatiale—Friedman developed an informational model of choice and decision, which he envisioned being facilitated by a typewriter-like machine that he called the FLATWRITER ▶ Fig. IV. A proto-configurator of sorts, this speculative machine asked the user to select room modules, equipment, and building components through the use of a keyboard with a fixed number of keys, and then printed out what Friedman speculated would be a thick book[45] displaying a "menu" of "all physically possible"[46] combinations of these elements. The menu would also present the user with metrics about the efficiency of each choice for their own daily habits and for the overall efficiency of the urban assemblage in which each choice would be inserted.

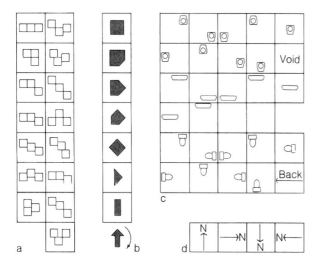

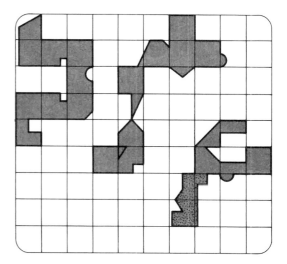

IV Some of the FLATWRITER's combinatorial
    possibilities, derived by considering elementary
    spatial configurations, shape, equipment
    placement, and building/equipment components

Habraken's and Friedman's proposals for self-decision building systems extrapolated on shifting practices in mass-produced housing and postwar planning that were already in effect. For example, in the late 1960s the French government implemented an experimental approach to housing that came to be known as *habitat évolutif* (evolutionary dwelling) as a response to the standardized mass housing approach of the *grands ensembles*.[47] The *habitat évolutif* experiments foregrounded the idea that a *combinatoire* (combinatory) of standardized elements offered a way out of mass housing's repetition and monotony by giving users the possibility of personalized combination within a finite set of prefabricated components. Responding to the *habitat évolutif* experiments, which usually involved experts guiding users through the combination of elements, Friedman promoted the FLATWRITER as enabling individuals to self-operate the system of configurational choices.

The Enumerative Imagination

Friedman's theories inspired early work on computer-aided participatory design by MIT's Architecture Machine Group—the Department of Architecture's first computing facility. The Architecture Machine Group collaborated with Friedman under a grant from the National Science Foundation to implement his participatory method in a system for *architecture-by-yourself*.[48] In describing the influence of Friedman's methods on the Architecture Machine Group's work, its founder Nicholas Negroponte warned readers against the theoretical shortcomings of "the particularly French notion of a 'banque de données' or what he [Friedman] calls a 'repertoire'"[49] in conceptualizing choice. Friedman's theory, he suggested, went beyond the combinatory of prefabricated elements customary in *habitat évolutif* examples or in Habraken's *support-infill system*. The problem with these approaches, he explained, was that "the offerings of a menu of solutions obviously cannot exceed the combinatorial product of the parts (which may be enormous)."[50] Negroponte argued that Friedman escaped this particular constraint by including in his repertoire "topologies that do not have a metric."[51] "It is the user's adding of this metric," he concluded, "that affords the limitless variety" ▶ Fig. V.[52]

Indeed, underpinning the FLATWRITER was a mathematically based theory of configuration that relied upon the representation of architectural floor plans through their underlying topologies—through their graphs. To construct these graphs, one placed a point at the center of each room shown in the plan and then drew a line between the rooms that were connected with a door. This representation, which was also known as the "adjacency graph," allowed one to enumerate all other possible floor plan layouts; one simply needed to count all possible connections between the graph's points. This rote combinatorial operation was a well-defined mathematical operation and could be easily performed by computers, at least for a small number of rooms. Using theorems from graph theory, one could also exclude nonplanar graphs (graphs with intersecting lines) that could not be resolved as single-level layouts and therefore required vertical circulation ▶ Fig. VI.

Viewed from the perspective of the mathematical techniques that it put to use, Friedman's participatory theory was in close alignment with a field of research that dominated early work on architecture and computing. This work went by the name of "configurational studies" or "plan morphologies." A central idea in these studies was the "dimensionless" representation of architectural plans[53] in which every room shown in the floor plan became a discrete grid cell of equal dimension to the other grid cells and information about how it connected to them. The shape and metric properties of an object—in this case the floor plan—were replaced by its underlying structure, its topology.

In his 1973 paper "Graph-Theoretic Representation of Architectural Arrangement" architectural researcher Philip Steadman

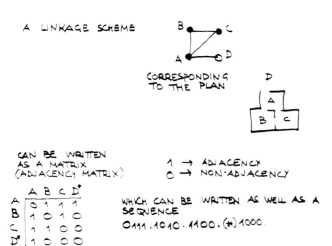

A LINKAGE SCHEME

CORRESPONDING
TO THE PLAN

CAN BE WRITTEN
AS A MATRIX
(ADJACENCY MATRIX)

1 → ADJACENCY
0 → NON·ADJACENCY

	A	B	C	D*
A	0	1	1	1
B	1	0	1	0
C	1	1	0	0
D*	1	0	0	0

WHICH CAN BE WRITTEN AS WELL AS A
SEQUENCE

0111 . 1010 . 1100 . (*) 1000 .

* DENOTES A LABEL DIFFERENT FROM THE OTHERS
(EXTERIOR SPACE)

V   Screenshot from the graph-based space planning
system implemented for the Architecture Machine
Group's Architecture-by-yourself project

distinguished between a "heuristic" and an "enumeration" approach to using graphs for representing floor plans. The "heuristic" approach found a layout that was permissible for a given set of constraints, whereas the "enumeration" approach was exhaustive. "*All* feasible solutions [emphasis in the original]," he argued, could be identified "once and for all"[54] and their record possibly published in book form. Steadman argued that such enumerative processes could motivate research endeavors such as the establishment of a "precise" correlation of governmentally set housing standards (dimensional or otherwise) with the "variety of allowable plan types"[55] or the exploration of the relationship between prefabrication systems and spatial arrangement possibilities. Much of the early work on computer-aided architectural design revolved around developing algorithms for *enumerating* possible *configurations*[56] derived from this initial topological description of a dimensionless shape. Architects were manipulating objectiles long before they talked about objectiles.

Recognizing the dependency of an enumerative and configurative imagination upon a mathematical object, the graph, is significant. This is not only because counting line (relation) permutations among immutable points (objects) gives a visual handle to a specific conception of open-endedness operative in configurative definitions of participation, but also because it provides a critical heuristic for assessing these definitions' limitations. In theories of participatory architectural design, the graph was promoted as an objective substructure defining extents of permissible choices and supporting superimpositions of subjective meanings and aesthetic choices. This is congruent with the "support-infill" or "infrastructure" model of design: the designer authors a featureless skeleton, an infrastructure, that delimits the possibilities of user choices. This skeleton is either a topology that is made concrete through the assignment of metric properties by the user or a set of components that have specific permissible rules of combination. By subjugating choice and possibility under an abstract, invariant structure, graphs tamed it under the certainty of a combinatorial universe in which topology, the abstract realm of structures, came before and above geometry, the surface of appearances. Rather than abolishing authorial control, participation-as-configuration displaced it to the realm that postwar architects saw as the prime site of theory and representation: architecture's organizational diagram, an informational skeleton made visible and operational through the mathematical object of the graph.

Conclusion

In 1996, writing on "virtual" (i.e., digital) worlds, media theorist Lev Manovich identified a "shift from creation to selection" as a constitutive condition of their aesthetics. "The modern subject," he wrote, "proceeds through life by selecting from numerous menus and catalogs of items." Manovich argued that this shift in subjectivity—what Toffler had tellingly termed "the configurative 'me'" or the "modular 'me'"[57]—also carried implications for creativity. "The great text of culture from which the artist created his own unique 'tissue

47 Kenny Cupers, *The Social Project: Housing in Postwar France* (Minneapolis: University of Minnesota Press, 2014).

48 Guy Weinzapfel and Nicholas Negroponte, "Architecture-by-Yourself: An Experiment with Computer Graphics for House Design," in *Proceedings of the 3rd Annual Conference on Computer Graphics and Interactive Techniques* (New York: SIGGRAPH, 1976), 74–78, doi.org/10.1145/563274.563290.

49 Ibid., 115.

50 Negroponte, *Soft Architecture Machines*, 115.

51 Ibid.

52 Ibid.

53 Philip Steadman, *Architectural Morphology: An Introduction to the Geometry of Building Plans* (London: Pion Ltd., 1983).

54 Philip Steadman, "Graph-Theoretic Representation of Architectural Arrangement," in *The Architecture of Form*, ed. Lionel March (London: Cambridge University Press, 1976), 103.

55 Ibid., 105.

56 Charles Eastman, "Through the Looking Glass—Why No Wonderland?: Computer Applications to Architecture in the USA," *Computer-Aided Design*, no. 6 (1974): 119–24.

57 Toffler, *The Third Wave*, 405.

of quotations' was bubbling and shimmering somewhere below the consciousness," Manovich warned, and was becoming "externalized" and therefore "greatly reduced" through digital menus driving the creative processes.

There is a story to be told about the democratizing potential of the "digital" for architecture—a potential that stems precisely from a quality of being *digit-al*: a kit of discrete parts combinable and recombinable based on *logic-s* in the plural, logics of multiple individuals or their collectivities. And yet there is a vexing sense in which configurative approaches to design—piecing fixed digital or physical parts together—promote a limited understanding of open-endedness, limited precisely because they assume all design possibilities to be enumerable before any action takes place. In this essay I have given claims about the digital's participatory and interactional potential a specific visual and conceptual handle: the graph. This handle represents both the basis for the configurative workings of methods striving to fulfill this potential and the limits of the enumerative imagination that validates them. We may then begin to contemplate limits of "aggregatory," combinatorial, modular imaginations of participation, arguing that they do not democratize architecture but confine possibilities within a very particular structural abstraction of architecture, its skeletal diagram. We may also then start speculating about alternative imaginations of democratization, which embrace perspectives, positionalities, and ways of seeing as opposed to relying on combinatorial operations of physical or digital parts.

One possibility might be to consider British philosopher Owen Barfield's quasi-spiritual urge for an immersion in the world of perceptual surface—or "participation," as he termed it—as a way to enrich one's capacity for discovery. Instead of a passive selection from preset menus of possibilities, this other mode of participation posits a perceptually active engagement either in the process of design or of inhabitation as an emancipatory practice. How to retheorize participation and its relationship to architectural computation is a question for another time. Yet even to begin asking it requires awareness of the historical and technical specificity of participation's complicated relationship to design as a digital, discrete, blocks-like process.

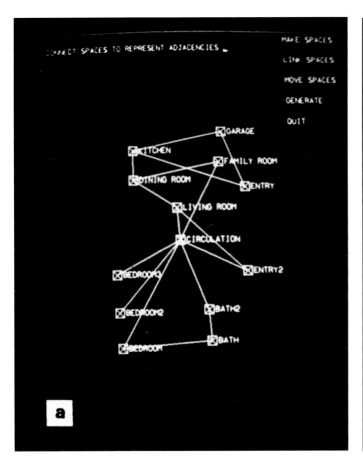
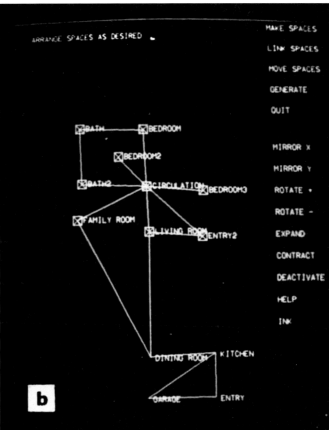

VI A schematic architectural plan mapped one-to-one
to a labeled planar graph, and then translated to an
adjacency matrix and binary code

URBAN 5

Nicholas Negroponte,
Architecture Machine Group

1967

SOFTWARE
URBAN 5 (programmed in FORTRAN)

HARDWARE
IBM 2250, model 1 Graphics Display Unit,
IBM 360/67 mainframe computer

PURPOSE OF SOFTWARE
design, human–computer interaction

The computer program URBAN 5 was an early experiment in design collaboration between human and machine. It was ultimately abandoned and considered a failure by its makers. One of the Architecture Machine Group's main interests was to develop a computer program that would be able to think, learn, and communicate. Rather than being a mere graphical tool, it was meant to acquire new skills and eventually to design on its own. URBAN 5 was based on 10 × 10-foot (3 × 3 m) cubes that could be placed on a screen and modified three-dimensionally. Each cube had up to ten different characteristics, such as transparency or accessibility, which could be adjusted by the user. Different display modes enabled the user to execute operations such as manipulating the topography or other physical elements. In addition, the program could simulate growth scenarios. An important part of the project was the idea of individualization. URBAN 5 was meant to observe the user's behavior and design methodology. Communication between human and machine would work in two ways: graphically by drawing with a light pen on the screen, and by entering sentences in English on a keyboard. The result was intended as a dialogue that worked in an informal way, allowing even inexperienced users to design without preexisting knowledge. In a next step the program was supposed to collect information gained from these interactions and acquire additional skills to support the designer by making suggestions or by outlining conflicts in the design. In reality, however, the program was unable to depart from its preset conditions as its constraints were based on fixed assumptions about architectural design. It was unable to evolve by itself and its reactions were based on a predefined catalog of answers.—*Franziska Mühlbauer*

Negroponte, Nicholas. *The Architecture Machine* (Cambridge, MA: MIT Press, 1970). ● Llach, Daniel Cardoso. "Inertia of an Automated Utopia: Design Commodities and Authorial Agency 40 Years after 'The Architecture Machine.'" *Thresholds* 39 (2011): 39–44. ● Steenson, Molly Wright. *Architectural Intelligence: How Designers and Architects Created the Digital Landscape* (Cambridge, MA: MIT Press, 2017). ● Vrachliotis, Georg. "Architekturmaschine. Individualisierungssyteme." *Arch+*, December 2018, 36–43.

| Computer setup for URBAN 5: buttons for switching modes, screen to interact
with light pen, and keyboard for language-based dialog

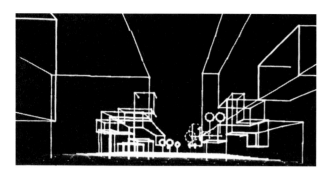

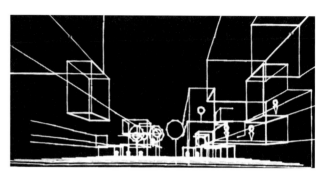

URBAN5

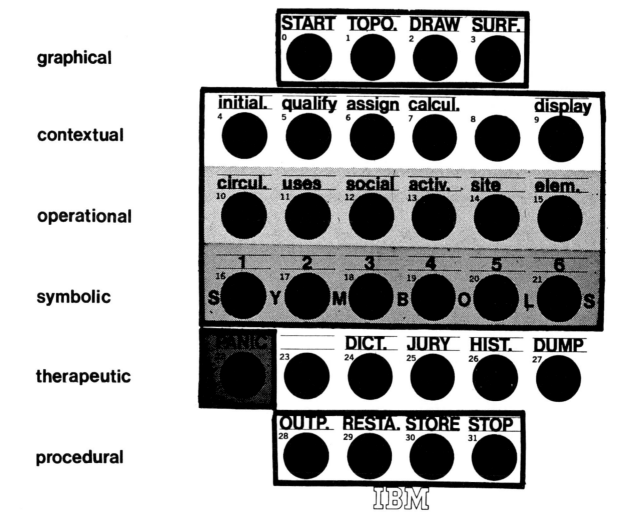

graphical

contextual

operational

symbolic

therapeutic

procedural

TED, MANY CONFLICTS ARE OCCURRING

II   Screenshots of a street view in URBAN 5
III Control pad showing different design modes
IV The program alerts a user to design problems.

Aspen Movie Map

*Michael Naimark, Peter Clay,
Bob Mohl, Architecture Machine Group*

1978—1980

SOFTWARE
Ramtek 9000 Series Graphic Display System,
Quick and Dirty Animation System (QADAS)

HARDWARE
optical videodisc and player (MCA Corporation),
touch-sensitive cathode-ray monitor (Elographics)

PURPOSE OF SOFTWARE
interactive image display

As one of the first hypermedia systems, the Aspen Movie Map enabled user-controlled virtual travel on a touchscreen monitor through the city of Aspen, Colorado. Michael Naimark and Bob Mohl were graduate students at MIT in 1978 when undergraduate Peter Clay proposed "mapping" the hallways of MIT with a 16mm film camera and transmitting the footage frame by frame onto an optical laser disc. Together with a computer program that allowed control of speed and direction in the digitized hallway, it resulted in the prototype for what became the Aspen Movie Map.

Later that year Nicholas Negroponte, director of the Architecture Machine Group, and Andrew Lippman as the project's principal investigator secured funding from the Cybernetics Technology Office of the Defense Advanced Research Projects Agency (DARPA) to develop a larger virtual map to teach soldiers how to familiarize themselves with a new territory quickly and realistically. During the fall and winter months of 1978–79 an interdisciplinary group of Architecture Machine faculty and graduate students, a wildlife cinematographer, and a psychologist traveled through Aspen to gather data and visual material. Four cameras mounted on top of a jeep took photos every ten feet (3 m), capturing the city's streets and facades. At the time, a laser disc could contain thirty minutes of film, equivalent to 54,000 single photos. For the Movie Map the team hacked the hardware to make every single photo accessible at random: the user could choose her way. The facades and mountain panorama were texture-mapped onto a 3-D virtual model, programmed in QADAS. The model also worked as a "local" interface for multimedia data that could be accessed through hyperlinks. Historical photographs, numeric data, and short videos could be shown when the user "arrived" at several buildings.

The Movie Map was exhibited at MIT for the first time in 1979. There, it was projected and accompanied by two cathode-ray tube monitors, and the user could navigate the map with a joystick, which was later replaced by the touchscreen monitor, while sitting in an Eames Lounge Chair.—*Sina Brückner-Amin*

Naimark, Michael. "A 3D Moviemap and a 3D Panorama." *SPIE Proceedings*, vol. 3012 (1997). ● Naimark, Michael. "Aspen the Verb: Musings on Heritage and Virtuality." *MIT Presence Journal* 15, no. 3 (2006): 330–35. ● Naone, Erica. "Déjà View." *MIT Technology Review* 111, no. 6 (2008). Accessed January 16, 2020. www.technologyreview.com/s/411453/d-j-view/.

Texture-mapped houses in the virtual 3-D model

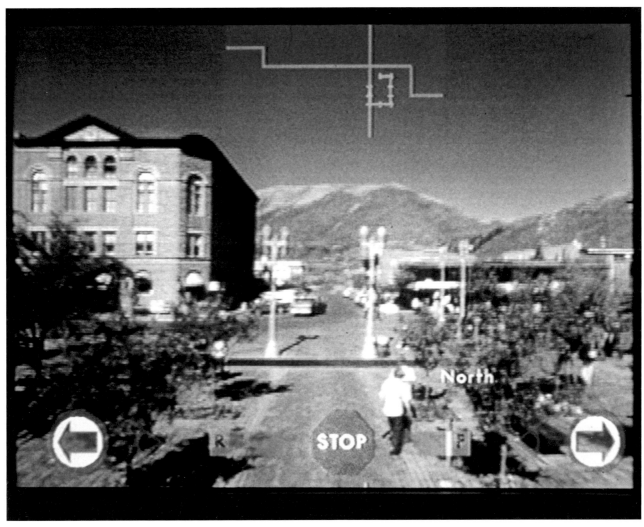

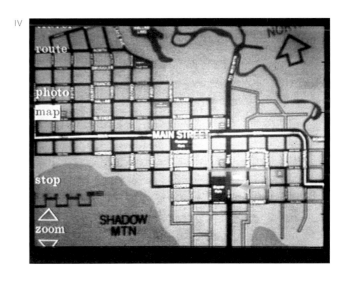

II   Aspen Movie Map and interface
III Street view with interface superimposed
IV   Interactive plan of Aspen

The Walter Segal Model

John Frazer, Julia Frazer, John Potter

1982

SOFTWARE
Shape Processor Language (John Frazer,
Julia Frazer, Paul Coates, Anne Sott),
scan software written in BASIC

HARDWARE
circuit board with machine-readable pin
connections, 32k Commodore PET

PURPOSE OF SOFTWARE
self-build design blocks

The Walter Segal Model project was a computer program intended for laypeople. It was based on a physical model and displayed the designs on a screen and allowed them to be checked for feasibility. Walter Segal created his most well-known and influential residential buildings as part of the self-build housing movement of the early 1980s. Material and labor inputs were reduced to the absolute minimum on these simple timber houses, so that the future residents could erect them in the shortest possible time. The single- or two-story detached homes were built in groups of about ten on urban plots in the London borough of Lewisham. This approach gave rise to neighborhood self-build groups, who helped one another construct their homes. Although the houses may originally have been intended to be subsidized rented homes, many of them were later bought by their tenants. Segal's simple building system, in which a timber frame was fabricated out of standard-format plywood boards, enabled the self-builders to design their house themselves by combining different modules. Segal devised a plug-in model that made the design process intuitive and comprehensible for the lay participants.

In 1982, John and Julia Frazer together with John Potter developed an electronic version of this plug-in model. The configuration of this model could be transferred to a computer program by means of electronic plug-in contacts. The computer program then checked the position of all components and the building design for feasibility, before producing floor area and cost figures. The system was also capable of generating the drawings required for construction. The Frazers had explored the idea of using physical models as user interfaces and data input devices for many years. The attractiveness of this idea was obvious: it was very difficult to display 3-D volumes in real time on a monitor in those days. Moreover, the plug-in model provided an intuitive user interface and a direct means of linking an input device to the object being designed. Segal's modular timber buildings were an ideal case study for this type of model interface. A manageable number of modules could be arranged in many different ways on a circuit board. In this respect, the model was reminiscent of early chess computers, which were being developed at the same time and recognized and analyzed arrangements of physical game pieces on a chessboard. It

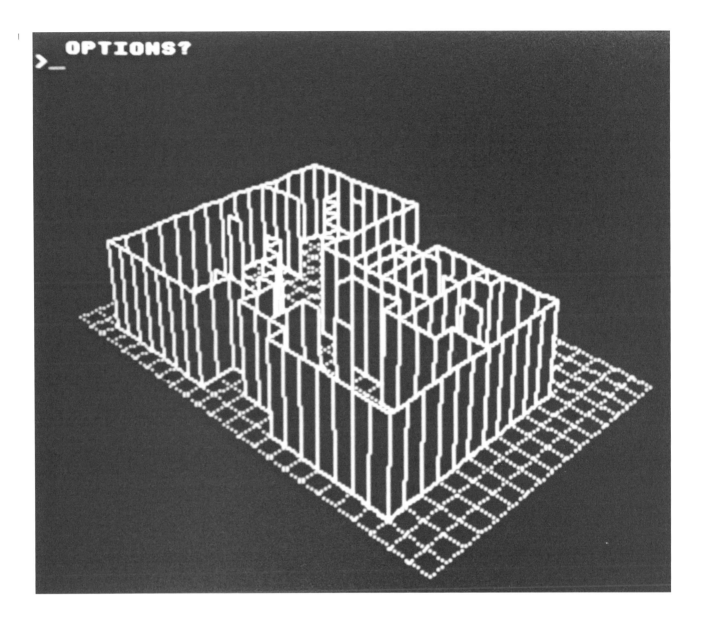

| Virtual model, created using the data read from the physical model

is not surprising, therefore, that the Segal plug-in model would make design resemble a game. As a design tool, it encouraged the trial-and-error approach and creativity. Its strengths lie mainly in its enjoyable operation, comprehensibility, and ease of use.
—Johannes Müntinga

McKean, John. *Learning from Segal: Walter Segal's Life, Work and Influence.* Basel: Birkhäuser Verlag, 1989. ● Frazer, John. *An Evolutionary Architecture.* London: Architectural Association, 1995. ● Grahame, Alice. *Walters Way and Segal Close.* Zurich: Park Books, 2017.

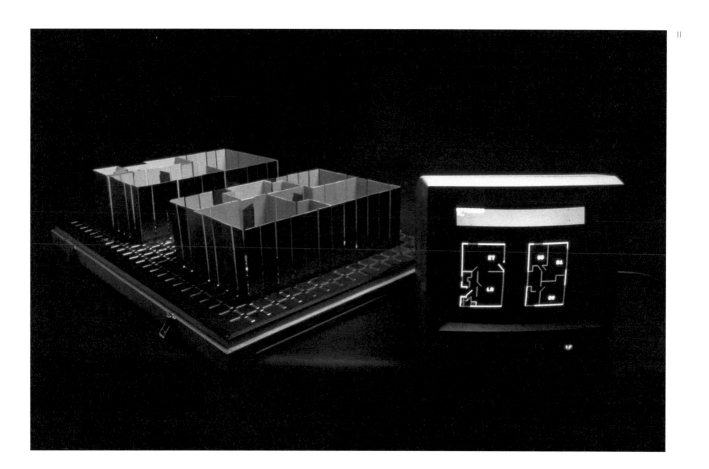

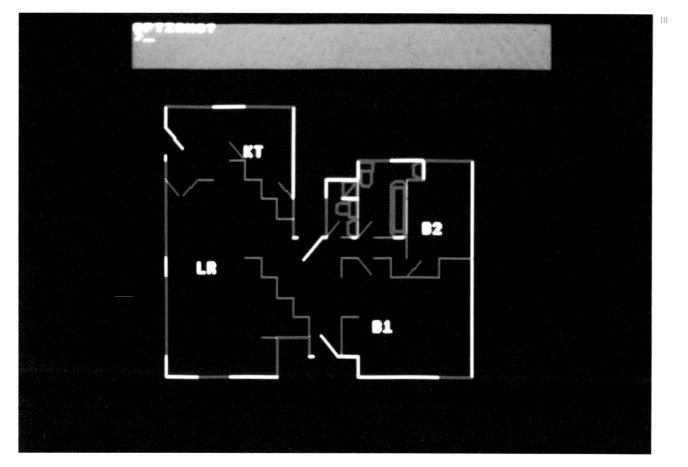

IV

WALLS	TYPE OF WALL	NO.	COST £
	Facing brick / cavity / blockwork	2	£ 88.32
	Facing brick / cavity insulation / blockwork	9	£ 447.12
	Facing brick / cavity / thermal block	10	£ 469.20
	Facing brick / cavity insulation / thermal block	6	£ 314.64
	Steel frame / cladding & insulation	4	£ 220.80
	Timber stud with plasterboard and skin both sides	6	£ 149.04
	Lightweight concrete block plastered both sides	9	£ 223.56
	Total :	46	£ 1912.68

Press a key to continue

V

II   Plug-in model in use, connected to a computer
III Schematic layout plans generated by the computer program
IV   Computer-generated cost estimate: element type, number of pieces, and price
V   Plug-in model being built

ARMILLA

Fritz Haller, Jupp Gauchel,
Christoph Mathys, Ludger Hovestadt,
Angelika Drach, Volkmar Hovestadt,
Peter Raetz

1982—present

SOFTWARE
ARMILLA, programmed in Knowledge Craft
(LISP), Byron (for facilities management)

HARDWARE
Unix computer

PURPOSE OF SOFTWARE
building information modeling, facilities
management

ARMILLA represented an early attempt at creating building information modeling software by integrating space, structure, and building appliances into a single digital model. The software was named after a fictitious city in Italo Calvino's 1972 book *Invisible Cities* that consisted solely of piping: "[Armilla] has nothing that makes it seem a city except the water pipes that rise vertically where the houses should be and spread out horizontally where the floors should be: a forest of pipes that end in taps, showers, spouts, overflows."[1] As in Calvino's city, Haller's software makes mostly hidden technical installations visible and autonomous.

ARMILLA was developed by Fritz Haller and his team at Karlsruhe University as a tool for planning with Haller's modular building system MIDI and applied in projects such as Kantonsschule Solothurn (1993). Haller had developed a number of construction systems of different scales, ranging from entire cities to buildings (MINI, MIDI, and MAXI) and to his well-known USM furniture system. The steel construction system MIDI visually integrated piping for water, air, and electricity in a floor framework of one-meter height and was intended for multistory "technical" buildings such as schools, office buildings, laboratories, and hospitals. In anticipation of expected changes in their use, ideas of flexibility and efficiency were put forward in the planning, prefabrication, and assembly of building elements.

ARMILLA was developed in response to this modular building system and followed its grid logic that connected all individual elements. Rather than applying piping systems as a last step in the design process, ARMILLA integrated them in the layout of the structure and thus made them independent of the specific project. Early on, Haller saw the potential of developing ARMILLA as a digital tool for the planning of technical appliances. The layered analog drawings based on a set of rules were translated into a combination of CAD visualization techniques and artificially intelligent programming. ARMILLA software set out not only to execute the planner's design decisions but to assist in the design, for instance by detecting conflicting pipe routes. Later versions developed along different paths, from a plug-in for Vectorworks to proposing a "naive interface" or a complete digital copy of the building, so that after completion its technical equipment could be monitored from a distance, further linking digital and physical space.—*Gerlinde Verhaeghe*

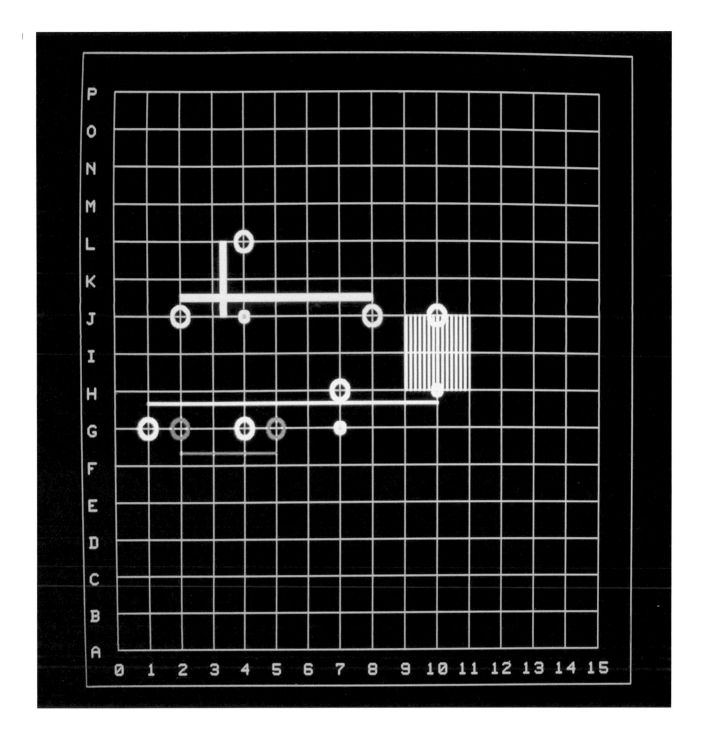

I Early version of ARMILLA based on a digitized grid

1 Italo Calvino, Invisible Cities (Orlando, FL: Harcourt, 1974), 49–50. ● Wichmann, Hans. *System-Design: Fritz Haller. Bauten-Möbel-Forschung.* Basel: Birkhäuser Verlag, 1989. ● Krippner, Roland. "MIDI-ARMILLA." In *Exemplarisch. Konstruktion und Raum in der Architektur des 20. Jahrhunderts*, edited by Winfried Nerdinger, 118–21. Munich: Prestel, 2002. ● Vrachliotis, Georg. "Modell, Werkzeug und Metapher. Fritz Hallers Architekturforschung." In *Fritz Haller—Architekt und Forscher*, edited by Laurent Stalder and Georg Vrachliotis, 78–91. Zurich: gta Verlag, 2015.

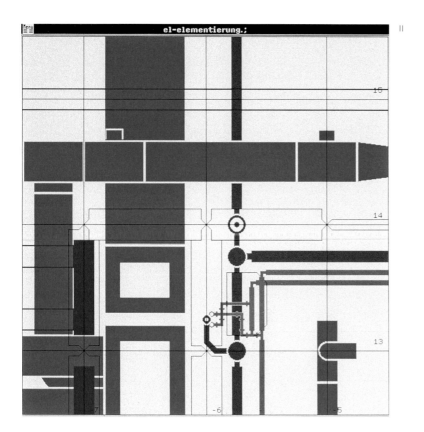

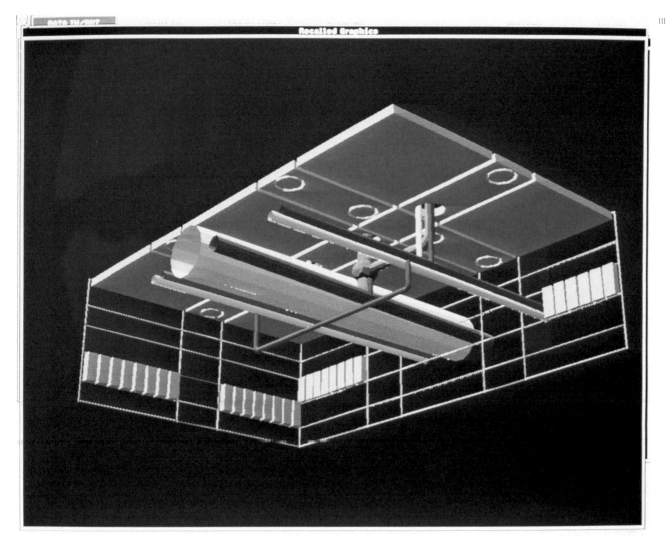

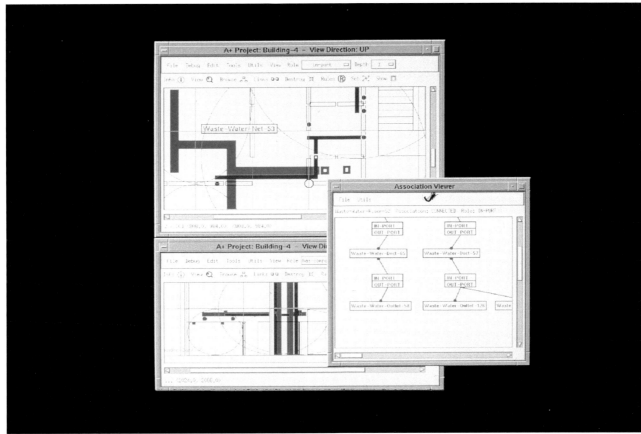

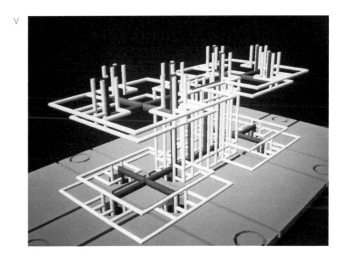

II Later version of ARMILLA
III Three-dimensional view of pipes
IV Software interface of ARMILLA
V Three-dimensional model of piping system for a building

H₂Oexpo

Lars Spuybroek, Joan Almekinders,
Peter Heymans, Maurice Nio,
William Veerbeek, Jan van der Windt
(Buro Zonneveld)

1993—1997

SOFTWARE
AutoCAD 11, LISP

PURPOSE OF SOFTWARE
construction drawings, rendering

H_2Oexpo is Lars Spuybroek's first building and an early attempt to create a liquid, interactive, and computer-controlled interior. The pavilion is one of the first completely topologically implemented buildings and a digital experiment that adapts to the movements of visitors. Also known as the Freshwater Pavilion, H_2Oexpo is located in the Delta Park Neeltje Jans, a theme park at the mouth of the Scheldt, and merges into the smaller Saltwater Pavilion of Kas Oosterhuis. H_2Oexpo is a 60-meter-long tube that has been deformed based on external parameters such as wind direction, the position and height of the surrounding sand dunes, and the anticipated movements of visitors. The pavilion allows visitors not only to experience water in its various manifestations but also to move like water through a curved tube. The shape of the pavilion consists of individual ellipses—smaller ones at the entrance and exit, larger ones in the middle—which Spuybroek deformed and scaled by incorporating the slightly undulating floor level. Using this technique, he designed a series of cross sections, which were prefabricated in steel and connected by horizontal beams, and then the whole pavilion was covered with silver-colored film. As a programmed movement architecture, it is a built manifesto of Spuybroek's concept of the fusion of perception and activity in architecture. The relationships between the horizontal carrying and vertical application of loading—or, as Spuybroek intended, between acting in the horizontal and perceiving in the vertical—are neutralized by the complete curvature. Like drops of water flowing through a double-curved tube, visitors interact with the pavilion by its stimulation of their locomotive and perception systems. Behind this is Spuybroek's neurologically founded concept of the body as a flexible perceptual apparatus that is constantly reshaping itself. According to the architect, topologically interpreted architecture and the human body share this fundamental characteristic. Spuybroek worked intensively on making architectural materials more flexible in order to transfer the metaphysical content of his concept into forms that unfold in space, as if in a frozen state of movement. His objective was a "motor geometry" in which the abstract movement of the H_2Oexpo is related to the actual movement of visitors.[1] The lights, sounds, and images triggered by motion sensors,

I Visitors in the installation

such as a virtual stone falling into water, and water in the form of springs, fountains, and geysers, are part of a complex spatial system programmed to react to the visitors. Spuybroek, who initially designed by hand, switched to working with AutoCAD during the project phase. The digitally generated floor plans, sections, and models were used for the final design of the building and for transferring the dimensions to the steelwork contractor.—*Regine Heß*

1 Spuybroek, *NOX. Machining Architecture*, 36. ● Spuybroek, Lars. *NOX. Machining Architecture, Bauten und Projekte*. Munich: DVA, 2004. ● Heß, Regine. *Emotionen am Werk. Peter Zumthor, Daniel Libeskind, Lars Spuybroek und die historische Architekturpsychologie*. Vol. 12 of Neue Frankfurter Forschungen zur Kunst. Berlin: Gebr. Mann Verlag, 2013. ● *HtwoOexpo, Greg Lynn in Conversation with Lars Spuybroek*. Vol. 10 of Archaeology of the Digital. Montreal: Canadian Centre for Architecture, 2015. www.cca.qc.ca/en/events/34443/h2oexpo.

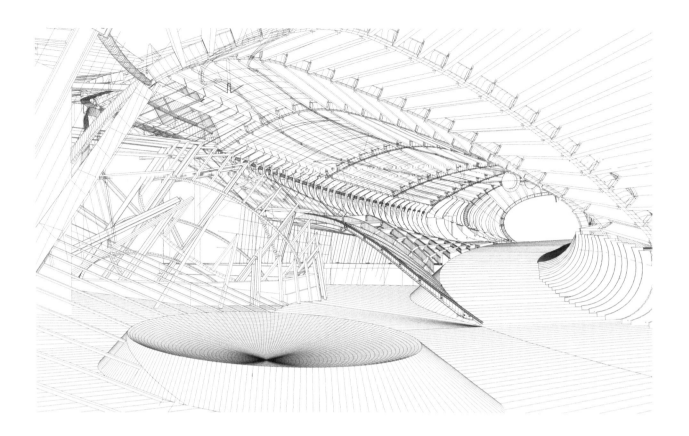

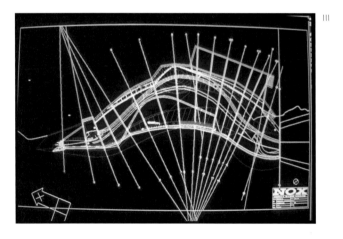

III

II Wireframe perspective of the interior
III 2-D drawing in AutoCAD
IV Interior with visitors, colored pencil on printed paper, 1994

The Virtual House Competition

ANY, with FSB—Franz Schneider Brakel GmbH + Co KG

1997

ARCHITECTS
Eisenman Architects, Herzog & de Meuron Architekten, Toyo Ito & Associates, Studio Daniel Libeskind, Ateliers Jean Nouvel, Foreign Office Architects

PHILOSOPHERS
John Rajchman, Gilles Deleuze, Éric Alliez, Erik Oger, Elizabeth Grosz, Paul Virilio

JURY
Akira Asada, Kurt Forster, Rebecca Horn

The competition for the virtual house is a perfect example of the linking of architecture and philosophy as promoted by the Anyone Corporation, bound with a euphoria for the digital. The Anyone Corporation was founded in 1990 in New York by the editor Cynthia C. Davidson, her husband Peter Eisenman, and the architects Arata Isozaki and Ignasi de Solà-Morales Rubió as a network of architects and theorists to stimulate an interdisciplinary architectural discourse. The journal *ANY* appeared between 1993 and 2000. The competition entries from the six invited architecture offices were presented on March 20–21, 1997, in Berlin and later publicized in the *ANY* double edition 19/20. Issue 19 was devoted to the virtual in philosophy, with the French theorist Gilles Deleuze as its focus. Issue 20 presented the designs for the virtual house. The concept of the competition was developed by philosopher John Rajchman. Because Deleuze wrote in *L'actuel et le virtuel* (1995) that every actual is surrounded by the virtual, i.e., by not yet conceived alternative developments that could unpredictably become real in thought, Rajchman called for a house that would be open to the unpredictable. At the same time, however, there were the following precise requirements: the building should be 200 square meters maximum, accommodate one to four people and a domestic pet, enclose space, offer protection, and be buildable.

The architectural design offices taking part understood virtuality in a variety of very different ways. Herzog & de Meuron placed the virtual in the digital and imaginative by creating a website with photographs that had accompanied one of their architecture projects. Eisenman Architects understood virtuality as a potential from which novel forms could arise. They developed a digital force field with the influencing vectors that deformed two grids in an unpredictable manner. This was based on the idea that only a computer program without subjective objectives could produce unknown forms. Foreign Office Architects interpreted virtuality as a breaking of conventions. For example, a Möbius strip–like structure would eliminate division into functional spatial units and the distinction between the building and the ground, and change its external appearance, adapting to a given landscape through the digital generation of a camouflage pattern.

The jury decided not to award a prize but considered, among other things, the Eisenman Architects project to be the winner.

| Presentation rendering of Foreign Office Architects'
virtual house in a Black Forest setting

The Herzog & de Meuron website entry was criticized in the absence of the architects by the jury, who felt that it could not be interpreted as a virtual house. The resulting misunderstanding is particularly interesting with regard to the perception of the Anyone Corporation as a self-appointed architectural elite. Herzog & de Meuron subsequently stated that their design had been ignored and ridiculed: "The ANY jury uses virtuality simply as a means to advance and market a particular architectural stance to the cost of other architects."[1] — *Frederike Lausch*

1 FSB, *Das virtuelle Haus* (Cologne: FSB, 1998), 156. ● "The Virtual House." ANY, no. 19/20 (September 1997). ● FSB. *Das virtuelle Haus*. Cologne: FSB, 1998. ● Deleuze, Gilles. "Das Aktuelle und das Virtuelle." In *Deleuze und die Künste*, edited by Peter Gente and Peter Weibel, 249–53. Frankfurt am Main: Suhrkamp, 2007.

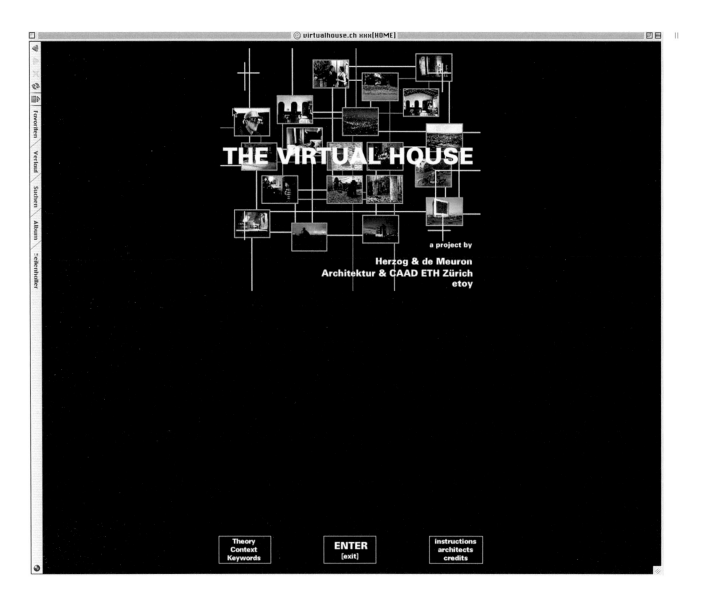

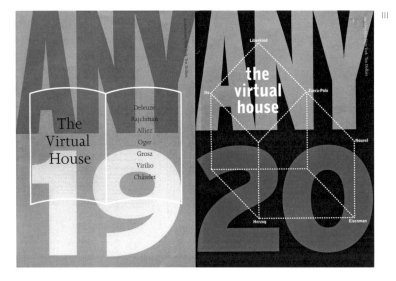

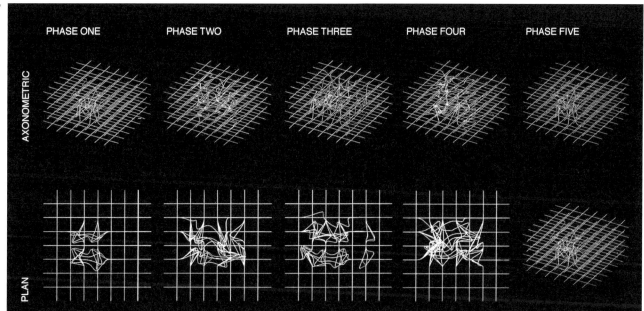

PHASE ONE PHASE TWO PHASE THREE PHASE FOUR PHASE FIVE

AXONOMETRIC

PLAN

II   Homepage of Herzog & de Meuron's website www.virtualhouse.ch
III Cover of the *ANY* double issue No. 19/20
IV Visualization of the design process by Eisenman Architects

Guggenheim Virtual Museum

Asymptote Architecture

1999—2001

SOFTWARE
Alias|Wavefront, Maya, Cosmo VRML, Photoshop, Premiere, Macromedia Flas

HARDWARE
Silicon Graphics RealityEngine

PURPOSE OF SOFTWARE
morphing, shape-finding, construction of virtual architecture

The Guggenheim Virtual Museum was the first attempt at creating an interactive and immersive architectural space for a museum on the Internet. It was commissioned in 1997 by the Bohen Foundation as part of the expanding network of "Global Guggenheims" under the Guggenheim's controversial director, Thomas Krens. The project was supported by a $1 million program to commission and display interactive, born-digital art. The first artwork on display was Brandon by media artist Shu Lea Cheang. For the design, Hani Rashid and Lise Anne Couture took the architecture of the existing Guggenheim spaces as a starting point for creating shape-shifting forms: Frank Lloyd Wright's Guggenheim Museum in New York was morphed in red and Frank Gehry's Guggenheim Bilbao in blue. As in their digital sketchbook *I-Scape,* for which they sampled found images of shoes, cars, and buildings, they created forms that were continually stretched into one another. Even though the virtual museum was using a traditional program for its spaces, including an atrium and galleries, its architecture deviated from previous attempts at creating Cartesian space online. Here, the abstract, three-dimensional forms were no longer stable but changed as the user moved through them. The interiors were a colorful collage of texture-mapped surfaces, text, and digital artwork. The museum included access to content from the Guggenheim's locations in Berlin, Bilbao, New York, and Venice as well as a broad range of digital media. Computer screens were the portals through which visitors gained access to the virtual spaces. Movement was simulated by scrolling, rotating, zooming, and clicking. The museum would have been accessible on the Internet as well as through a terminal in the Guggenheim Center for Art and Technology in SoHo. In addition to designing the virtual gallery, Asymptote created an ambitious website, www.guggenheim.com, which would have included access to the virtual exhibition, reproductions of artwork from the collections of the Guggenheim and several international partners, as well as commercial features such as a gift shop and educational material. The website was scheduled to open in September 2001 but was canceled in the aftermath of 9/11. — *Teresa Fankhänel*

Rashid, Hani, and Lise Anne Couture. *Asymptote: Flux*. New York: Phaidon, 2002.
●Rashid, Hani. "Learning from the Virtual." *e-flux. Post-Internet Cities*. Accessed November 4, 2019. www.e-flux.com/architecture/post-internet-cities/140714/learning-from-the-virtual/.

I–II View of the atrium

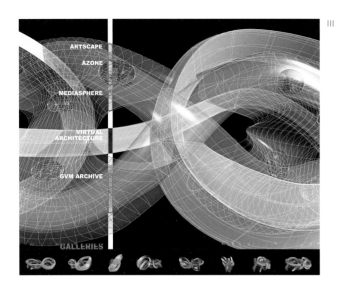

ARTSCAPE
AZONE
MEDIASPHERE
VIRTUAL
ARCHITECTURE
GVM ARCHIVE
GALLERIES

III

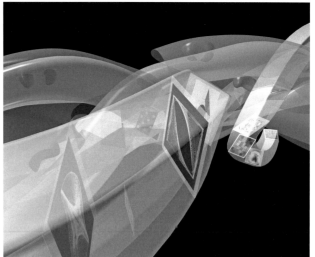

IV

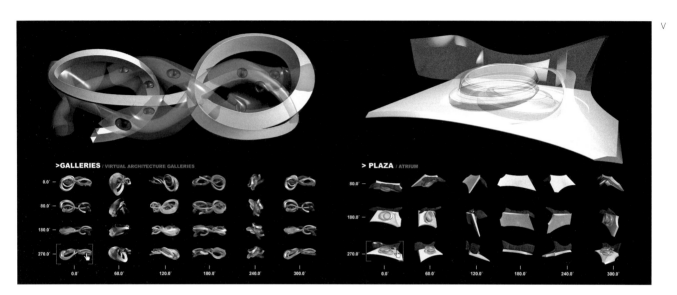

V

>GALLERIES / VIRTUAL ARCHITECTURE GALLERIES

0.0° —
80.0° —
180.0° —
270.0° —

0.0°　　60.0°　　120.0°　　180.0°　　240.0°　　300.0°

> PLAZA / ATRIUM

80.0° —
180.0° —
270.0° —

0.0°　　60.0°　　120.0°　　180.0°　　240.0°　　300.0°

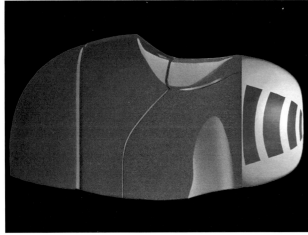
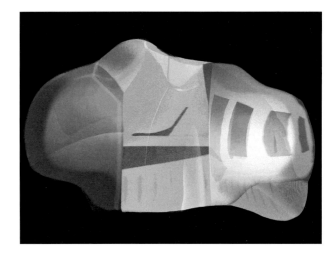
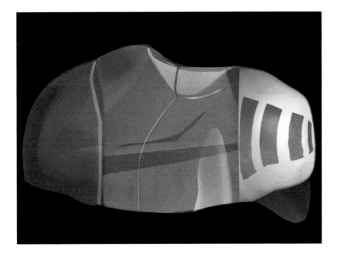
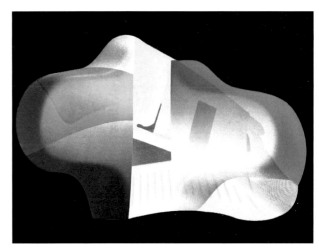
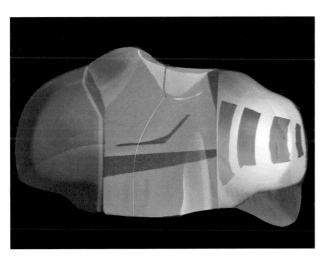

VI

III   Interface for navigating the Guggenheim Virtual Museum
IV   Artwork on display in the virtual galleries
V   Interface for rotating and navigating through the galleries and plaza
VI   Still images of texture mapping and morphing of shapes

Barclays Center

SHoP Architects (design architect), Hunt Construction Group (design builder), Ellerbe Becket/AECOM (architect of record), Thornton Tomasetti (structural engineer)

2009—2012

SOFTWARE
Grasshopper, CATIA 3DEXPERIENCE, Navisworks, SigmaNEST

HARDWARE
PC, Microsoft Windows

PURPOSE OF SOFTWARE
3-D-modeling, fabrication instructions, progress tracking

With the building of the Barclays Center, SHoP Architects demonstrated how effective communication via apps opens new ways to convey ideas and the progress of a project to customers. The New York firm SHoP Architects was founded by Gregg Pasquarelli, Christopher Sharples, Coren Sharples, Kimberly Holden, and William Sharples in 1996. Their nontraditional approach to practice employs both entrepreneurship and technology, with the aim of bridging the gap between design and construction. SHoP implemented this philosophy when they were called on to further develop the plans of Ellerbe Becket for the Barclays Center, an arena for the Brooklyn Nets. SHoP conceived the final design through a virtual model–based process. After the geometry was established using the 3-D programs Rhinoceros and CATIA, the fabrication instructions for each of the 12,000 unique facade elements were exported directly from the model. The result is a sculptural building whose facade is divided into three bands that flow along the form of the building. A glass band separates two bands of weathered steel latticeworks that relate the structure to the brownstone buildings of Brooklyn. Transparency allows interior-exterior connections on the ground floor, making it possible to see the scoreboard in the sunken arena from outside the building. These connections are strengthened by the entrance plaza, whose canopy features a giant oculus lined with LED screens, turning it into both an attraction and a gathering space.

The integration of the arena with its surroundings was particularly important for the success of the project, which had a difficult start in terms of public opinion. Homes had to be demolished to clear the site for the arena, the project faced economic problems, and Frank Gehry, the initial architect, was dropped from the project. When SHoP Architects entered the picture, they managed to alleviate anxiety about the project with an app showing the progress on the construction site via a virtual model, tracking each element all the way from manufacture to assembly. SHoP were among the first architects to employ the all-digital design approach when they built the Camera Obscura at Mitchell Park in 2005. They continue to push boundaries using these methods. A notable current project is the Botswana Innovation Hub under construction in Gaborone, Botswana, which surpasses the Barclays Center in element count and complexity.—*Tonderai Koschke*

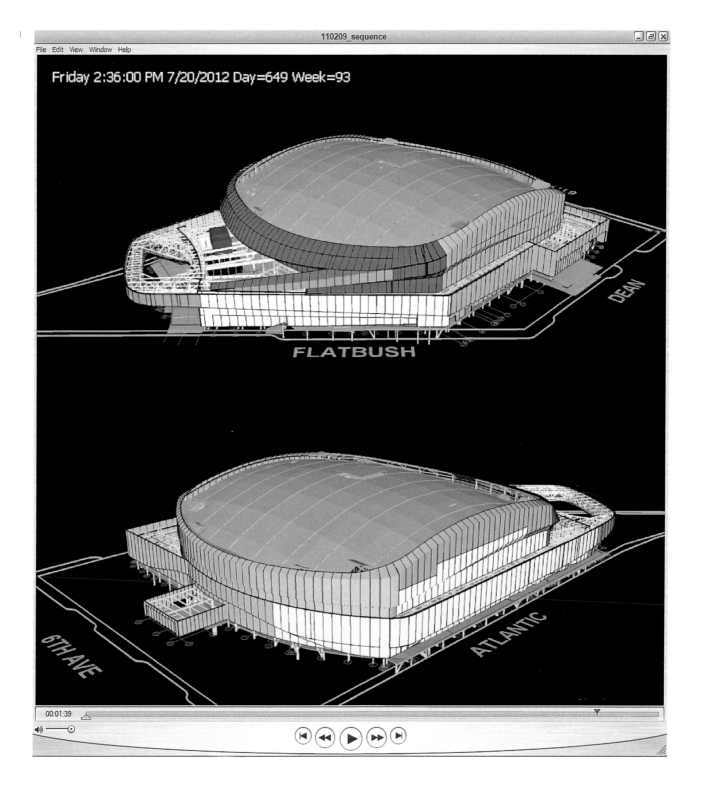

Friday 2:36:00 PM 7/20/2012 Day=649 Week=93

DEAN

FLATBUSH

6TH AVE

ATLANTIC

00:01:39

| Graphic progress updates

Gonchar, Joann. "Beauty and the Behemoth." *Architectural Record*, December 2012, 102–6. ● Wessner, Gregory. "Interview: Gregg Pasquarelli." Architectural League NY. Accessed November 25, 2019. archleague.org/article/interview-gregg-pasquarelli/.

II   Each element tracked by app
III 12,000 unique elements
IV   Steel latticework "mega-panel"

Hyper-Reality

Keiichi Matsuda

2016

SOFTWARE
After Effects, Mocha, PFTrack, Cinema 4D

PURPOSE SOFTWARE
augmented reality interface, postproduction

"How do I install ad blocker?" is the most frequent comment under Keiichi Matsuda's six-minute short film *Hyper-Reality* on the video portal YouTube. In 2016, the British-Japanese artist, designer, and filmmaker, working with the Colombia-based studio Fractal, designed a very real vision of the future in which its garish, fast-paced importunity both fascinates and disturbs, and upon closer consideration reveals a dystopian critique of media and society.

Set in the Colombian city of Medellín and seen from the perspective of forty-two-year-old JobMonkey worker Juliana Restrepo, the film immerses the viewer in hyperreality. Sitting on a bus, Juliana closes a Candy Crush–like video game and groans when she receives a call from her job agent. The view out of the bus is obscured and instead a virtual interface of advertising and information appears. It shows which jobs are waiting, her rating point status, where she has to get off the bus, and lastly that her number of friends is too small. Her frustrated Google queries—who was she, where was she going, and could she start again—are never answered. It is the same in the city center: virtual advertisements for tampons and banks are written into her field of view. She is reminded that city traffic presents real dangers when a warning notice saying "Clear the area" appears on the road.

Juliana buys food for one of her customers in the Éxito supermarket. She is helped by a virtual dog sitting on the front of her trolley and drawing her attention to special offers, loyalty points, and weight-reducing products in a croaky voice. Between the chiller cabinets for butter and yogurt, the virtual world comes to a halt, the displayed information starts to flicker and soon disappears completely, and Juliana is no longer recognized by the electronic shopping adviser. Her account has been hacked. She stands in a dismal, drab supermarket aisle, lost, and worried about her loyalty points. After a few seconds the system restarts; everything lights up in bright colors again. She needs to have her biometric information verified in order to get her account fully working again. On the way there, she is injured by a mugger with a knife. Her virtual world and her real world collapse, both at the same time. However, Juliana still has her belief in God. On the opposite side of the road, a statue of Mary offers help. An advertising banner carried by angels pops up above the statue: "Find your path!"—"Start again!"—"Join Catholicism!" There is no escape. Juliana is already one level up.

I–II *Hyper-Reality*

Matsuda impressively blurs the boundaries between virtual and physical space in *Hyper-Reality* and shows a new urban world that spills out colorfully, brightly, and interactively into urban transport, public space, and supermarkets. The street scenes were filmed with a GoPro, which made the video appear even more alien because of the camera's wide-angle lens. Was this the reason people feared Google Glass in 2012, or is it actually the future of augmented reality? Medellín is the perfect location for *Hyper-Reality*. The Alumbrado navideño, a Christmas world of flashing flowers, animals, houses, and Santa Clauses created out of millions of LEDs, has taken place there every year since the 1990s. All very real.—*Philipp Sturm*

Peleschak, Kevin. "Making the Wildly Successful Dystopian Augmented Reality Short, 'Hyper-Reality.'" *Motionographer*, August 15, 2016. Accessed January 6, 2020. motionographer.com/2016/08/15/making-the-wildly-successful-dystopian-augmented-reality-short-hyper-reality/.

IV

III *Hyper-Reality*
IV Christmas festival Alumbrado navideño, Medellín, 2013

London Developers Toolkit

You+Pea
(Sandra Youkhana, Luke Pearson)

2020

SOFTWARE
Unity, Qubicle, MagicaVoxel

HARDWARE
Windows PC

PURPOSE OF SOFTWARE
interactive computer game

The London Developers Toolkit is a satirical app centered on the domination of the London skyline by the residential skyscrapers of the super-rich. The app was developed by the British architectural office You+Pea. Using playful elements, the application asks users to produce architecture based on "napkin sketches" and then parameterize it, thus allowing nonarchitects to create their own totemic structure. At the beginning of the game, players are invited to "Press SPACE to enter the SweetieCorp London Developers Toolkit." This gives them access to the main interface accompanied by the tune of "In Too Deep" by Genesis in an 8-bit chiptune musical style. On the left-hand side a first skyscraper design is visible. It is depicted with colored 3-D cubes, which make reference to the computer game *Minecraft*. Pressing the Repeat key allows the building to be varied at random, with two tiny helicopters flying around the six-section tower each time. The changing stock market graphics and flashing matrices contribute to the serene mood.

Pressing the unignorably large Play button in the middle displays two pixelated busts of men in gray suits, the Sweetie Brothers. They greet the players and ask them to use their mouse to trace napkin sketches from some of the world's most famous architects. This is the first of three steps in the skyscraper generator. The next screen shows satirical silhouettes, such as a walkie-talkie—a reference to the controversial London skyscraper 20 Fenchurch Street by Rafael Viñoly. With this step successfully completed, the player has to parameterize the tower. The individually adjustable parameters are Luxury, Extravagance, and Excess. However, the total should not exceed 100 percent, otherwise it would simply be too expensive! In the final step, the men in suits ask the player to memorize a sequence of boroughs illuminated on a London street map. The Sweetie Brothers also add that these boroughs would like to resemble Dubai. Finally, the players can gaze in wonder at their self-generated, unique, and iconic building. To match this, the name generator "name.gen/xtravagance" supplies a random project name such as Excalibur, Zenith, or the Cornichon—an allusion to the 30 St. Mary Axe skyscraper designed by eminent architect Norman Foster and popularly known as the Gherkin. After the player has gone through all the steps, promotional material can be produced to attract the affluent by clicking on

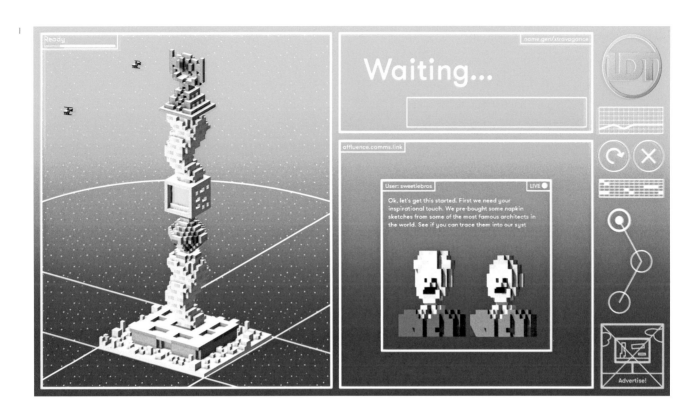

Digital investors: the Sweetie Brothers

the unlocked Advertise! button. In addition to the font and color of the building name, the background, architectural context, accessory figures, and visual effects can be set. Clicking on the Render! button reveals a visualization of the latest piece of personalized London star architecture! The real estate landscape of Britain's capital city receives harsh criticism in a futuristic gaming context. Sections of the game highlight problems caused by the unrestrained building mania of real estate sharks; there is also some specific criticism of individual buildings. The flying banknotes and fireworks displayed during the final step—the advertising of the building—satirize this system. The game parodies this form of "sham participation." Such dystopian development with inexorably rising housing costs has long become a real threat to people on average earnings.—*Lluis Dura*

Luke Caspar Pearson. "London Developers Toolkit." Alephograph (website). Accessed January 26, 2020. alephograph.com/london-developers-toolkit/. ● You+Pea. "London Developers Toolkit." You+Pea (website). Accessed January 25, 2020. youandpea.com/london-developers-toolkit/.

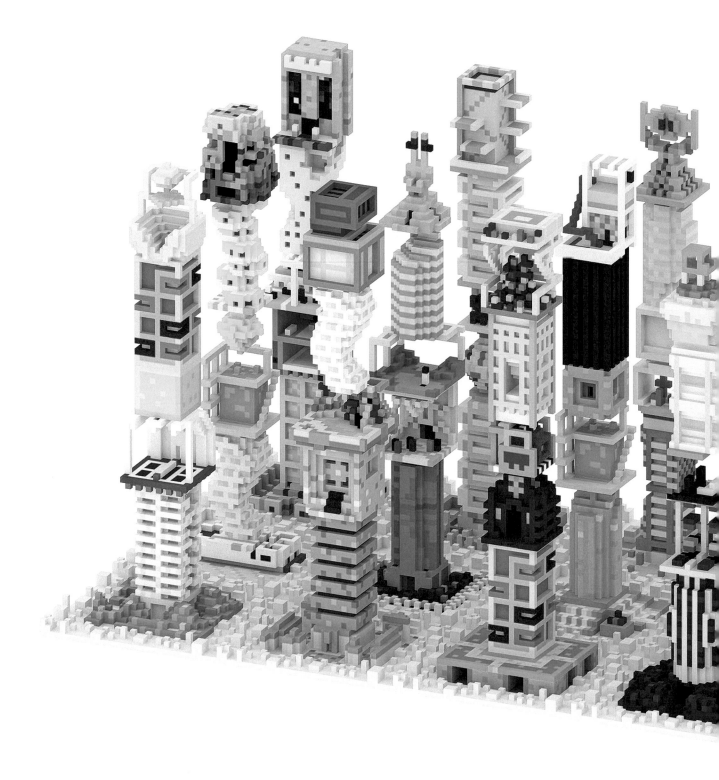

III

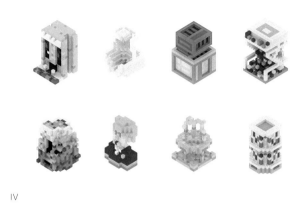

IV

II Skyscraper city London
III The end of the game: "Advertise!"
IV Skyscraper components

Transcribed Nature

Atelier Oslo

2020

SOFTWARE
Unreal Engine, Ikinema Orion

HARDWARE
gaming PC, Windows, HTC Trackers, HT Vive, headphones

PURPOSE OF SOFTWARE
3-D modeling, virtual reality experience

The installation *Transcribed Nature* is an updated social and multisensory experiment produced for the Architekturmuseum der TUM. The Norwegian architectural firm Atelier Oslo was established in 2006. Partners are Nils Ole Bae Brandtzæg, Marius Mowe, Jonas Norsted, and Thomas Liu. They were one of thirty-two offices that were invited to take part in the exhibition at the Nordic Pavilion at the Venice Biennale in 2012. In 2013 they were commissioned to create the work *Corporeal Room,* a 1:1 installation as part of the exhibition *Under 40*, in the Sverre Fehn Pavilion, by the National Museum—Architecture in Oslo. In the period 2015–19 Atelier Oslo was one of three partners in the cross-disciplinary and design-based research project "Mediascapes—Architecture Museums and Digital Design Media." The two other partners were the Department of Education, University of Oslo and the National Museum of Art, Architecture and Design. The project was financed by the Research Council of Norway.

As the main case study they executed the exhibition experiment *The Forest in the House: Explorations of Parallel Realities* (2018). The exhibition invited a diverse audience to a multisensory experience of architecture, using VR technology and digital sound in a full-scale physical installation. The experiment encompassed new insights into VR, real architectural elements, motion and senses, social experience, meaning making, and informal learning in architecture exhibitions.

Transcribed Nature is based on the previous social and multisensory experiment, adjusted to the gallery space at the Architekturmuseum and using updated technology. The installation uses spatial qualities from the forest that are transcribed into architectural elements in VR and in a physical installation. Nature is transformed into basic architectural elements: trees are transformed into columns, the forest floor into terraced levels, while the branches and leaves become ceilings with skylights. By creating a meeting between the elements of architecture and nature, the architects of Atelier Oslo want to create an architecture that is varied and informal, awakening curiosity and giving a sense of belonging.

The installation is a collaboration between Atelier Oslo, the National Museum of Art, Architecture and Design, Oslo (Birgitte Sauge), and the Architekturmuseum der TUM.

Birgitte Sauge, Thomas Liu

I–II *Forest in the House*, view of installation, 2018

Sauge, Birgitte, et al. "Born Digital Architectural Projects: Imagining, Design-
ing and Exhibiting Practices." In *Designs for Experimentation and Inquiry:
Approaching Learning and Knowing in Digital Transformation*, edited by Åsa
Mäkitalo et al., 87–109. London: Routledge, 2019. ● Sauge, Birgitte, et al.
"Telling the Whole Story: Curating, Designing, and Researching Virtual Archi-
tectural Experiences in an Exhibition Experiment." In *Experimental Museology:
Institutions, Representations, Users*, edited by Marianne Achiam, Kirsten
Drotner, and Michael Haldrup. London: Routledge, forthcoming.

III

IV

III   *Forest in the House*, VR view, 2018
IV   *Transcribed Nature*, 2020

Architectural Software Timeline

Architectural Software Timeline

Philip Schneider and
Teresa Fankhänel

Drawing

Digital drawing: the creation of digital, infinitely scalable vector drawings

In the 1950s, the US military developed devices to allow the interactive use of computers. These systems were the foundations for the first computer-aided design programs (CAD). Drawings could be modified in real time using an input device, a computer program, and a graphical user interface. In 1960, US military technology manufacturer Itek developed the first commercial CAD program, the Electronic Drafting Machine. At almost the same time, between 1961 and 1963, Ivan Sutherland wrote the drawing program Sketchpad as part of his dissertation "Sketchpad: A Man–Machine Graphical Communication System" at MIT. This allowed the user to give drawing commands to the computer using a light pen and also had simple parametric functions.

Aircraft manufacturers saw the advantages of digital drawing at an early stage. Technical drawings could be done more quickly and were easier to edit than their manual counterparts. In 1965, Lockheed began the development of Project Design for the design of supersonic aircraft. Emerging from this in 1972, CADAM was new in that it was a virtual 2.5-dimensional working space that allowed two-dimensional drawings for machine-controlled production to be created quickly. CADAM was licensed to IBM in 1974 to establish the software on the European market; one of the first users was the French aircraft manufacturer Dassault Aviation. Building on the capabilities of CADAM, Dassault integrated DRAPO (Définition et Réalisation d'Avions Par Ordinateur) into its manufacturing facilities in 1975 to control machines for automated production of complex engineering components with angular cutouts and doubly curved surfaces used to clad aircraft fuselages. The program UNISURF, developed by Pierre Bézier to allow a more precise digital representation of curves for the car manufacturer Renault, was bought by Dassault in 1972, with subsequent wide-ranging effects on architecture. This technology allowed pioneering new geometries in the 1990s, the most well-known being blob architecture. While CADAM remained two-dimensional—extending to the drawing of contours—the desire for three-dimensionality came to the fore in 1978. Dassault developed CATIA for creating 3-D models. New software programs for two-dimensional drawing appeared in the 1980s, among them AutoCAD and other well-known programs such as today's Vectorworks and Illustrator.

Modeling

Modeling: the creation and processing of digital three-dimensional objects

3-D computer modeling had its start in the aerospace, automotive, and film industries. In 1967, MAGI (Mathematical Applications Group, Inc.) brought out SynthaVision, the first program that used constructive solid geometry to allow the intersection and combination of three-dimensional objects and the creation of complex geometric shapes. MAGI's achievements became known through the animations in the Disney film *TRON* (1982).

Aircraft manufacturer Dassault Aviation started developing CATI (Conception Assistée Tridimensionnelle Interactive) in 1978, integrating three-dimensional functions for the first time. Renamed CATIA in 1981, the program is still one of the leading modeling software packages for engineers. The Yost Group was founded in 1988. One of its members, Tom Hudson, wrote the code for Solid States, a wireframe display application. The Yost Group was then working for Autodesk on THUD, a predecessor of 3ds Max. 3D Studio 1 appeared two years later. It was renamed 3ds Max in 2006 and is still being further developed today.

At the same time, architects were beginning to see the potential for 3-D modeling. In 1984, Peter Eisenman met Christos Yessios at Ohio State University, where he was working on the 3-D program TEKTON. Yessios and Eisenman ran a course together in 1987 in which the computer and TEKTON, since renamed ARCHIMODOS, were the primary design tools. Based on this experience, Yessios founded AutoDesSys in 1988, which brought out form·Z 1.0 two years later. The program was a void modeler. Instead of modeling the external shape of objects (solid modeling), the program manipulates voids, making it a suitable tool for architects, who mainly concern themselves with spaces.

Another architectural office that shaped the future for 3-D modeling in the early 1990s was Frank Gehry Partners. In order to create architecture composed of complex sculptural forms, the designers were looking for a method to digitalize physical models and check that they could be constructed. Based on these requirements, Gehry Partners began the design of El Peix in 1992, working with CATIA, which was capable of creating the necessary mathematically precise representations. Architecture offices could not function as they do today without 3-D models. Through Building Information Modeling (BIM), they are now the basis of projects and of all the additional project drawings, renderings, and animations.

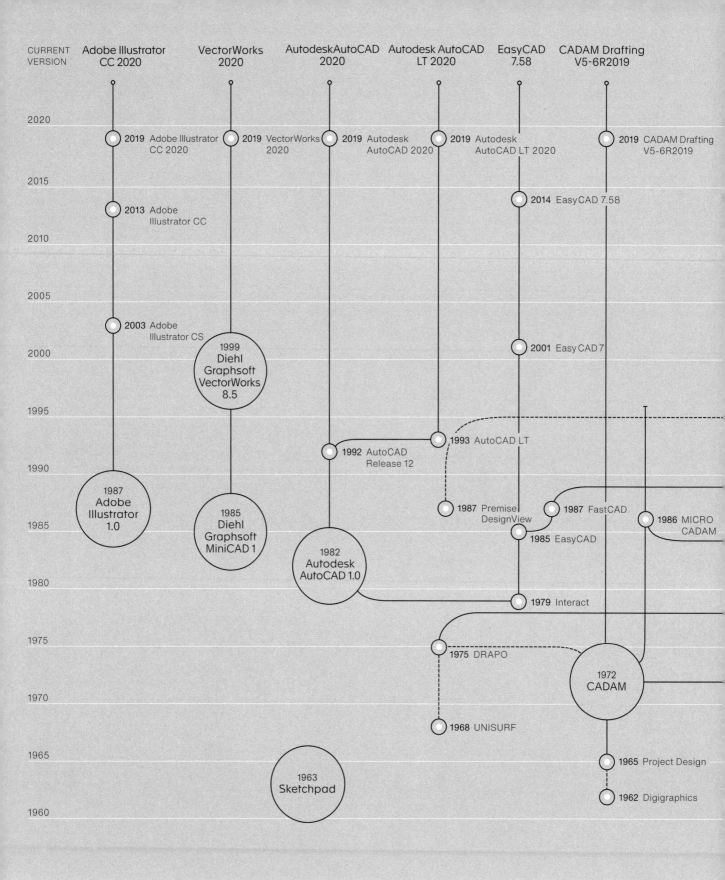

Adobe Illustrator CC 2020	VectorWorks 2020	AutodeskAutoCAD 2020	Autodesk AutoCAD LT 2020	EasyCAD 7.58	CADAM Drafting V5-6R2019

2020

2019 Adobe Illustrator CC 2020

2019 VectorWorks 2020

2019 Autodesk AutoCAD 2020

2019 Autodesk AutoCAD LT 2020

2019 CADAM Drafting V5-6R2019

2015

2014 EasyCAD 7.58

2013 Adobe Illustrator CC

2010

2005

2003 Adobe Illustrator CS

1999 Diehl Graphsoft VectorWorks 8.5

2000

2001 EasyCAD 7

1995

1993 AutoCAD LT

1992 AutoCAD Release 12

1990

1987 Adobe Illustrator 1.0

1987 Premise DesignView

1987 FastCAD

1986 MICRO CADAM

1985 Diehl Graphsoft MiniCAD 1

1985 EasyCAD

1985

1982 Autodesk AutoCAD 1.0

1980

1979 Interact

1975

1975 DRAPO

1972 CADAM

1970

1968 UNISURF

1965

1965 Project Design

1963 Sketchpad

1962 Digigraphics

1960

Drawing

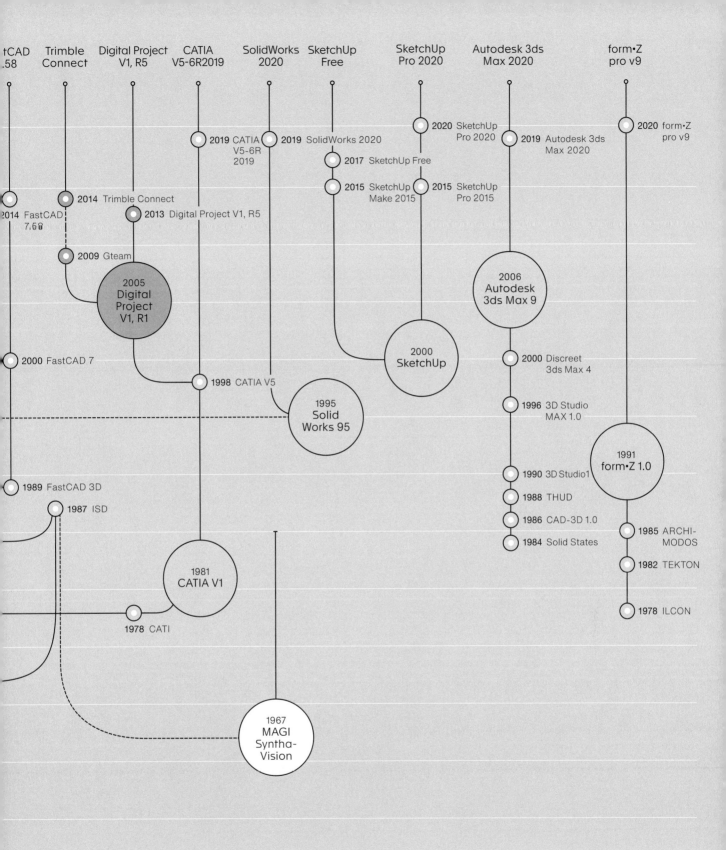

| tCAD .58 | Trimble Connect | Digital Project V1, R5 | CATIA V5-6R2019 | SolidWorks 2020 | SketchUp Free | SketchUp Pro 2020 | Autodesk 3ds Max 2020 | form·Z pro v9 |

2020 SketchUp Pro 2020

2020 form·Z pro v9

2019 CATIA V5-6R 2019

2019 SolidWorks 2020

2019 Autodesk 3ds Max 2020

2017 SketchUp Free

2015 SketchUp Make 2015

2015 SketchUp Pro 2015

2014 Trimble Connect

2014 FastCAD 7.60

2013 Digital Project V1, R5

2009 Gteam

2005 Digital Project V1, R1

2006 Autodesk 3ds Max 9

2000 FastCAD 7

2000 SketchUp

2000 Discreet 3ds Max 4

1998 CATIA V5

1996 3D Studio MAX 1.0

1995 Solid Works 95

1991 form·Z 1.0

1989 FastCAD 3D

1990 3D Studio1

1987 ISD

1988 THUD

1986 CAD-3D 1.0

1985 ARCHI-MODOS

1984 Solid States

1981 CATIA V1

1982 TEKTON

1978 CATI

1978 ILCON

1967 MAGI Syntha-Vision

Modeling

○ Milestone ○ Rendering ○ Scripting ○ Modeling
○ Drawing ○ Analysis ○ Animation
○ Program — develops into ---- absorbed by ⊢ end of program

Architectural Software Timeline

Rendering

Rendering: the simulation of light reflections, textures, and other visual surface effects to create pixel images

The development of rendering technology is closely linked to the history of modeling and animation software. With the invention of vector-based 3-D modeling in the late 1960s, it became possible to turn modeled objects into illuminated, color pixel images, known as computer-generated images (CGI), which could be displayed on ordinary screens such as televisions. By 1966, MAGI (Mathematical Applications Group, Inc.) had developed ray casting, an algorithm for simulating radioactive radiation. In 1967, this technology was integrated into the first version of SynthaVision for simulating lighting situations. While ray casting—a simplified version of today's well-known ray tracing—had existed before, SynthaVision marked its first commercial application.

As with modeling, it was the film and advertising industries that accelerated the use of computer-generated images. MAGI was among the companies invited by Disney to work on *TRON*. They created a fifteen-minute animated sequence for the film, which appeared in 1982. Industrial Light & Magic, the film studio founded by George Lucas, produced almost photo-realistic animations for films during the 1980s and 1990s, including *The Abyss* (1989), *Terminator II* (1991), and *Jurassic Park* (1993). Programs such as Alias—today's version is known as Maya—and Softimage were used to make the animated virtual scenes in these films as realistic as possible and allow them to be linked with real filmed scenes. Texture mapping, invented by Jim Blinn and Martin Newell in 1976, was used extensively for projecting digital photographic images onto three-dimensional objects.

Today, render engines and texture mapping are integrated into almost all 3-D software: 3ds Max, Cinema 4D, Maya, and Blender. Even engineering programs such as CATIA can do this. Today rendering is no longer just the creation of pixel images in 3-D software. In architecture these images are post-processed using image-editing software such as Photoshop. Many visualization studios, among them Mir (Norway), Brick Visual (Budapest), and Lucia Frascerra (London), use this workflow to create photo-realistic images for architectural presentations.

Animation

Animation: the programming of moving digital objects to create moving images

The development of animation software began with the emergence of new data carriers and screens in the 1980s that could display and store image sequences. *TRON* appeared in movie theaters in 1982. It was the first film to have extensive animations created using SynthaVision. Images generated individually on the computer were then photographed on the screen with analog cameras and sequenced to make moving pictures. Very few programs were originally intended for creating animations. One of them was Alias, now Maya, which was developed in 1985 to better represent curves and surfaces in the automotive industry. After its advantages had been recognized by filmmakers, Alias was offered in two different versions from 1990—Studio for product design and PowerAnimator for animations. Maya 1.0 was a combination of programs, including PowerAnimator and Wavefront Explorer. This software was further developed by Autodesk from 2005 and is a standard program today. The development of Softimage was an exception. David Langlois developed the program in 1989 as the first complete animation solution capable of modeling, animating, and rendering objects. Following its sale to Autodesk, development stopped in 2014 in favor of Maya and 3ds Max. George Lucas's film studio Industrial Light & Magic and special effects studios such as Disney, Pixar, and Sony Pictures used these programs to produce several milestones in the history of animation. Films with animated special effects have been produced since the late 1980s: *Abyss* (1989), *Terminator II* (1991), *Jurassic Park* (1993), and *Forrest Gump* (1993). *Toy Story* (1995) was the first film to be created completely on the computer.

Today there are hardly any Hollywood films that do not use the continuously expanding possibilities of photo-realistically rendered animations. 3ds Max, Blender, Cinema 4D, and even architecture-related programs such as ArchiCAD and Revit have animation tools—integrated or accessible via plug-ins. Since the first experimental use of moving shapes in architecture in the 1990s, animations have become an essential constituent of design and project presentations.

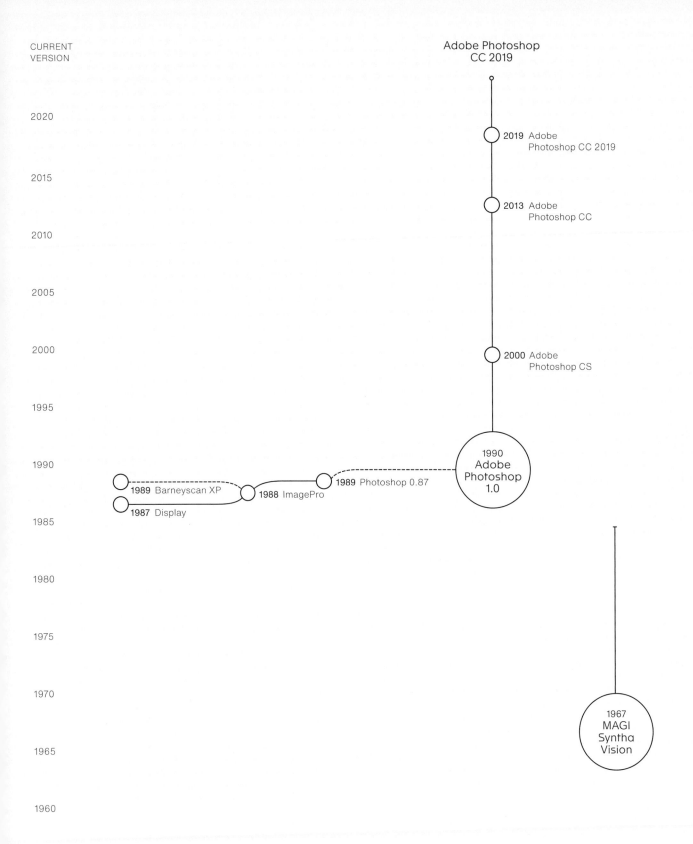

Adobe Photoshop
CC 2019

2020

2019 Adobe
Photoshop CC 2019

2015

2013 Adobe
Photoshop CC

2010

2005

2000

2000 Adobe
Photoshop CS

1995

1990

1990
Adobe
Photoshop
1.0

1989 Barneyscan XP

1989 Photoshop 0.87

1988 ImagePro

1987 Display

1985

1980

1975

1970

1967
MAGI
Syntha
Vision

1965

1960

Rendering

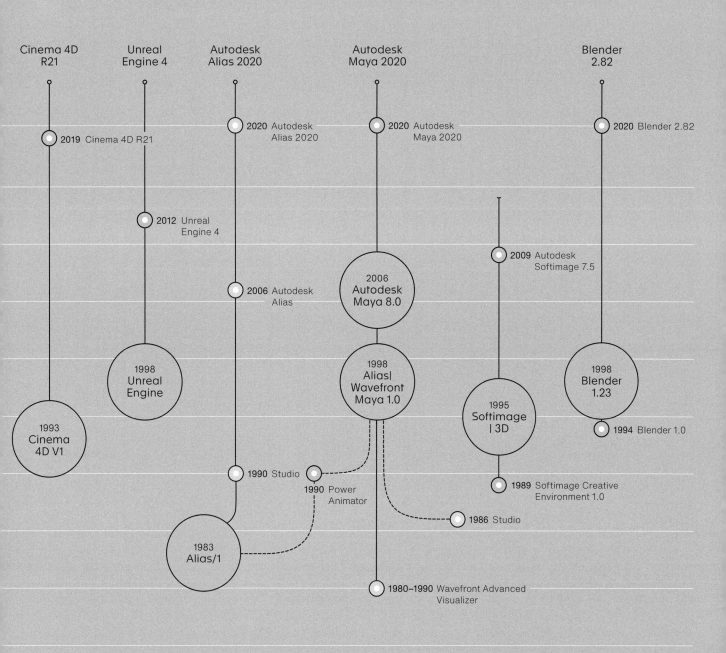

Cinema 4D
R21

Unreal
Engine 4

Autodesk
Alias 2020

Autodesk
Maya 2020

Blender
2.82

2019 Cinema 4D R21

2020 Autodesk
Alias 2020

2020 Autodesk
Maya 2020

2020 Blender 2.82

2012 Unreal
Engine 4

2009 Autodesk
Softimage 7.5

2006 Autodesk
Alias

2006
**Autodesk
Maya 8.0**

1998
**Unreal
Engine**

1998
**Alias|
Wavefront
Maya 1.0**

1998
**Blender
1.23**

1995
**Softimage
| 3D**

1993
**Cinema
4D V1**

1994 Blender 1.0

1990 Studio

1989 Softimage Creative
Environment 1.0

1990 Power
Animator

1986 Studio

1983
Alias/1

1980–1990 Wavefront Advanced
Visualizer

Animation

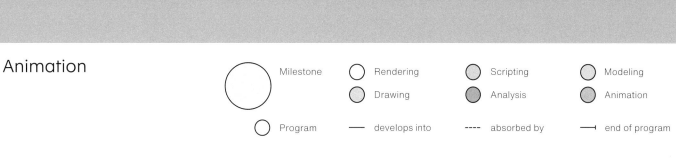

Milestone ⃝ Rendering ⃝ Scripting ⃝ Modeling

⃝ Drawing ⃝ Analysis ⃝ Animation

⃝ Program —— develops into ---- absorbed by ⊢ end of program

Architectural Software Timeline

Scripting

Scripting: the manual programming of complex digital commands through a programming interface

Scripting has existed since the first computer and is an alternative term for programming. Until 1983, when the Apple Lisa came onto the market, programming was a prerequisite in order to use a computer. User interfaces for software and operating systems have developed so much since then that programming skills are no longer essential. However, scripting continues to find use for the implementation of new, complex, or repetitive command structures and enables the realization of new ideas developed in-house.

Based on programming interfaces called Application Programming Interfaces (API), software manufacturers seek to induce third-party providers and users to develop additional applications for their programs. Autodesk in particular adopted this approach, introducing AutoLISP for AutoCAD, a customized programming language for the drawing program, in 1986. 3ds Max followed this trend in 1997 with the integration of MAXScript. Maya has been able to be controlled by Maya Embedded Language (MEL) since it came onto the market in 1998.

Visual programming interfaces offer a less demanding alternative. Like electrical circuits, they connect programming modules together while the program is written automatically in the background. The possibilities are more limited compared with those of a full programming language, but they are usually adequate for most architectural purposes. The best-known of these programming interfaces is Grasshopper, which has continued to be developed by David Rutten since 2007 and is available as an add-on module for Rhinoceros. In the meantime, ArchiCAD is also offering an interface with Grasshopper. The equivalent software Revit by Autodesk has an integrated option in the form of Dynamo.

Architecture offices also take part in the development of this new script-based technology. Earlier attempts by John Frazer in the 1960s at the Architectural Association laid the foundations for new computer-aided design methods. Since the 1990s, Frank Gehry and his colleagues have developed their own add-on modules based on CATIA, which are now available commercially as the stand-alone software Digital Project. With the growing interest in parametric design since the early 2000s, similar approaches have enjoyed a boom, and architectural practices, including Zaha Hadid Architects with ZHCODE, have set up their own departments to develop in-house programs.

Analysis

Analysis: the performance-based evaluation of digital 3-D models (structural engineering, ventilation, building components)

In the context of architecture, analysis is based on BIM (Building Information Modeling), which is based on the principle of a centralized, virtual building model. Architects use BIM, for example, to obtain an overview of the number of components and for sending relevant data to engineers or component manufacturers. Analysis tools are also increasingly important for engineers. Computer simulations produced by methods such as finite element analysis can determine the precise behavior of structures under loads.

In 1961, Recheninstitut im Bauwesen (RIB) in Stuttgart integrated an IBM computer into the structural analysis of bridges. Next came Georg Nemetschek, who wrote computer programs for use in his structural engineering office in Munich. Nemetschek formed Nemetschek Programmsystem GmbH and brought out Allplan, a CAD system for engineers and architects, in 1984. Since then, the Nemetschek software platform has expanded to include Allplan Architecture and Allplan Engineering. Meanwhile, in Communist Hungary, Gábor Bojár founded GRAPHISOFT in 1982 to develop a comprehensive 3-D solution for architects. This turned out to be complicated, with computers from the West being contraband under the terms of an economic embargo. In spite of this, RADAR (Räumliche Darstellung für Architekten), a software package for the Apple Lisa, was launched in 1984. This developed into ArchiCAD (1986), which now belongs to the Nemetschek Group and is one of the most important BIM programs on the European market.

Since the construction of El Peix in Barcelona in 1992, CATIA has been used in Frank Gehry's architectural office for the efficient exchange of technical drawings with engineers and manufacturers. The program proved an enormous advantage, since the project's complex shapes and support structures demanded accurate documentation. After the digital workflow had proved successful, the newly formed Gehry Technologies developed software such as Digital Project (2005) in cooperation with Dassault Systèmes. Today, this program is used for complex architectural projects by offices such as Zaha Hadid Architects, Ateliers Jean Nouvel, Asymptote Architecture, and Diller Scofidio + Renfro. The well-known software package Revit followed relatively late, with similar developments. In 2000 the market saw the introduction of Revit 1.0 (Revise Instantly), which was acquired by Autodesk in 2002.

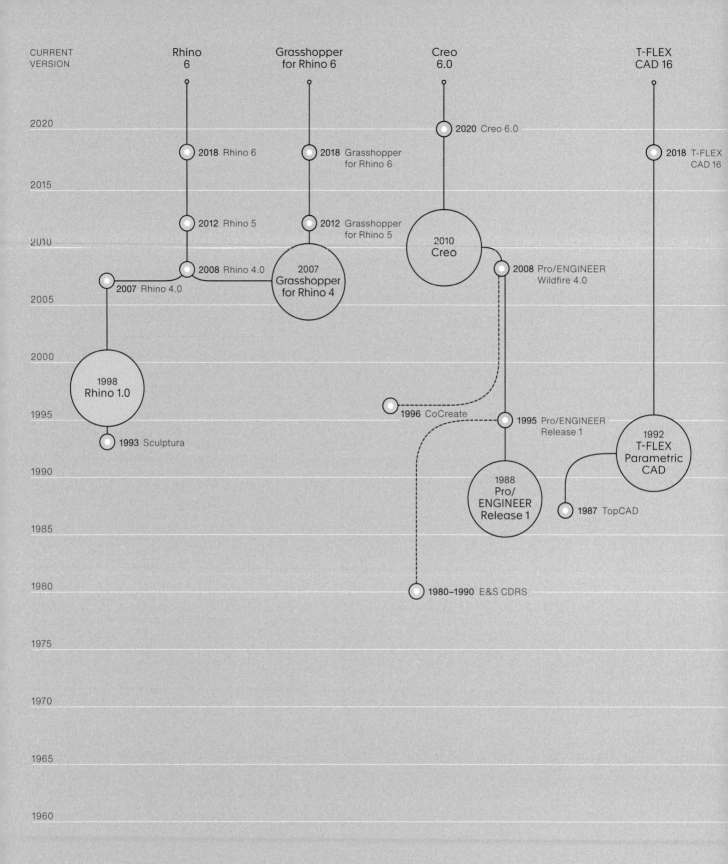

| | Rhino 6 | Grasshopper for Rhino 6 | Creo 6.0 | T-FLEX CAD 16 |

2020

2020 Creo 6.0

2018 Rhino 6   **2018** Grasshopper for Rhino 6   **2018** T-FLEX CAD 16

2015

2012 Rhino 5   **2012** Grasshopper for Rhino 5

2010   2010 Creo

2008 Rhino 4.0   2007 Grasshopper for Rhino 4   **2008** Pro/ENGINEER Wildfire 4.0

2007 Rhino 4.0

2005

2000

1998 Rhino 1.0

1996 CoCreate   **1995** Pro/ENGINEER Release 1

1995

1993 Sculptura   1992 T-FLEX Parametric CAD

1990   1988 Pro/ ENGINEER Release 1

1987 TopCAD

1985

1980   **1980–1990** E&S CDRS

1975

1970

1965

1960

Scripting

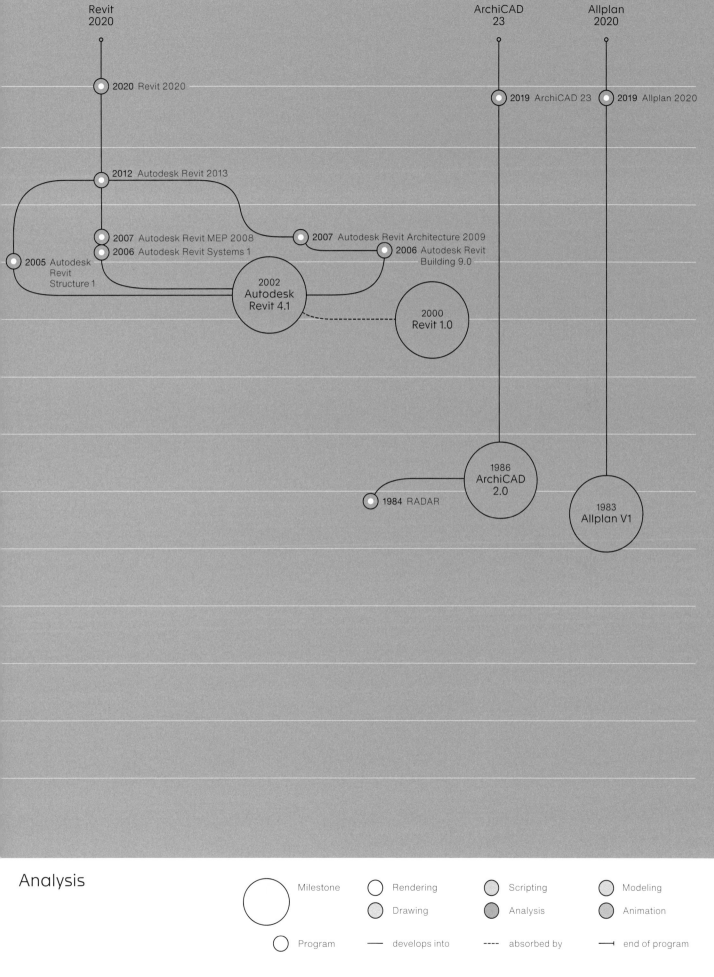

Revit
2020

ArchiCAD
23

Allplan
2020

2020 Revit 2020

2019 ArchiCAD 23

2019 Allplan 2020

2012 Autodesk Revit 2013

2007 Autodesk Revit MEP 2008

2007 Autodesk Revit Architecture 2009

2006 Autodesk Revit Systems 1

2006 Autodesk Revit Building 9.0

2005 Autodesk Revit Structure 1

2002
Autodesk
Revit 4.1

2000
Revit 1.0

1986
ArchiCAD
2.0

1984 RADAR

1983
Allplan V1

Analysis

Milestone

Rendering

Scripting

Modeling

Drawing

Analysis

Animation

Program

develops into

absorbed by

end of program

237

Appendix

Biographies

Roberto Bottazzi is an architect, researcher, and educator based in London. He is director of the Master in Urban Design program at the Bartlett School of Architecture, University College London, and author of *Digital Architecture beyond Computers: Fragments of a Cultural History of Computational Design* (Bloomsbury, 2018). His research on the impact of digital technologies on architecture and urbanism has been presented and exhibited internationally.

Mollie Claypool is an architecture theorist. She is director of Automated Architecture Ltd (AUAR), a design and tech consultancy, and codirector of Design Computation Lab at the Bartlett School of Architecture, University College London. She was a 2019 Fellow in Automation in the South West Creative Technology Network and is coauthor of the recent book *Robotic Building: Architecture in the Age of Automation* (Edition DETAIL, 2019).

Teresa Fankhänel is a curator at the Architekturmuseum der TUM and assistant professor at the Chair of Architectural History and Curatorial Practice at the Technical University of Munich. She is the curator of the exhibition *The Architecture Machine*.

Andres Lepik is a professor of architecture history and curatorial studies at the Technical University of Munich and director of the Architekturmuseum der TUM. Previously he worked as a curator at Neue Nationalgalerie, Berlin, and at the Architecture and Design Department at MoMA, New York. He was Loeb Fellow at Harvard's Graduate School of Design.

Anna-Maria Meister is a professor of architecture theory and science at the Technical University of Darmstadt and works at the intersection of architecture's histories and the histories of science and technology. Meister received a joint PhD in the History and Theory of Architecture and the Council of the Humanities from Princeton University, holds a degree in architecture from Columbia University, New York, and was a fellow at the Max Planck Institute for the History of Science, Berlin. Meister publishes her research internationally and is cocurator of the collaborative project Radical Pedagogies.

Molly Wright Steenson is senior associate dean for research in the College of Fine Arts and associate professor at Carnegie Mellon University. She is the author of *Architectural Intelligence: How Designers and Architects Created the Digital Landscape* (MIT Press, 2017) and the coeditor of *Bauhaus Futures* (MIT Press, 2019).

Felix Torkar is an architecture historian. He holds a BA and MA in art history from Freie Universität Berlin and has worked as a curatorial assistant at the Deutsches Architekturmuseum. A recipient of a doctoral fellowship from the Wüstenrot Stiftung, he is currently writing his PhD on Neobrutalism at FU Berlin.

Theodora Vardouli is an assistant professor at the Peter Guo-hua Fu School of Architecture, McGill University, Montreal. Her research examines histories and contemporary practices of architectural computing with a focus on their mathematical underpinnings. She is coeditor of *Computer Architectures: Constructing the Common Ground* (Routledge, 2019) and cocurator of the exhibition *Vers un imaginaire numérique* (Centre de design de l'UQAM, 2020).

Georg Vrachliotis is a curator, writer, professor of architecture theory, and director of the saai | Archive for Architecture and Civil Engineering at the Karlsruhe Institute of Technology. He was dean of the Faculty of Architecture from 2016 to 2019. He previously taught and conducted research at the Institute for the History and Theory of Architecture (gta) at the ETH Zurich.

Acknowledgments

After almost two years of research and travel, visits to private and public archives, and countless stimulating conversations, the exhibition and the accompanying catalog finally emerge as the fruit of international collaboration.

We would like to take the opportunity to thank in particular the many architects, collectors, researchers, and developers who generously opened their doors and hard disks to grant us free access to their work. Without their knowledge and willingness to answer all our possible and impossible questions, this exhibition would never have come about: Dennis Allain, Asymptote Architecture (Hani Rashid, Oscar Cuevas), Atelier Oslo (Thomas Liu), Balmond Studio (Sarah Balmond), Barkow Leibinger (Frank Barkow, Tim Berge, Polina Goldberg), Richard and Oskar Beckmann (Archiv Otto Beckmann), Ruth Berktold (Munich University of Applied Sciences), Brick Visual (Judit Huszár), Daniel Cardoso Llach (Carnegie Mellon University), Jana Čulek (Studio Fabula), Diller Scofidio + Renfro (Christine Noblejas), Dyvik Kahlen Architects (Christopher Dyvik, Max Kahlen), Eisenman Architects (Erdem Tuzun), Foreign Office Architects, Franken Architekten (Bernhard and Nicole Franken), Lucia Frascerra, John and Julia Frazer, Gehry Partners (Meaghan Lloyd), Werner Goehner (Cornell University), Donald Greenberg (Cornell University), Zaha Hadid Architects (Shajay Bhooshan, Nils-Peter Fischer), Herzog & de Meuron (Fabrizia Vecchione), Ludger Hovestadt (ETH Zurich), Reinhard König (Bauhaus-Universität Weimar), Ole Petter Larsen, Thomas Leeser (Leeser Architecture), Johannes Leitich, Studio Libeskind (Amanda de Beaufort), Greg Lynn FORM (Greg Lynn, Walker Hart), Keiichi Matsuda, Mir, Erika Mühlthaler (Munich University of Applied Sciences), MVRDV, Michael Naimark, Nicholas Negroponte, Michael Noll, Norbert Palz (Berlin University of the Arts), Preston Scott Cohen, Reiser + Umemoto (Jesse Reiser and Nanako Umemoto, Jasmine Lee), Gilles Retsin (The Bartlett School of Architecture, UCL), Carola Scheil, Dennis Shelden (Georgia Institute of Technology), SHoP Architects (Chris Sharples, Rachel Lexier-Nagle, Nadine Berger), Karl Sims, Skidmore, Owings & Merrill (Karen Widi), Tang & Yang (Ming Tang), Bernhard Többen (Hannover University of Applied Sciences and Arts), Leila Topić (Museum of Contemporary Art, Zagreb), Heiko Worner, Manfred Wolff-Plottegg, You+Pea (Luke Pearson, Sandra Youkhana), David Zeltzer.

Many institutions have actively and patiently supported us in preparing this exhibition: Architectural Association School of Architecture Archive (Edward Bottoms), Canadian Centre for Architecture (Mirko Zardini, Martien de Vletter, Rafico Ruiz, Tim Klähn, Stefana Breitwieser), Deutsches Architekturmuseum (Oliver Elser, Wolfgang Welker), ETH Zurich gta Archives (Almut Grunewald), FRAC Centre, Het Nieuwe Instituut (Floor van Ast, Elza van den Berg, Suzanne Mulder, Frans Neggers), Kunsthalle Bremen (Christine Demele, Tanja Borghardt), Leibniz Supercomputing Centre of the Bavarian Academy of Sciences and Humanities (Elisabeth Mayer, Thomas Odaker, Dieter Kranzlmüller), MIT Libraries Distinctive Collections (Nora Murphy), MIT Media Lab (Jimmy Day, Alexandra Kahn, David Robertson, Ellen Hoffman), MIT Museum (Gary Van Zante, Daryl McCurdy), Museum of Modern Art (Paul Galloway, Evangelos Kotsioris), Nasjonalmuseet for kunst, arkitektur og design (Birgitte Sauge), saai | Archive for Architecture and Civil Engineering (Georg Vrachliotis), Siemens Historical Institute (Frank Wittendorfer), Ungers Archive for Architectural Research (Anja Sieber-Albers).

In addition to our external partners, we express our thanks to our colleagues at the Faculty of Architecture, Technical University of Munich (TUM), above all Frank Petzold, Richard Junge, and their coworkers at the Chair of Architectural Informatics for their help and support. We are also grateful to Martin Luce and Gabriele Zechner from the Dean's Office of the Faculty of Architecture for the payment of part of our travel costs. We would also like to express our special thanks to the President of the TUM, Thomas Hofmann, for his interest in this topic, which is so important for the Architekturmuseum.

A great debt of thanks is owed to all the numerous authors of the catalog, who researched individual projects, often entailing meticulous detective work, or developed the broader contexts in the essays: Roberto Bottazzi, Mollie Claypool, Anna-Maria Meister, Molly Wright Steenson, Felix Torkar, Theodora Vardouli, and Georg Vrachliotis for taking part in our conference and the essays in the book. Laura Altmann, Sina Brückner-Amin, Lluis Dura, Myriam Fischer, Clara Frey, Stefan Gruhne, Jia Yi Gu, Regine Heß, Tonderai Koschke, Evangelos Kotsioris, Frederike Lausch,

Thomas Liu, Anna-Maria Mayerhofer, Franziska Mühlbauer, Johannes Müntinga, Birgitte Sauge, Philip Schneider, Franziska Stein, Philipp Sturm, Julian Trummer, Gerlinde Verhaeghe, Heike Werner, and Sina Zarei for the project texts.

The external participants at the conference "Pixels, Vectors, and Algorithms: The Digital Revolution in Architecture" on October 11, 2019, at the TUM are thanked for their critical questions and new research contributions: Alex Blanchard, Galo Cañizares, Dennis Chau, Ariel Genadt, Evangelos Kotsioris, Malgorzata Starzynska.

Sincere thanks are due to the student participants at the master's seminar in the summer semester 2019 at the Chair of Architectural History and Curatorial Practice for their excellent questions and their contributions to the preparation of the exhibition.

Last but not least, we would like to thank our friends and colleagues who have discussed the topic of the exhibition extensively and critically with us: Joseph Bensimon, Nathalie Bredella, Chris Dähne, Oliver Elser, Myriam Fischer, Marcelo della Giustina, Kevin Graf Schumacher, Stefan Gruhne, Max Hallinan, Frederike Lausch, Aliza Leventhal, Elena Markus, Johannes Müntinga, Martin Prade, Stéphanie Quantin, Franziska Stein, Philipp Sturm, Gerlinde Verhaeghe, Tim Walsh, Matthew Wells, and Heike Werner.

We would like to thank the team at the Architekturmuseum, who, as always, provided professional support for this project: Laura Altmann, Vera Simone Bader, Katrin Bäumler, Marlies Blasl, Andreas Bohmann, Sina Brückner-Amin, Anton Heine, Martina Heinemann, Regine Heß, Thomas Lohmaier, Anja Schmidt, Thilo Schuster, and Ester Vletsos.

We would also like to thank student assistants Philip Schneider, Clara Frey, Anna-Maria Mayerhofer, and Franziska Mühlbauer for their outstanding work and enormous personal commitment.

We thank the designers of the book and the exhibition graphics, Jonas Beuchert, Tilman Schlevogt, and Johanna Wenger from PARAT.cc., for their creative collaboration, and Florian Bengert for his excellent work on the conception and implementation of the exhibition architecture and his in-depth immersion in the content for the project.

We would like to thank Birkhäuser Verlag, especially Katharina Holas, Ulrich Schmidt, Amelie Solbrig, and Baharak Tajbakhsh, for the realization and supervision of the book.

Our thanks are also due to Martin Schnitzer for his personal commitment to supporting the exhibition as well as the Nemetschek Group for their financial support. Great thanks also go to the Gerda Henkel Foundation, which has financially supported our research at the Chair of Architectural History and Curatorial Practice since the beginning of the project and made publication possible through a grant for printing costs. We are grateful for the support by the Förderverein Architekturmuseum TU München for the exhibition and book. We thank the Freunde der Pinakothek der Moderne (PIN) for its generous support of the exhibition. Finally, we would like to thank Philip Kurz and Verena Gantner from the Wüstenrot Stiftung for their critical questions and financial assistance for the catalog and exhibition.

Teresa Fankhänel and Andres Lepik

Illustration Credits

4   Roberto Bottazzi, drawing: Philip Schneider
5   Dürer, Albrecht. *Underweysung der Messung, mit dem Zirckel un Richtscheyt*. Nuremberg, 1525. Creative Commons License
6   Courtesy of SOM | © Skidmore, Owings & Merrill LLP 1984
7   Richard Voss
8–9 Marjan Colletti

Movement, Time, and Architecture
1   © Copyright 1965 A. Michael Noll. Conceived and programmed by A. Michael Noll at Bell Telephone Laboratories, Inc. in 1965
2, 5 Architekturmuseum der TUM
3   Whitted, Turner. "An Improved Illumination Model for Shaded Display." *Commun. ACM* 23, 6 (June 1980), 343–49, fig. 7. doi. org/10.1145/358876.358882
4   © 1991 / STUDIOCANAL—All Rights Reserved
6   © Franken Architekten
7   © Boeing, p42271
8   Asymptote Architecture

Cornell in Perspective
1–4 Donald Greenberg

Skeleton Animation System
1–2 David Zeltzer

9 Cities
1–2 *Nine Cities* video courtesy of SOM | Skidmore, Owings & Merrill LLP 1984
3, 5 Architekturmuseum der TUM, Courtesy of SOM | Skidmore, Owings & Merrill LLP 1984
4   Weingarten, Nicholas. "DRAW3D." *16th Design Automation Conference Proceedings*. New York: IEEE, 1979, 136.

Locomotion Studies
1–3 Courtesy Karl Sims

Eyebeam Atelier
1–2 Leeser Architecture
3   Diller Scofidio + Renfro
4   © Reiser + Umemoto, 2001

Arctic
1–2 Lucia Frascerra

Villa R
1–4 Dyvik Kahlen

Prince Claus Bridge
1   © mir.no
2   Courtesy National Gallery of Art, Washington, DC
3   © Royal Museums of Fine Arts of Belgium, Brussels, photo: J. Geleyns—Art Photography

The Elephant and the Corsair
1–5 © Dennis Allain

Hilma af Klint Museum
1–4 Jana Čulek / Studio Fabula
5   Courtesy of the Hilma af Klint Foundation. Photo: Moderna Museet, Stockholm

Sørli Visitor Center
1–2 Brick Visual

CHAPTER 4

Playing Architect
1   *Block'hood* screenshot. Video game by Jose Sanchez, Plethora Project
2   Architekturmuseum der TUM
3, 5 Electronic Arts Inc.
4   Electronic Arts Inc., Vincent Ocasla
6   © 2019 Ubisoft Entertainment. All Rights Reserved. *Assassin's Creed* is a trademark of Ubisoft Entertainment in the US and/or other countries

Computing Choice
1   © Michael_Kirkham
2   Gramazio Kohler Architekten
3   Cross, Nigel, ed. *Design Participation: Proceedings of the Design Research Society's Conference*. London: Academy Editions, 1972.
4   Friedman, Yona. "The Flatwriter: Choice by Computer." *Progressive Architecture*, March 1971, 100–101. © VG Bild-Kunst, Bonn 2020
5   Friedman, Yona. *Toward a Scientific Architecture*. Cambridge, MA: MIT Press, 1975, 31, fig. 16. © VG Bild-Kunst, Bonn 2020
6   MIT Media Lab, Architecture Machine Group

URBAN 5
1–4 Negroponte, Nicholas. *The Architecture Machine: Toward a More Human Environment*. Cambridge, MA: MIT Press, 1970, 80, 76, 74, 85. © Massachusetts Institute of Technology, by permission of The MIT Press

Aspen Movie Map
1,3,4 MIT Media Lab
2   MIT Media Lab, Courtesy of Bob Mohl

The Walter Segal Model
1–5 John Frazer, Julia Frazer, photo: John Frazer

ARMILLA
1–5 gta Archives / ETH Zurich, Fritz Haller

H₂Oexpo

1–4 Lars Spuybroek Fonds, Canadian Centre for Architecture, Gift of Lars Spuybroek, © Lars Spuybroek

The Virtual House Competition
1   Foreign Office Architects Fonds, Canadian Centre for Architecture, Gift of Farshid Moussavi and Alejandro Zaera-Polo, © Foreign Office Architects
2   © Herzog & de Meuron
3   "The Virtual House." *ANY*, no. 19/20 (1997).
4   Eisenman Architects, The Virtual House, 1997. Design proposal for Virtual House Competition organized by *ANY* magazine, New York

Guggenheim Virtual Museum
1–6 Asymptote Architecture

Barclays Center
1–3 © SHoP Architects
4   © SHoP Architects, photo: Bruce Damonte

Hyper-Reality
1–3 Keiichi Matsuda
4   Philipp Sturm

London Developers Toolkit
1–4 London Developers Toolkit, a game by You+Pea

Transcribed Nature
1–2 Annar Bjørgli / The National Museum of Art, Architecture and Design
3   Mediascapes—Architecture Museums and Digital Design Media
4   Atelier Oslo

Imprint

CATALOG

This book is published in conjunction with the exhibition *The Architecture Machine. The Role of Computers in Architecture* at the Architekturmuseum der TUM, Munich, from October 14, 2020 to January 10, 2021.

Editors Teresa Fankhänel and Andres Lepik
Managing editor Teresa Fankhänel
Editorial assistant Philip Schneider
Reproductions Ester Vletsos

The exhibition and catalog were supported by:
PIN. Freunde der Pinakothek der Moderne
Wüstenrot Stiftung
Gerda Henkel Stiftung
Förderverein Architekturmuseum TU München
Nemetschek Group
Dekanat der TUM

Printed with the support of Gerda Henkel Stiftung, Düsseldorf

Essays
Roberto Bottazzi, Mollie Claypool, Teresa Fankhänel, Anna-Maria Meister, Molly Wright Steenson, Felix Torkar, Theodora Vardouli, Georg Vrachliotis

Project texts
Laura Altmann, Sina Brückner-Amin, Lluis Dura, Teresa Fankhänel, Myriam Fischer, Clara Frey, Stefan Gruhne, Jia Yi Gu, Regine Heß, Frederike Lausch, Tonderai Koschke, Evangelos Kotsioris, Thomas Liu, Anna-Maria Mayerhofer, Franziska Mühlbauer, Johannes Müntinga, Birgitte Sauge, Philip Schneider, Franziska Stein, Philipp Sturm, Julian Trummer, Gerlinde Verhaeghe, Heike Werner, Sina Zarei

Content editor Katharina Holas, Birkhäuser Verlag, A-Vienna
Production editor Amelie Solbrig, Birkhäuser Verlag, D-Berlin
Translation from German into English Raymond Peat, GB-Aberdeen
Copyediting John Arthur Sweet, CA-Montreal
Proofreading Alun Brown, A-Vienna
Graphic design PARAT.cc, D-Munich
Lithography DZA Druckerei zu Altenburg GmbH, D-Altenburg
Printing DZA Druckerei zu Altenburg GmbH, D-Altenburg
Paper IGEPA Profibulk 1.3, 150 g
Typefaces Apax (Optimo), Helvetica Now (Monotype)

Library of Congress Control Number 2020931338

Bibliographic information published by the German National Library
The German National Library lists this publication in the Deutsche National-bibliografie; detailed bibliographic data are available on the Internet at http://dnb.dnb.de.

ISBN 978-3-0356-2154-9
German Print-ISBN 978-3-0356-2155-6

© 2020 Architekturmuseum der TUM
© 2020 Birkhäuser Verlag GmbH, Basel

Birkhäuser Verlag GmbH, Basel
P.O. Box 44, 4009 Basel, Switzerland
Part of Walter de Gruyter GmbH, Berlin/Boston

9 8 7 6 5 4 3 2 1

www.birkhauser.com

EXHIBITION

Director Andres Lepik
Curator Teresa Fankhänel
Assistant Philip Schneider
Student assistants Franziska Mühlbauer, Clara Frey
Exhibition design Florian Bengert / BNGRT
Graphic design PARAT.cc, Munich
Installation Andreas Bohmann, Thomas Lohmaier
Conservator Anton Heine
Archive and registrar Anja Schmidt, Thilo Schuster
Office Marlies Blasl, Martina Heinemann, Tanja Nyc
Press Vera Simone Bader
Public relations Teresa Fankhänel, Clara Frey

Architekturmuseum der TUM inside the Pinakothek der Moderne
Barer Str. 40
80333 Munich
www.architekturmuseum.de

An exhibition by Architekturmuseum der TUM

Loans
Dennis Allain, Asymptote Architecture, Atelier Oslo, Balmond Studio, Barkow Leibinger, Archiv Otto Beckmann, Brick Visual, Canadian Centre for Architecture, Daniel Cardoso Llach, Matthias Castorph, Jana Čulek, Diller Scofidio + Renfro, Dyvik Kahlen Architects, ETH Zurich gta Archives, FRAC Centre, Franken Architekten, Lucia Frascerra, John and Julia Frazer, Donald Greenberg, Het Nieuwe Instituut, Kunsthalle Bremen, Thomas Leeser, Studio Libeskind, Greg Lynn FORM, Keiichi Matsuda, Mir, MIT Media Lab, MIT Museum, Museum of Modern Art, Nasjonalmuseet for kunst, arkitektur og design, Reiser + Umemoto, saai | Archive for Architecture and Civil Engineering, Carola Scheil, SHoP Architects, Siemens-Archiv, Karl Sims, Skidmore, Owings & Merrill, Tang & Yang, Ungers Archiv für Architekturwissenschaft, Heike Werner, Manfred Wolff-Plottegg, You+Pea